FIGURES FROM AMERICAN HISTORY

ALEXANDER HAMILTON

BY

HENRY JONES FORD

FIGURES FROM AMERICAN HISTORY

Now Ready

THOMAS JEFFERSON
By David Saville Muzzey

JEFFERSON DAVIS
By Armistead C. Gordon

STEPHEN A. DOUGLAS
By Louis Howland

ALEXANDER HAMILTON
By Henry Jones Ford

Further volumes will follow at short intervals, the list including WASHINGTON, LINCOLN, WEBSTER, GRANT, LEE, CLEVELAND, and others.

———

CHARLES SCRIBNER'S SONS, PUBLISHERS

ALEXANDER HAMILTON

BY

HENRY JONES FORD
PROFESSOR OF POLITICS, PRINCETON UNIVERSITY

NEW YORK
CHARLES SCRIBNER'S SONS
1920

PREFACE

LITTLE material is available for a biography of Alexander Hamilton beyond that collected by his son, John Church Hamilton, and his grandson, Allan McLane Hamilton. Much that once existed was lost. Tuckerman's "Life of General Philip Schuyler" relates that many letters from Hamilton and other political papers were burned by a son of one of Schuyler's executors, because he regarded them as containing expressions too personal to be exposed to any risk of publicity. The loss to American history is as great as that inflicted by Charles Thomson, secretary of the Continental Congress, when he destroyed his memoirs for a like reason. A bowdlerized style of writing history and biography was once in vogue that made such suppression of truth seem actually meritorious, and damage was done that can never be repaired. Hamilton's reputation has suffered greatly by it. His career was too vivid and salient, his statesmanship too incisive, his self-revelation too candid to admit of the bowdlerizing process, and he cannot be judged fairly unless all is brought out and put in the scales. Such has been my aim in the present work. My special acknowledgments are due to my friend, Mr. Charles R. Williams, of Princeton, for his care in verifying references, in correcting the proofs, and for helpful criticism.

PRINCETON, March 23, 1920.

CONTENTS

CONTENTS

ALEXANDER HAMILTON

ALEXANDER HAMILTON

CHAPTER I

BIRTH AND FAMILY CONNECTIONS

At present the term West Indies suggests something foreign and remote. Such was not the case when Alexander Hamilton was born in Nevis, one of the chain of islands known as the Lesser Antilles. The British possessions in this quarter were considered to be an integral part of the newer England that had been planted in the western world. A compilation of laws published in 1704, for the use of "gentlemen trading to or concerned in her Majesty's plantations," mentions them in the order, Virginia, Jamaica, Barbados, Maryland, New England, New York, Carolina. In our own time the Lesser Antilles seem rather farther away than Europe, since a quick and regular ferry has been established across the Atlantic. But in the colonial period intercourse between the Antilles and the mainland was easier than between the different colonies on the mainland. The brigantines, which were the usual means of conveyance, made the voyage with speed and comfort, as compared with the conditions of land travel at that

1

time.   People looking about for places in which to
settle would naturally include the West Indies in
their survey of American opportunities.   Thus it
was that the Reverend Hugh Knox, who did so
much for Hamilton's early education, found his
way there.   He arrived in America from Ireland in
1753, studied for the ministry under the Reverend
Aaron Burr, at Newark, New Jersey, and after or-
dination went to St. Croix as pastor to the settlers
there.   To view Hamilton's birthplace as it was
then regarded, Nevis should be thought of simply as
an outlying American colony.

Nevis is one of the group known as the Leeward
Islands, the northernmost of the Lesser Antilles.
It has an area of only fifty square miles, almost
round in form, the centre, a peak of 3,200 feet, rising
so gradually that, viewed from the sea, the island
looks like a perfect cone.   Settled originally from
St. Kitts, Nevis has been a British colony since
1628.   Here Alexander Hamilton was born, January
11, 1757.

At that time the West Indies figured grandly in
the world's affairs.   With slave labor and with the
demand then existing for their products, the islands
were reservoirs of wealth for whose possession all the
powers of western Europe had contended, producing the diversity of national ownership that has
come down to our own times.   The great planters
lived in magnificent style.   Nowhere probably in

the western world was there such a display of luxurious dress, fine equipage, and profuse hospitality as in the West Indian capitals. The fame of this grandeur was world-wide. It was a theme that inspired poetic fancy, and the great West Indian staple was the subject of an epic that ranked as a notable poem in its day, but is now preserved from oblivion only by references to it in Boswell's *Life of Johnson.* The author, Doctor James Grainger, while on a visit to the West Indies, married the widow of a Nevis planter. He wrote a poem in four books on the cultivation of the sugar-cane, which was published in England in 1764. His account of the way in which the cane suffered from attacks of vermin began with a line over which Doctor Johnson made merry:

"Now, Muse, let's sing of rats."

But this appeared only in the first edition, and the poem was received with so much favor that piratical editions of it were printed. Grainger eventually settled in St. Kitts, where he died in 1766. Hamilton, who was then nine years old, must have known the poet, as St. Kitts and Nevis are so close together that they form one community. With the decay of the sugar interest the social grandeur of Hamilton's age passed away. The great stone mansions of the wealthy planters were built with a solidity that might have insured their perpetuity in any other climate, but with the decline of prosperity many became untenanted, windows would be broken, there would be no one to close the storm-shutters, and, when the tremendous blasts of a West Indian hurricane gained admittance to the interior, away would go the roof, and only the walls would be left standing, soon to be buried in tropical thickets. Now lizards frisk and land-crabs scuttle in the ruins of houses that were brilliant social centres in Hamilton's day.

A circumstance that was brought up against Hamilton in his political career—particularly by John Adams—was the illegitimacy of his birth. The bare legal fact is indisputable, but it is far from meaning what that fact would ordinarily imply. It was a result of the lax conditions of the times, which produced irregular social consequences in all the American colonies, and it was the habit to make allowances for them. One may be sure that the great patroon, General Schuyler, would never have given his daughter to Hamilton if a social stigma had actually rested upon him. Scottish and Huguenot families were prominent in the British occupation of the Lesser Antilles, and Alexander Hamilton came of both these stocks. Among the Huguenot families was one originally named Faucette, which became Englished as Fawcett. John Fawcett, who settled in Nevis, was a medical practitioner until his gains were large enough to enable him to retire from professional work and live as a wealthy planter. His wife Mary, of whose family there is apparently no record, was twenty years younger and had means of her own. They built a great house on their country estate and had also a town house for occupancy when the Captain-General was holding his official court in Nevis and the fashionable season was at its height. After twenty years of married life, when Doctor Fawcett had become gouty and irritable, his wife demanded and obtained a separate maintenance. The only child left at home at the time of the separation was Rachel, born after her sisters had grown up. The mother moved to an estate she owned on St. Kitts, taking with her Rachel, then four years old. Great care was taken with Rachel's education, and she was proficient in languages and in the young-lady accomplishments of the day—painting, singing, and ability to play the harp and the guitar. She is described as having fair hair with a reddish tinge, sparkling gray eyes, a complexion of the marked whiteness which seems almost peculiar to the sheltered gentlewomen of the tropics, with features finely modelled and full of vivacity and charm. She became the mother of Alexander Hamilton, but that was after an unhappy experience producing conditions from which she escaped by an irregular union.

When she was sixteen her mother arranged for her a marriage with John Michael Levine, a Dane of

wealth and social position, who had come to St.
Croix with the idea of buying an estate there and
settling down to the life of a planter. The wedding
was a fashionable event, followed by a trip to
Europe, Mrs. Fawcett accompanying the bridal
couple. After remaining long enough to see her
daughter presented at court and splendidly received
in Copenhagen society, Mrs. Fawcett returned to
the West Indies, the Levines following some months
after. Meanwhile the young bride had had some
revulsion of feeling which turned her against her
husband. Watching her chance, she ran away to
her mother, boarding a ship just as it was leaving
St. Croix for St. Kitts, while her husband was attending some state function. The differences between them—whatever they were—were never settled, and she never returned to her husband, but a
boy born after the separation was turned over to
the father's care while still a small infant.

After some years of the forlorn life of a grass-
widow the young woman met James Hamilton and
the two fell deeply in love. He was the fourth son
of Alexander Hamilton, of Grange, in Ayrshire,
Scotland, who was the fifteenth in descent from
David Hamilton, who had a charter of land from
his uncle, Alan Hamilton, of Lethberd, confirmed by
the overlord, Archibald, Earl of Douglas, January 29,
1411. Like many another cadet of ancient Scottish
lineage, James Hamilton had emigrated in search of

better opportunities for advancement than he could find at home. He reached St. Kitts, where he had a kinsman, William Hamilton, an old friend of the Fawcetts. William was a man of local eminence, a physician, a planter, and a member of the Council. James Hamilton was a well-educated and well-born Scottish gentleman. When the two met he was about twenty-one and Rachel Levine was about twenty. The two met often in society, for Rachel's friends stood by her and she moved in the best circles. Mrs. Fawcett died and a beautiful, attractive, accomplished young woman was left alone. The two wanted to marry and could not. Efforts to free Rachel were unavailing. Finally the two decided to unite outside of the law. The circumstances of the case received much indulgent consideration, but the investigations made by Mrs. Atherton on the spot show that the couple experienced social censure. This explains the inconvenient arrangement made for their married life. Rachel had through inheritance from her father a place in Nevis, to which they moved, although Hamilton's business was in St. Kitts and he had to cross the two-mile strait between the two islands almost daily. But the kinsfolk and old friends of the Fawcetts and Hamiltons stood by the young couple, their home was hospitable and attractive, they drew about them a circle of friends, and obtained a recognized position in Nevis society.

The circumstances should be viewed not only with regard to local conditions but also with regard to the general conditions then existing as to marriage law in the British Empire. The old canon law, which admitted of the annulment of marriage entered into by an inexperienced girl under duress, had been overthrown, and secular jurisprudence had not yet extended its cognizance to such situations. From the traditional information collected by Mrs. Atherton it appears that Rachel had been much averse to the marriage with Levine and gave way only under pressure. The only way in which she could have obtained divorce was by a special act of Parliament, always a matter of great expense and difficulty, and quite unattainable in St. Kitts. It is plain that the behavior of James Hamilton and his consort stood quite apart in moral quality from that which commonly attends an irregular union. Rachel always had the position of an honored wife, and received social recognition as such. In later years the Hamiltons of Scotland were glad to claim relationship, but there is no evidence of their interest until Alexander Hamilton had become famous.

But, while his birth and rearing had none of the disadvantages which the term illegitimate might suggest, he did experience some of the inconveniences of poverty, not, however, to a greater extent than was probably a help in fortifying his character. James Hamilton went into business in St. Kitts, had trouble with his partners, withdrew from the firm, and set up for himself. His wife sold her St. Kitts estate to provide him with capital, which was sunk in unsuccessful enterprises, and the family was impoverished. Peter Lytton, husband of one of Rachel's elder sisters, gave James Hamilton the position of manager of a cattle estate on St. Croix, and he moved there with his family. The Hamiltons were kindly received by the Lyttons and also by the Mitchells, the family into which the other sister had married. But James Hamilton made a failure of his management, fell out with his brother-in-law, and in the third year after the family settlement in St. Croix he went to St. Vincent in search of employment. He kept in correspondence with his wife, but was never able to re-establish his household, and his family became dependent upon his wife's relatives. The Lyttons took Mrs. Hamilton and her children into their own home, allotting to her use an upstairs wing of their great mansion. Two years passed by, and James Hamilton had not succeeded in doing any better in business than to earn a small salary; then came a final severance through the death of Mrs. Hamilton, February 16, 1768. She was then only thirty-two years old. James Hamilton lived for many years after, remaining on St. Vincent, where he died on June 3, 1799. Notwithstanding his separation from his family, his famous son regarded him with affection. A letter has been

preserved from Alexander Hamilton to his brother,
written from New York, June 23, 1785, in which he
said:

But what has become of our dear father? It is an age
since I have heard from him or of him, though I have
written him several letters. Perhaps, alas, he is no more,
and I shall not have the pleasing opportunity of contributing to render the close of his life more happy than
the progress of it. My heart bleeds at the recollection of
his misfortunes and embarrassments. Sometimes I flatter myself his brothers have extended their support to
him; and that he now enjoys tranquillity and ease. At
other times I fear he is suffering in indigence. Should he
be alive, inform him of my inquiries; beg him to write to
me, and tell him how ready I shall be to devote myself
and all I have to his accommodation and happiness.

Eventually Alexander Hamilton invited his father
to make his home with him. In a letter of June 12,
1793, the father wrote: "My bad state of health has
prevented my going to sea at this time." Moreover, the war between England and France made
travel dangerous. But he added: "We daily expect
news of a peace, and when that takes place, provided
it is not too late in the season, I will embark in the
first vessel that sails for Philadelphia." The letter
sent "respectful compliments" to Mrs. Hamilton
and the children, and closed with wishes of health
and happiness to his "dear Alexander," subscribed

by "your very affectionate father, James Hamilton."
Although the elder Hamilton lived for six years after
the date of that letter, he was never well enough to
attempt the voyage, and the two never met after
the son left the West Indies. That they corre-
sponded regularly is attested by Hamilton's letter
of 1797 to a Scotch kinsman, in which he said:

It is now several months since I have heard from my
father, who continued at the island of St. Vincent's. My
anxiety at this silence would be greater than it is were it
not for the probable interruption and precariousness of
intercourse which is produced by the war. I have strongly
pressed the old gentleman to come and reside with me,
which would afford him every enjoyment of which his
advanced age is capable; but he has declined it on the
ground that the advice of his physicians leads him to fear
that the change of climate would be fatal to him. The
next best thing for me is, in proportion to my means, to
endeavor to increase his comforts where he is.

From the same letter it appears that the Lyttons
and the Mitchells, who lived in affluence during
Hamilton's boyhood, were then in straitened circumstances. Hamilton's expense-book, July 1, 1796,
records a donation of one hundred dollars to Mrs.
Mitchell. This book also records money sent to
Hamilton's father and younger brother, to the
amount of several thousand dollars, during the
years 1796 to 1799, when Hamilton was himself in

difficulties over the insufficiency of his income to sustain expenditure required by his position. Little is known about the career of Hamilton's younger brother, except that he remained in the West Indies and was obscure in character and fortune.

CHAPTER II

A PICKED-UP EDUCATION

ALEXANDER HAMILTON was eleven years old when his mother died; his brother James was five years younger. Alexander's education seems to have been desultory, but he learned to speak French fluently. That language has always had a commercial value in the Lesser Antilles that brings it into extensive use, and a clever child is apt to pick up some knowledge of it. Hamilton acquired fluency by continual practice with his mother. In other studies he was helped by the Reverend Hugh Knox, who was a frequent visitor at the Lytton mansion, and who lent the boy books and took an active interest in his progress. After his mother's death Alexander went to live with his aunt, Mrs. Mitchell. Her husband had made a fortune in the slave trade; he owned a large general store and also plantations yielding sugar, molasses, and rum. He had a town house in Christianstadt, and, living there, Hamilton was now able to go regularly to school with Knox, who lived in the same town. He was one of a small class of students to whom the Presbyterian pastor gave lessons in Latin and mathematics, but Hamilton could not have gone far in his studies, as he was only twelve years old when he went to work for Nicholas Cruger, proprietor of a large general store. Such rudiments of learning as he had received were steadily improved by assiduous reading. Evidence of his youthful ambition is given by a letter from Hamilton to his chum, Edward Stevens, saying:

. . . for to confess my weakness, Ned, my ambition is prevalent, so that I contemn tne grovelling condition of a clerk, or the like, to which my fortune condemns me, and would willingly risk my life, though not my character, to exalt my station. I am confident, Ned, that my youth excludes me from any hopes of immediate preferment, nor do I desire it; but I mean to prepare the way for futurity. I'm no philosopher, you see, and may be justly said to build castles in the air; my folly makes me ashamed, and beg you'll conceal it; yet Neddy, we have seen such schemes successful, when the projector is constant.

This letter, which is a stock quotation in Hamilton biographies, is usually presented as evidence of precocious ambition, but this is not really a remarkable circumstance. Nothing is more common than for youth to have such dreams. Alexander Hamilton hit the mark, but myriads have had like aims who missed the mark and settled down to obscure fortunes. The letter is a remarkable one to have been written by a boy not yet thirteen, but it is remarkable not so much for its declaration of purpose as for its revelation of the writer's character. Its youthful pomposity attests his familiarity with the literary models of the age. The style is a clever boy's imitation of the rolling periods of the eighteenth-century historians and essayists. Hamilton turned out to be one of the small class of men of whom it has been justly said that they appear as levers to uplift the earth and roll it into another course, but they do not attain to such rare functions by the high range of their ambition but by the large development of their powers. "The grovelling condition of a clerk" which he contemned was probably of great value as a discipline; for nothing braces the mind so much as training in ability to apply its powers to disagreeable tasks. Certain it is that Hamilton put his mind to his work as a clerk with energy and success, and it was by doing well what was then in his sphere of opportunity that larger prospects were opened. His ability was such that his employer trusted him with important affairs, and in 1770 he was left in charge of the business while Mr. Cruger was on a trip to America. The diversified experience which Hamilton obtained in business management, and the habits of accuracy and circumspection which trading pursuits tend to develop, were good training for the career which made him famous.

Hamilton's desire for a college education was well known to friends and relatives. They had the means to gratify that desire, and withheld it rather from inattention or from inertia than from positive unwillingness. A chance event produced a concentration of influence that was decisive. In August, 1772, a terrible hurricane swept St. Croix, causing great wreckage and ruin. Hamilton wrote an account of it which was published in a St. Kitts newspaper, there being no English newspaper in St. Croix. It attracted much attention and caused a strong sentiment that so clever a youth ought to have the best advantages. Arrangements were then made by his aunts for sending him to America for a college education. There have been many instances of such benefactions to promising youths in West Indian annals, but the case of Alexander Hamilton is the most illustrious. He sailed on a vessel bound to Boston, which was reached in October, 1772, and he at once took passage for New York. He never returned to the West Indies, but spent the rest of his life in the United States.

It has been generally assumed in biographies that Hamilton's interest in the American struggle was excited by the influences of his collegiate career, but it is probable that he brought that interest with him, for the same issues were quite as absorbing to thought in the West Indies as on the American continent. Indeed, the constitutional temper which was manifested in those times has been better preserved in the West Indies than in continental America. As the English in Ireland have preserved the

Shakesperian pronunciation that has been lost in England itself through phonetic change; as Nova Scotia has preserved seventeenth-century customs that have died out in Scotland itself; as one may find in the West Indies features of the seventeenth-century organization of local government that have disappeared in the mother country; so too one may note relics of political thought, characteristic of all the American colonies in Hamilton's boyhood, still preserved in the West Indies, although now extinct in the United States through the political transformations it has experienced. St. Kitts and Nevis have lost the representative assemblies they possessed in Hamilton's day, and the local legislature is now nominated by the Crown. But Barbados still manages its own affairs under a charter of the same type as was originally granted to Virginia and Massachusetts, and while these have long since adopted other constitutional arrangements, the Barbados charter is still in operation and the colonial assembly occupies the same position and displays the same constitutional spirit as was evinced by the Virginia House of Burgesses and by the Massachusetts General Court in the colonial period. An instance of this spirit, displayed in 1816, may be exhibited as a specimen of political doctrine which was clamorous throughout the West Indies during Hamilton's boyhood. A bill had been introduced in the British House of Commons providing for a local official, with fees fixed by imperial authority. This proposal was denounced by the Barbados Assembly in terms that exactly reproduce what was common doctrine in all the American colonies when Hamilton was a child. The speaker of the Barbados Assembly declared:

There is a right which every British subject possesses, destroyed by no lapse of time or circumstance, namely, that as the burdens of the people are borne by the great mass of the community, they cannot be imposed without the consent of those who represent the interests and sympathize with the wants of the bulk of the people. It matters not on what soil an Englishman may have fixed his hut, or in what uncongenial climate he may earn a precarious subsistence; the pittance of his industry is safe, except for the aids for the general benefit voted by the power of the representative system.

American legislative bodies have been reformed out of all likeness to their original pattern, and the representative assembly has declined to a singularly humble and subordinate position in the constitutional scheme, so it is now rather in Barbados than anywhere in the United States that such a constitutional atmosphere is preserved as that in which Alexander Hamilton grew up. The Stamp Act, which was the beginning of the series of measures that provoked the American Revolution, was passed in 1765, when Hamilton was eight years old. One may be sure that he often heard it discussed, for resentment was as keen and protests were as emphatic in the West Indies as on the mainland. In St. Kitts the people burned all the stamped papers sent to the island and made the official distributors resign. These measures were carried out in a systematic way, with a show of orderly procedure. Those taking part in them moved over to Nevis in a body to assist the settlers there to do likewise. In both islands the Stamp Act was defeated by solid resistance. The issues that culminated in the American Revolution were thus familiar knowledge in the islands and gave as strong a tincture to the ideas and prepossessions of the rising generation as on the American continent. When during this troublous period Alexander Hamilton arrived in New York to begin his college education, he was already an ardent American patriot.

He brought with him letters of introduction which obtained for him access to the best society, into which he was received with the easy hospitality of the times. The bright, clever, attractive West Indian lad soon made friends of lifelong value. The support of the Livingston and Schuyler families was the basis of the power which Hamilton acquired in New York politics and acquaintanceship with members of these families began while he was attending Francis Barber's grammar school at Elizabethtown, New Jersey. This school had no provision for lodgers and students boarded around as they themselves arranged. It was a common thing for those well introduced to be invited into the homes of the neighboring gentry. In this way Hamilton lived for some time with the family of Elias Boudinot, already a prominent man in New Jersey politics. Another of the friends made by Hamilton in this period was William Livingston, at whose house, Liberty Hall, he stayed frequently, meeting there men who became eminent. Among them was John Jay, who married one of Livingston's daughters. Livingston himself became governor of New Jersey during the Revolution.

In biographies of Hamilton written by his own descendants it is asserted that he went to Barber's school to prepare for Princeton, that in little over a year he was ready and would have entered there except for the fact that President Witherspoon refused him permission to go through in shorter time than was allowed by the curriculum. There is no record at Princeton of the application Hamilton is said to have made, but so many circumstances harmonize with the family tradition that it may be regarded as well authenticated. It is quite characteristic of Hamilton's nature and of his circumstances that he should have desired to get his college degree as soon as possible. It cannot be doubted that it was his original intention to go to Princeton. The Reverend Hugh Knox, his first instructor, was a Princeton man; so was Barber, under whose tuition

Hamilton placed himself; so too was Boudinot, with whom he lived. That, after all, he should have turned aside to King's College, New York, was certainly an afterthought, and the only probable explanation of it is that he was refused the privilege he desired of passing from class to class as he was able to qualify.

King's College, the germ of Columbia University, did not then rank with Princeton in reputation or in equipment. The maintenance of the regular curriculum was the work of only one man, the Reverend Doctor Myles Cooper, who gave the courses in Latin, Greek, English, mathematics, and philosophy. Hamilton took them all. In company with his friend, Edward Stevens, who was studying medicine, Hamilton also attended the lectures of Doctor Samuel Clossey, who had the chair in anatomy. The only other known member of the faculty was Doctor Peter Middleton, who lectured on chemistry. Hamilton entered as a private student, attached to no particular class but allowed to attend any. He applied himself to his studies with great diligence, employing a tutor and scheduling his days so that no time should be wasted. But, after all, he never finished his college course and was not graduated, as the outbreak of the Revolutionary War caused the college to be deserted for the camp. Hamilton, like many other young men at that time, was prematurely withdrawn from study and thrown into war and politics by the pressure of events. The prominent dates show how brief were his opportunities for systematic education. He arrived in New York October, 1772; in the autumn of 1773 he entered King's College; in 1774 the Continental Congress held its first session, and in that same year Hamilton began his career as a public speaker and a pamphleteer. But a student animated by definite purpose and pursuing it with steady, concentrated effort can do a great deal in two years, and there is ample evidence that Hamilton acquired sound scholarship, and with it the power of applying his mind with energy and success to any task. He kept on with his studies after he left college to join the army. A pay-book kept by Hamilton in 1776, as commander of a New York company of artillery, is interspersed with notes and reflections upon political philosophy and public finance, and it contains a list of books which is given below just as he wrote it:

> Rousseau's Emilius.
> Smith's History of New York.
> Leonidas.
> View of the Universe.
> Lex Mercatoria.
> Millot's History of France.
> Memoirs of the House of Brandenburgh.
> Review of the characters of the principal Nations of Europe.
> Review of Europe.
> History of Prussia.

History of France.
Lassel's Voyage through Italy.
Robinson's Charles V.
Present State of Europe.
Grecian History.
Baretti's Travels.
Bacon's Essays.
Philosophical Transactions.
Hobbes' Dialogues.
Plutarch's Morals.
Cicero's Morals.
Orations—Demosthenes.
Cudworth's Intellectual System.
Entick's History of the late War.
European Settlements in America.
Ralt's Dictionary of Trade and Commerce.
Winn's History of America.
Montaigne's Essays.

Hamilton's military career interrupted but did not suspend his studies. He resumed them whenever he had any spare time, and in this way he turned to good account the long spells of leisure which camp life often allows. It will be seen later that during military service he found time to develop the ideas which eventually he applied to the organization of the government and to the management of public finance.

CHAPTER III

THE OUTBREAK OF THE REVOLUTION

In its traditions King's College was stanchly loyalist; the faculty deplored the movements of colonial sentiment, and conditions became so uncongenial to Doctor Clossey that in 1774 he resigned and went back to England. President Cooper added the weight of his authority to some solemn warnings issued by conservative leaders, and soon had his students arrayed against him. At a mass meeting held on July 6, 1774, in what is now known as City Hall Park, to stir up New York opinion in favor of joint action with the other colonies against British dealings with Massachusetts, Hamilton, then only seventeen years old, was one of the speakers. Doubtless the opportunity was conferred in recognition of the presence of a body of collegians in the crowd, and as a means of enlisting their support, but he spoke with a power that made a distinct impression. At this period he began to write for Holt's *Journal*, and his criticisms of British policy in its columns attracted the notice of leading men. There is a reference to them in John Jay's correspondence.

The chief source of information on the details of Hamilton's behavior at this time is Robert Troup, born the same year as Hamilton, his classmate in

college and his comrade in arms. He ought, therefore, to be a good witness, but he did not commit his
recollections to writing until after Hamilton's death,
and when his statements are collated with facts of
record it becomes evident that they are not always
accurate. Troup supplied his recollections to several inquirers. The earliest extant statement from
him is preserved in the collection of Hamilton papers
in the Library of Congress. It bears date March 22,
1810, and is addressed to the Reverend Doctor John
Mason, who attended Hamilton on his death-bed.
In it Troup says:

The General, in his sentiments on government, was
originally a monarchist. He was versed in the history of
England, and well acquainted with the principles of the
English constitution, which he admired. Under this bias
towards the British monarchy, he took a journey to Boston, soon after the destruction of the East India tea by
people in disguise and called the Mohawk Indians, when
the public mind was in a state of violent fermentation.
Whilst at Boston his noble and generous heart, agitated
by what he saw and heard, listed him on the side of America. From Boston he returned to New York a warm
Republican, and quite an enthusiast for resisting the
claims of the British Parliament; and his enthusiasm impelled him first to advocate the cause of America with
his pen and afterwards to vindicate it with his sword.

This account of a Boston trip has been adopted
and enlarged upon by subsequent biographers, but,

all things considered, it is probable that no such trip took place, and that—writing after the lapse of thirty-six years—Troup has confused with subsequent events the mention he doubtless heard Hamilton make of visiting Boston when he first landed in America. The Boston tea riots took place December 16, 1773, at a period when Hamilton was in his first term at King's College, applying himself to his studies under a schedule strictly controlling his time. It is quite unlikely that he would break away to make the then long and tedious trip from New York to Boston unless there was some strong occasion for it, and no such occasion is known. Troup's account of Hamilton's motives is demonstrably false, although his errors are such as naturally occur if recollections are not carefully checked off by exact records. Internal evidence shows that there was no such change in Hamilton's views at this time as the account assumes. He was originally a monarchist, but so was every one else. Up to July 4, 1776, the general attitude was that of loyalty to the crown, combined with denial of the legislative authority of the English Parliament over the colonies. "The most valid reasons can be assigned for our allegiance to the King of Great Britain," wrote Hamilton in his pamphlet *The Farmer Refuted*, "but not one of the least force, or plausibility, for our subjection to parliamentary decrees." In the same pamphlet he expressed an ardent wish that the differences between "the parent state and the colonies" may be reconciled, and he declared: "I am a warm advocate for limited monarchy, and an unfeigned well-wisher to the present royal family." Just such views were held in the British West Indies in Hamilton's childhood. The Reverend Hugh Knox, Hamilton's pastor and teacher at St. Croix, was in full sympathy with them, as is attested by his letters to Hamilton. In 1777 Mr. Knox prepared and sent to the Continental Congress for publication, an argument in favor of the American cause entitled, *An Address to America by a Friend in a Foreign Government.*

A statement made by Hamilton himself is cited as evidence that he experienced a change of heart through a trip to Boston. In the "Advertisement" prefaced to *The Farmer Refuted* he remarked that it is a fair query, How can he be sure that his views are not the result of prejudice? and he answers: "Because he remembers the time, when he had strong prejudices on the side he now opposes. His change of sentiment (he firmly believes) proceeded from the superior force of the arguments in favor of the American claims." The style of this utterance is merely that of the exordium, an introduction meant to prepare the reader's mind for the statement and argument that follow. Hamilton was simply conforming to a rhetorical pattern then taught in the schools. The language used does not point to ideas recently caught up, but rather to those of gradual development. It was such as one would use who had inherited strong loyalist prejudices, and had had to surrender them under the instructions of experience, and this might well have been Hamilton's West Indian experience. People do not speak of "remembering a time" when referring to a recent event, such as that Boston trip would have been had it taken place.

The internal evidence supplied by Hamilton's writings demonstrates that he did not write in any spirit of affection for New England. At that time New England was not in high repute with its neighbors. Hamilton took care to distinguish between New England behavior and the nature of the constitutional issues. He does not express approval of the Boston tea riots, but he complains that, "instead of trying to discover the perpetrators, and commencing a legal prosecution against them, the Parliament of Great Britain interfered in an unprecedented manner, and inflicted a punishment upon a whole province." He argues that it is not to be supposed that the colonies were acting merely out of sympathy with Massachusetts, for "had the rest of America passively looked on, while a sister colony was subjugated, the same fate would gradually have overtaken all." It was the habit of Tory pamphleteers to cite New England traits and happenings to the discredit of that section, and it is noticeable that Hamilton does not attempt to refute such charges but simply avoids them as being beside the point. His argument is that all the colonies have a common interest in defending charter rights against aggression. "Hence, while our ears are stunned with the dismal sound of New England's republicanism, bigotry, and intolerance, it behooves us to be on our guard."

To view Hamilton's literary activities in their proper setting, it should not be supposed that producing a political pamphlet was then any extraordinary performance. In the eighteenth century it rained pamphlets whenever there was a political storm. The newspaper press had begun to be a medium for the expression of public opinion; it was not yet an organ of public opinion. The traditional view was that it was a gross indecency for newspapers to indulge in political comment, but the Revolutionary movement suppressed such scruples, and communications on public affairs from Cato, Camillus, Decius, Senex, Agricola, and such-like classical worthies frequently appeared in the newspapers. That would do for short pieces, but when an argument was drawn out to any length the pamphlet was the ordinary recourse. It was the fashion of the times either to figure as one of the great men of antiquity or else to speak as a rural sage. The celebrated *Farmer's Letters* of John Dickinson in 1768 were so called because they purported to come from "a farmer" who had "received a liberal education" and was accustomed to spending much of his time in a library which he thought "the most valuable part of his small estate." Hence he had acquired a greater knowledge of history, law, and political institutions than is usually attained by men of his class; and therefore he felt moved to offer his thoughts upon the situation. So, too, when the Reverend Doctor Seabury produced his pamphlet, *Free Thoughts on the Proceedings of the Continental Congress,* he signed it "A Westchester Farmer." In reply Hamilton produced a pamphlet in December, 1774, entitled *A Full Vindication of the Measures of Congress from the Calumnies of Their Enemies.* Doctor Seabury rejoined in a pamphlet entitled *Congress Canvassed by a Westchester Farmer.* Hamilton replied in a pamphlet entitled *The Farmer Refuted ; or, a More Comprehensive and Impartial View of the Disputes Between Great Britain and the Colonies, Intended as a Further Vindication of the Congress.*

In reading these pamphlets, the one produced before Hamilton was eighteen, the other a little after, one is not at all surprised that Doctor Cooper found it hard to believe that such a youth could have produced such "well-reasoned and cogent political discussions." That phrase exactly characterized them. Not only do they make a remarkable exhibition of precocious ability, but, on making no allowance for the youth of the author, they stand in the first rank of the political pamphlets of the Revolutionary period. The *Full Vindication* is about 14,-000 words in length. There is more strut in the style than was characteristic of Hamilton later on, but that is the only mark of juvenility in the production. The deep analysis and the logical coherence that are the specific traits of Hamilton's state papers are well marked in these products of his youth. What could go straighter to the mark than this, in rejoinder to comment on so much fuss about a trifling impost? "They endeavor to persuade us," he said, ". . . that our contest with Britain is founded entirely upon the petty duty of three pence per pound on East India tea; whereas the whole world knows it is built upon this interesting question, whether the inhabitants of Great Britain have a right to dispose of the lives and properties of the inhabitants of America, or not." Reviewing the failure of remonstrance and petition, he pointed out that all that was left was a choice between non-importation and armed resistance. At that time Congress recommended non-importation. The aim of Hamilton's argument was to justify the measures of Congress, and he set systematically to work to show first that that policy was reconcilable with the strictest maxims of justice. Next he proceeded to examine whether it had also the sanction of sound policy. "To render it agreeable to good policy, three things are requisite. First, that the necessity of the times requires it; secondly, that it be not the

probable source of greater evils than those it pretends
to remedy; and, lastly, that it have a probability of
success." He drew out the argument under each of
these three heads with an amount of information
and with a soberness of estimate that are certainly
marvellous in one of his years. The bombast so
natural to youth on fire with patriotic indignation is
quite absent. He does not boast of American greatness, but he points out that, since Great Britain
could not send out a large army, "our superiority in
number would overbalance our inferiority in discipline. It would be a hard, if not impracticable
task, to subjugate us by force." On comparing the
anticipations of military and economic conditions
made in this pamphlet with those which actually
ensued, it must be credited with remarkable prescience.

The succeeding pamphlet, *The Farmer Refuted*,
was a still more elaborate argument. It contained
over 35,000 words, and as originally published ran to
78 pages. It is marred by some of the smart personal allusions that inferior disputants are apt to import into controversy. Comparing his opponent to
one of the characters in Pope's *Dunciad*, he remarked:
"'Pert dullness' seems to be the chief characteristic
of your genius as well as his." Later on he makes
a much neater stroke, when, after citing some harsh
terms applied to himself by his opponent, he observed: "With respect to abuse, I make not the least

doubt but every reader will allow you to surpass me in that." However cleverly such gibes may be made, they are the cheapest stuff that can be employed in controversy; but at this period such stuff was used profusely by those who did not have Hamilton's excuse of youth.   In the main, the pamphlet is a solid and dignified argument resting upon historical and economic data of great fulness and exact pertinence.   The argument is devoted to stating, developing, and proving the thesis that to disclaim the authority of the British Parliament does not imply a breach of allegiance to the Crown.   This was the doctrine with which colonial resistance to imperial authority began.   It was a doctrine which admitted of fighting the King's troops while professing loyalty to the King, and this, of course, made it necessary to draw out some very fine distinctions.   Hamilton's pamphlet is as good a sample of legal ingenuity in this line as is to be found in any tract of the times. In addition to legal acuteness, the pamphlet is marked by observations upon the economic aspects of the struggle, displaying an ability to think precisely and correctly upon such matters which doubtless owed something to Hamilton's own commercial experience.   In contending that America had sufficient resources to provide for her own needs, he made a declaration that was prophetic of his own statesmanship.   "In such a country as this," he said, "there can be no great difficulty in finding business for all its inhabitants. Those obstacles which, to the eye of timidity or disaffection seem like *Alps*, would, to the hand of resolution and perseverance, become mere *hillocks*."

Not only his writings but also his conduct at this period shows that this youth of eighteen was as remarkable for the sobriety as for the power of his intelligence. It is characteristic of times of excitement that disorderly outbreaks of popular sentiment receive special indulgence. Riots become patriotic demonstrations; outrages upon persons and property become evidences of zealous devotion to the cause. At the same time that Hamilton was active in measures for organized resistance to British policy he was quite as active in opposing the rowdyism that attached itself to the movement. According to Troup, Hamilton intervened to save Doctor Cooper from attack by a mob. The story goes that as the mob approached Cooper's residence Hamilton and Troup ascended the steps, and Hamilton made a speech to the crowd "on the excessive impropriety of their conduct and the disgrace they were bringing on the cause of liberty, of which they professed to be the champions." Doctor Cooper, seeing Hamilton from an upper window, and not being able to hear what he was saying, mistook his purpose, and shouted to the mob: "Don't listen to him, gentlemen; he is crazy." The delay occasioned by Hamilton's resolute stand enabled Doctor Cooper to make his escape.

That on some occasion Hamilton did speak and act as Troup described need not be questioned. It was quite in keeping with his character. But that it had the decisive connection with Doctor Cooper's escape which appears in the traditional narrative is more than doubtful. J. C. Hamilton makes the incident a feature of the commotion which filled the city as a result of the shots fired by the man-of-war *Asia*, wounding several persons on the Battery. But this affair occurred on August 23, 1775. According to data in the New York colonial archives, the mob attack which drove out Doctor Cooper took place on the night of May 10, 1775, but he got word of the approach of the mob from a former pupil and took refuge in the house of a Mr. Stuyvesant, remaining there the next day until evening, when he took refuge with Captain James Montague, commanding the British man-of-war *Kingfisher*, which vessel conveyed Doctor Cooper to England.[1] This account is corroborated by Doctor Cooper's verses, written on the anniversary of his escape, published in the *Gentleman's Magazine* for July, 1776. In it he relates how he was roused from sleep by a "heaven-directed youth" and warned that a mob

[1] *Documents Relating to the Colonial History of the State of New York*, vol. VIII, p. 297.

was approaching. He says that they wrecked his
home, but

> "Meanwhile, along the sounding shore,
>   Where Hudson's waves incessant roar,
>   I take my weary way;
>   And skirt the windings of the tide,
>   My faithful pupil by my side,
>   Nor wish the approach of day."

There is nothing to indicate that the faithful
pupil who aided Doctor Cooper's escape was Hamilton, although it might have been. But there
is ample evidence that he condemned and opposed
the mob spirit. One of its targets was the printer,
James Rivington, from whose press Tory pamphlets
had been issued. So, too, had Whig pamphlets,
among them Hamilton's own productions; but Rivington was known to side with the Tories, and his
press was regarded as a centre of Tory influence.
But the blow did not fall upon him from his own
townsmen. On November 23, 1775, a company of
horsemen from Connecticut, commanded by Israel
Sears, rode into town declaring that they had come
to destroy Rivington's press. It is related that
Hamilton again interposed, and was so indignant at
this raid from another province that he even appealed to the people to resist the Connecticut ma-
rauders by force. The mob, however, followed the
lead of the raiders, and Rivington's establishment

was wrecked and pillaged. A few days later Hamilton wrote a long letter to John Jay, then a member of the Continental Congress, which gives signal evidence of his calm statesmanship. After referring to the raid on Rivington's press, he observed:

In times of such commotion as the present, while the passions of men are worked up to an uncommon pitch there is great danger of fatal extremes. The same state of the passions which fits the multitude, who have not a sufficient stock of reason and knowledge to guide them, for opposition to tyranny and oppression, very naturally leads them to a contempt and disregard of all authority. The due medium is hardly to be found among the more intelligent; it is almost impossible among the unthinking populace. When the minds of these are loosened from their attachment to ancient establishments and courses, they seem to grow giddy and are apt more or less to run into anarchy. These principles, too true in themselves, and confirmed to me both by reading and my own experience, deserve extremely the attention of those who have the direction of public affairs. In such tempestuous times, it requires the greatest skill in the political pilots to keep men steady and within proper bounds. . . .

This laying down of general principles was the preface to a practical recommendation, which was that troops should be stationed in New York, both to repress Tories and to preserve order. He suggested that they might be "raised in Philadelphia, the Jerseys, or any province except New England." Jay communicated Hamilton's views to Nathaniel

Woodhull, president of the Provincial Congress of New York, with some comments of his own condemning the New England exploit.

The notion that the forceful arguments produced by Hamilton at this period were improvisations inspired by the zeal of a new convert may be dismissed as unfounded. Constitutional views so mature and so well documented take time for their growth. The issues involved had been before Hamilton's mind from the time he was eight years old, and he had long been gathering information upon them. But, even so, one cannot read the pamphlets and letters without astonishment that a youth of eighteen, actively engaged in a popular movement and exposed to all of its excitements, should be able to keep such a cool head and to display such a combination of energy and sagacity. One must admit that here is clear evidence of genius, an outpouring of power and capacity beyond anything that might be expected from the circumstances of the case or be accounted for on any theory of heredity.

CHAPTER IV

IN THE STATE MILITIA

IT will be a view of Hamilton's position at this period that will best accord with known facts, if we regard the distinction now usually imputed to his youthful activities as being reflected upon them by his subsequent fame. He had certainly distinguished himself by his pamphlets, in the opinion of competent judges, but that did not constitute popular distinction. The force of argument and the dignity of style that mark those productions are better calculated to impress those who think than those who feel, and popularity belongs to those who can appeal most effectively to the feeling of the hour. The bulk of the literary output of the times consisted of sarcastic poems, personal quips, scurrilous tirades, burlesques, and facetiæ. Probably few people in turbulent New York at that time heard of Hamilton's pamphlets. They were known and admired in a restricted circle, but that circle included men of leadership and influence, whose good opinion was valuable. Besides the two pamphlets he wrote in reply to Doctor Seabury, he also produced a pamphlet in 1775, entitled *Remarks on the Quebec Bill*, which is shorter than its predecessors and is inferior to them in quality. It is plainly an appeal to Protestant bigotry. It discusses the policy of the British Government in Canada in support of a contention that "arbitrary power, and its great engine, the Popish religion, are, to all intents and purposes, established in that province."

According to Troup's reminiscences, Hamilton, Troup, and other students formed a military company in 1775, known as "Hearts of Oak." It was drilled and instructed by Major Fleming, who had been an adjutant in the British Army. It has been assumed on the strength of Troup's recollections that the Hearts of Oak participated in the removal of the cannon from the Battery in the course of which the British man-of-war *Asia* fired upon the crowd. Troup relates that during this bombardment "Hamilton, who was aiding in the removal of the cannon, exhibited the greatest unconcern, although one of his companions was killed by his side." It is entirely probable that the collegians were in the crowd at the Battery, and that they lent a hand to the efforts of the troops to remove the cannon; but contemporaneous chronicles make no mention of the participation of the Hearts of Oak in that affair. There were twenty-one cannon posted on the Battery, and the order for their removal was issued by the Provincial Congress of New York, that they might be transferred to forts then ordered to be constructed in the Highlands of the Hudson. Captain John Lamb, in command of a company of artillery, assisted by a detachment of infantry from Colonel John Lasher's battalion, performed this service, in the course of which shots were fired from the shore against a barge belonging to the *Asia*, killing one of her crew. The *Asia* retaliated by a bombardment that wounded three persons in the crowd and damaged neighboring property, but killed nobody. This took place on August 23, 1775. It may be doubted whether the Hearts of Oak were then in existence. Their motto, "Freedom or Death," inscribed on the hatbands which belonged to their uniform, suggests that they were one of the numerous volunteer military companies that sprang up after Montgomery used that watchword in the battle of Quebec, in which he was killed, December 31, 1775. A return of the militia companies in New York City made in August, 1775, does not mention the Hearts of Oak, but a return in 1776 mentions a corps of that name commanded by Captain John Berrian.[1]

The definitely established facts indicate that while the Continental Congress was taking the first steps in armed resistance to British policy, Hamilton was assiduously pursuing his studies, civil and military. Custis's *Reminiscences*, written in his old age and

[1] *Documents Relating to the Colonial History of New York*, vol. VIII, p. 601; *Memoirs of the Long Island Historical Society*, vol. III, p. 108.

showing marks of inaccuracy, relates that at one time Hamilton thought of returning to St. Croix. Custis, a stepson of Washington and an inmate of his household, saw and heard a great deal of Hamilton, and is not likely to be mistaken as to the bare fact, although the melodramatic setting he gives it is improbable. That such a notion occurred to Hamilton harmonizes with other facts in his situation at this period. He had come to America to get a college education with funds provided by his West Indian relatives for that purpose. After the flight of Doctor Cooper and under the distractions of the times King's College began to break up. It may well have occurred to Hamilton whether it was not his duty to return to the West Indies with his remaining funds. He decided that the circumstances warranted a conversion of his funds to new uses, and he applied for the command of a company of artillery which was included in the list of forces authorized by the New York Provincial Convention; was examined as to his fitness, and his commission was issued March 14, 1776. He employed the last of his funds in recruiting this company. On April 6 the treasurer of King's College was notified by a Committee of Safety that the building was needed for military purposes. The college library and other apparatus were then deposited in the City Hall, the remaining students were dispersed, and the college building was turned into an army hospital.

It is evident that Hamilton was already regarded as a youth of military promise, for Lord Stirling, who took command of the Continental forces in New York on March 6, 1776, requested Elias Boudinot to engage Hamilton for him as a member of his staff. Boudinot replied that "Mr. Hamilton had already accepted the command of artillery, and was therefore deprived of the pleasure of attending your Lordship's person as brigade major." It was a marked distinction for a youth of nineteen, but not an unusual one in those times when youths of education and intelligence were much in demand to supply staff service to the numerous militia generals.

Hamilton applied himself with characteristic thoughtfulness and diligence to drilling and exercising his company. Custis relates that in the summer of that year General Greene saw him drilling his company in the Fields (now City Hall Park) and was so impressed by his ability that he made his acquaintance, invited him to his quarters, and formed such an opinion of him that eventually he introduced him to Washington, with recommendations that bore fruit in Hamilton's appointment to Washington's staff. Hamilton's correspondence at this time attests his thoroughness in the discharge of his military duties. Several of his letters to the Provincial Congress are preserved, dealing with matters pertaining to the discipline and equipment of his company with intelligence and good judgment. The exact and cautious character of his observations is well illustrated by a communication in August, 1776, in which he recommends one of his sergeants for a commission, remarking that "he is a very good disciplinarian—possesses the advantage of having seen a good deal of service in Germany, has a tolerable share of common sense, and will not disgrace the rank of an officer and gentleman." The sergeant so recommended got his commission and made a good officer.

Hamilton's artillery company was among the forces with which Washington tried to oppose the British attack upon New York in August, 1776. Washington had a total force of 28,500 officers and men with which to oppose Howe's army of over 31,000. The American Army was composed of twenty-five regiments, recruited by order of the Continental Congress, and therefore the lineal predecessors of our present regular army, and in addition there were forty-six regiments or battalions of State militia. The militia officers had not the training or experience to look properly after their men, and there was so much sickness that on the day of the battle of Long Island Washington had only about 19,000 effectives, while Howe had over 24,000. Among Washington's troops uniforms were the exception, and most of the soldiers were dressed in citizens' clothes. For arms the troops had old flintlocks, fowling-pieces, rifles, and some good

English muskets. Lacking discipline, they of course also lacked cohesion.

In the battle, fought on August 27, the American troops were outflanked and defeated, and Lord Stirling and General Sullivan, on whose divisions the brunt of the attack fell, were both captured by the British, who took prisoner in all ninety-one American officers. Washington, who had remained in New York, uncertain where the attack would fall, hurried forward reinforcements as soon as news arrived of the British movements, and this brought Hamilton's company into the action. The American lines were crumpled up so that it was not possible to make a stand, but it appears that Hamilton's company acted as a rear-guard in the retreat, in the course of which he lost a field-piece and his baggage. One of Hamilton's chums fared even worse on that day. Lieutenant Robert Troup was one of a special patrol of five commissioned officers detailed to watch Jamaica Pass. Their watch was so poor that the whole party was surprised and captured, and thus the way was opened for the flanking movement that struck the American line unawares and produced a rout and a disorderly retreat.[1]

Washington, who possessed a mind that no calamity could stun and an energy of character that no circumstances could paralyze, exerted himself with

[1] See *Memoirs of the Long Island Historical Society*, vol. III, p. 177.

considerable success in rearranging his forces on new lines at Brooklyn. But some British men-of-war made their way into Flushing Bay and the American rear was exposed to possibilities of attack that made retreat advisable. This was so skilfully managed that the army was drawn back to New York without loss. Washington's situation was still very perilous, as his army was beginning to melt by the desertion of militia, who began to leave by groups and even whole companies. Scott's brigade, to which Hamilton's company was attached, was now posted on the East River front. Washington regarded the position as defensible if he had troops that could be depended upon. Writing to Congress on September 2, he said: "Till of late I had no doubt in my own mind of defending this place, nor should I have yet, if the men would do their duty, but this I despair of. It is painful, and extremely grating to me, to give such unfavorable accounts, but it would be criminal to conceal the truth at so critical a juncture." His best generals strongly advised evacuation of the city, and on September 12 the removal of the army to lines on Harlem Heights was begun, but was not completed by the 15th, when the British occupied the city. On that day Scott's brigade was still on the East River front, about the foot of what is now Fifteenth Street. A force of British, under cover of fire from five British frigates, made a landing in Kip's Bay, where some militia regiments were

posted.   They were seized with panic and ran away
in a manner which Washington described as "dis-
graceful and dastardly."   Scott's brigade had to
make an immediate retreat, or else it might have
been surrounded and captured.   General Putnam,
to whose division the brigade belonged, was in great
difficulties, and the escape of this division is attributed largely to the efforts of Aaron Burr, who was
one of Putnam's aides.   Burr, who knew the ground
thoroughly, led it over to the Bloomingdale road,
and after a circuitous march of about twelve miles
the division reached Harlem Heights with little loss,
to the joy of the other brigades, who had given it
up for lost.

It was on Harlem Heights that Hamilton first met
Washington, according to J. C. Hamilton, who relates that, "on the inspection of an earthwork he
was throwing up, the commander-in-chief entered
into conversation with him, invited him to his tent,
and received an impression of his military talent."
This account does not tally well with the account
given by Custis that Hamilton was recommended
to Washington by General Greene.   It is probably
an embellished version of the fact that Washington
met and talked with Hamilton in the course of his
arrangements for fortifying his lines.   In the circumstances that was almost inevitable.   But it is altogether unlikely that Washington had any time for
general conversation when he was working under

great pressure to rearrange his disheartened and demoralized forces. It was at this juncture that Washington made one of the strokes characteristic of his generalship. The British by this time thought the Colonials such easy marks that a force of about 300 had the temerity to push up to the lines, sounding bugle-calls of the sort used at a fox-hunt. Washington, who had a quick military eye, saw a chance to hearten his troops. Drawing the attention of the British by some weak skirmishing on their front, he sent out a flanking expedition which came near bagging them. As it was, they had to run and, reinforcements being thrown in by both sides, there was considerable of a battle, in which the British were beaten and had to retreat. This engagement, in which not more than 1,800 took part on the American side, became known as the battle of Harlem Heights. It was a smart affair, and Washington wrote that it "inspirited our troops prodigiously."

It is not likely that Hamilton took any part in this affair, as the brigade to which he belonged was not engaged. His work on Harlem Heights continued to be that in which Washington found him engaged, the fortification of his part of the line and careful preparation against possible attack. But no attack took place. Howe, who did his work leisurely but with professional competency, in a few weeks flanked Washington out of the Harlem Heights position by sending a force through Hell Gate to make a landing in Westchester County, threatening Washington's communications. Washington therefore moved to a new position, his right flank resting on the Bronx and his left flank on Chatterton's Hill. On October 28 the British made an attack, and, when it appeared that its chief weight would fall on the left flank, Captain Alexander Hamilton's two-gun battery was among the reinforcements sent to Chatterton's Hill. The attacking force, numbering about 4,000 men, were met by a fire before which they recoiled, but on moving up again they extended more to the left of the American position. The militia stationed there gave way, compelling a general retreat on the American side.

This affair on Chatterton's Hill is known as the battle of White Plains. On the American side not over 1,600 troops were engaged, and they inflicted severer losses than they sustained, but the effect was to cause Washington to make another masterly retreat. During the night he fell back to the heights of North Castle, occupying so strong a position that Howe decided not to attack. According to British historians, Howe concluded that Washington could not be induced to risk a decisive engagement, and that the Americans knew the country too well to be cut off, so he desisted from pursuit and turned to other operations, which were quite successful. On November 16 he attacked Fort Washington, on the Hudson, and Washington, who watched the fighting from Fort Lee, had the mortification of seeing the garrison forced to surrender. This disaster closed the campaign in the vicinity of New York, during which the American Army lost most of its artillery—218 pieces of all calibre—while 329 officers and 4,100 men were taken prisoner by the British.

Hamilton passed through all these gloomy experiences, and he and his little battery were in the remnant of the American Army that still clung to Washington's desperate fortunes. An anecdote obtained by Washington Irving from "a veteran officer of the Revolution" gives a glimpse of Hamilton in this retreat. Said this officer: "I noticed a youth, a mere stripling, small, slender, almost delicate in frame, marching beside a piece of artillery, with a cocked hat pulled down over his eyes, apparently lost in thought with his hand resting on the cannon, and every now and then patting it as he mused, as if it were a favorite horse, or a pet plaything."

One obtains another glimpse of Hamilton during this retreat through Custis's *Memoirs*. He relates that at the passage of the Raritan, near New Brunswick, Hamilton attracted the notice of the commander-in-chief, who while posted on the river bank, and contemplating with anxiety the passage of the troops, was charmed by the brilliant courage and admirable skill displayed by a young officer of artillery, who directed a battery against the enemy's advanced columns that pressed upon the Americans in their retreat by the ford. The general ordered Lieutenant-Colonel Fitzgerald, his aide-de-camp, to ascertain who this young officer was, and bid him repair to headquarters at the first halt of the army. According to Custis, who was so situated that he might have received the information from Washington's own lips, the personal regard of Washington for Hamilton dated from that incident.

From New Brunswick the American troops retreated by the road passing through Princeton. J. C. Hamilton quotes "a friend" as saying: "Well do I remember the day when Hamilton's company marched into Princeton. It was a model of discipline; at their head a boy, and I wondered at his youth; but what was my surprise when struck with his slight figure, he was pointed out to me as that Hamilton of whom we had already heard so much."

In the course of this campaign Washington adhered to his Fabian tactics, avoiding a general engagement and watchful of opportunity to make sudden counter-strokes. His great exploit was the surprise of the Hessians at Trenton, during their Christmas festivities, followed up by the battle of Princeton. Hamilton took part in these affairs, in which his company sustained losses reducing its strength to about thirty men. This force was among the fragments of the original army which still remained with Washington when he established his winter quarters at Morristown, early in January, 1777. During that winter Hamilton became one of Washington's secretaries, and on March 1, 1777, he was formally appointed an aide-de-camp, with the rank of lieutenant-colonel. Hamilton sent notice of this event to the New York Convention, advising them of the appointment, and asking instructions as to what should be done with the remnant of the company, suggesting that "the Continent will readily take it off your hands." The Convention replied that "it is determined to permit that company to join the Continental Army, for which you will take the necessary steps." This event closed Hamilton's service in the State militia and marked the beginning of his distinctly national career.

In taking up arms in the service of the American colonies Hamilton did not sever his relations with his West Indian relatives and friends. On February 14, 1777, he wrote to the Reverend Hugh Knox, at St. Croix, what Knox characterized as a "very circumstantial and satisfactory letter." It appears from Knox's reply, which has been preserved, that in this letter Hamilton mentioned his appointment on Washington's staff. Knox wrote that Hamilton's account of his services and advancement "has given high satisfaction to all friends here." The good clergyman was himself overjoyed. "Mark this!" he wrote; "you must be the Annalist and Biographer, as well as the Aide-de-Camp, of General Washington and the Historiographer of the AMERICAN WAR!" Mr. Knox pressed this point, saying: "This may be a new and strange thought to you: but if you survive the present trouble, *I aver*—few men will be as well qualified to write the history of the present glorious struggle. God only knows how it will terminate. But however that may be, it will be a most interesting story."

This letter, from the clergyman under whom Hamilton began his studies, is important in several ways. It testifies to the high opinion of Hamilton's abilities among those who had known him from his infancy. It shows that the sympathy of the West Indian set to which Hamilton belonged was strongly on the side that Hamilton had espoused, so that Hamilton's action was no severance of old ties. Mr. Knox expressed the hope that he would "justify the choice, and merit the approbation, of the *great and good General Washington*—a name which will shine with distinguished lustre in the annals of history—a name dear to the friends of the Liberties of Mankind!" When it is considered that Hamilton's letter must have borne a tale of disaster, it is evident that the clergyman's ardor in the American cause must have been deep and strong to express itself in such a way at such a time. It is a great pity that Hamilton's letter to which this was a reply has never been recovered. It would doubtless have supplied an exact account of Hamilton's activities in America up to the beginning of his personal association with General Washington.

CHAPTER V

AT HEADQUARTERS

HAMILTON's reports made in closing his connection with the State militia mention sickness as having caused delay in submitting them. A letter from a Provincial committee, dated April 2, 1777, says that they are sorry to hear of his "indisposition." The letter from Mr. Knox of April 21, 1777, congratulates Hamilton upon his "recovery from a long and dangerous illness." It also appears that General Washington was ill about the same time. A letter of Gouverneur Morris, March 26, 1777, refers to the "universal joy" it caused "to hear of the General's recovery."

When Hamilton was appointed aide-de-camp he had just turned twenty, while Washington had just turned forty-five. The physical contrast between them was very marked. Washington was six feet two inches tall, with unusually large limbs. Hamilton was only about five feet seven, just the height of Napoleon Bonaparte. His hair—a lock of which I have examined—was sandy red, and authentic accounts leave no doubt that his complexion was of the ruddy Scottish type. William Sullivan, a Massachusetts Federalist lawyer, politician, and historian, gave this account of Hamilton's appearance as a guest at a dinner-party in December, 1795: "He was under middle size, thin in person, but remarkably erect and dignified in his deportment. His hair was turned back from his forehead, powdered and collected in a club behind. His complexion was exceedingly fair, and varying from this only by the almost feminine rosiness of his cheeks. His might be considered, as to figure and color, an uncommonly handsome face. When at rest, it had a rather severe and thoughtful expression; but when engaged in conversation, it easily assumed an attractive smile. He was dressed in a blue coat with bright buttons; the skirts of his coat were unusually long. He wore a white waistcoat, black silk small clothes, white silk stockings. The gentleman, who received him as a guest, introduced him to such of the company as were strangers to him; to each he made a formal bow, bending very low, the ceremony of shaking hands not being observed."

This description of Hamilton's looks and bearing at the age of thirty-eight will do quite well for him at the age of twenty, for his sense of personal dignity was as strongly marked then.

Timothy Pickering, who was Washington's adjutant-general in 1777, said that Washington was then unhandy with his pen. "When I first became acquainted with the General," Pickering related, "his writing was defective in grammar, and even in spelling, owing to the insufficiency of his early education; of which, however, he gradually got the better in the subsequent years of his life, by the official perusal of some excellent models, particularly those of Hamilton; by writing with care and patient attention; and reading numerous, indeed multitudes of, letters to and from his friends and correspondents."

The year in which Pickering first became acquainted with Washington was the same year in which Hamilton was appointed aide-de-camp, so it exhibits Washington as he was when Hamilton's service began. Washington had difficulty in getting a military secretary to his liking, or else found it hard to retain an aide-de-camp assigned to that function. The duties were heavy and multifarious, for, in addition to directing the army under his immediate command, Washington was charged with a general supervision of military arrangements. What government there was was an improvised thing without proper organs, and he was expected to act as a sort of secretary of war without means for executing that office. A view of the difficulties into which he was plunged is afforded by a letter of April 23, 1776, from Washington to Congress: "I give in to no kind of amusement myself, and consequently those about me can have none, but are confined from morning till evening, hearing and answering the applications and letters of one and another, which will now, I expect, receive a considerable addition, as the business of the northern and eastern departments, if I continue here, must, I suppose, pass through my hands. If these gentlemen had the same relaxation from duty as other officers have in their common routine, there would not be so much in it. But to have the mind always upon the stretch, scarce ever unbent, and no hours for recreation, makes a material odds. Knowing this, and at the same time how inadequate the pay is, I can scarce find inclination to impose the necessary duties of their office upon them."

From the account Pickering gives of the battle of the Brandywine, September 11, 1777, it appears that Robert H. Harrison of Maryland was then serving as military secretary, although Hamilton's staff appointment took effect the previous March. At this time Hamilton's staff duties were not so confining but that he could take part in expeditions of a skirmishing character. On September 18 he went with a small party of horse to destroy some stocks of flour in some mills on the Schuylkill, which the British were likely to seize. Hamilton took the precaution of securing a flat-bottomed boat in case a sudden retreat should be necessary. It turned out to be a wise arrangement, as the British were at hand, and as Hamilton and his men rowed across the river they were fired upon, "by which means," wrote Hamilton, "I lost my horse—one man was killed and another wounded." That Hamilton kept his wits about him in this exciting situation is shown by the fact that he at once dispatched a message to John Hancock, President of Congress, saying: "If Congress have not left Philadelphia they ought to do it immediately without fail." The same night he sent another message to the same effect, calling attention to the advance of the British, and remarking: "This renders the situation of Congress extremely precarious, if they are not on their guard." The effect of this warning, in which Hamilton acted on his own judgment, was to cause Congress to adjourn to Lancaster, about sixty miles west of Philadelphia. Hamilton himself went to Philadelphia to bring off all the supplies he could before the British arrived, and on the 22d he sent another report to President Hancock, at Lancaster, saying that "every appearance justified the supposition" that the enemy was about to cross the river to the Philadelphia side. As it turned out, the British occupation of Philadelphia took place on September 26.

The indications are that it was not until after this affair that Hamilton attained the position of intimacy and influence with Washington he certainly occupied before the year was out. Washington found in him a secretary always apt and ready, clear-headed and well informed. In addition to his intellectual qualifications, Hamilton possessed an advantage which he probably owed to his commercial training. His handwriting was beautifully distinct and legible. His original papers preserved in the Library of Congress are, in sheer mechanics, on a level with the work of a professional engrossing clerk. It was inevitable that having found such a treasure Washington would make steady use of it, and it is evident that he got into the habit of trusting much to Hamilton's ability and good judgment.

Custis gives an intimate account of scenes at headquarters. Washington was attended throughout the war by his body-servant, Will Lee, a stout, active negro who was a famous horseman. Billy, as everybody called him, always slept in call of his master. It was Washington's practice to turn over in his mind every morning the business to be attended to during the day, and sometimes he would lie on his couch thinking over matters after his aides had been dismissed for the night. When dispatches arrived, or when he had reached some conclusion requiring immediate action, the word would go to Billy: "Call Colonel Hamilton."

It is noticeable that after Hamilton took charge complaints of clerical difficulties cease to appear in Washington's familiar letters. It is also a plain inference that Hamilton was able to organize and systematize the work so that he himself was not engulfed by it, for from time to time he was employed by Washington on important missions. Washington's own letters certify this fact. When the news of Burgoyne's surrender reached Washington, October, 1777, he sent Hamilton to confer with General Gates, bearing a letter saying: "Our affairs having happily terminated at the northward, I have, by the advice of my general officers, sent Colonel Hamilton, one of my aides, to lay before you a full state of our situation. . . . From Colonel Hamilton you will have a clear and comprehensive view of things, and I persuade myself you will do all in your power to facilitate the objects I have in contemplation." This was certainly an important trust to confide to a youth of twenty. Although necessarily occupied most of the time by staff duties, it appears that Hamilton was eager to be where the fighting was going on. Custis relates an incident of the battle of Monmouth, June 28, 1778, which has doubtless received some melodramatic color in its transmission, but the main facts are quite in keeping with the characteristics both of Hamilton and Washington. The behavior of General Lee had upset Washington's plans and left the army exposed to great peril. Washington was so incensed that he called Lee to his face "a damned poltroon." Lafayette, who was present, says it was the only time he "ever heard General Washington swear." Hamilton leaped from his horse and, drawing his sword, said: "We are betrayed; your Excellency and the army are betrayed, and the moment has arrived when every true friend of America and her cause must be ready to die in their defence." Hamilton was not in the habit of using such stilted language, but that he suspected treachery and sprang to meet it is quite probable. Washington's part in this anecdote bears the stamp of authenticity, both as to words and action. "Pointing to the Colonel's horse that was cropping the herbage, Washington calmly observed, 'Colonel Hamilton, you will take your horse.'"

One outcome of the discussion over General Lee's behavior was a duel between him and Colonel Laurens, in which Hamilton acted as Laurens's second, and Major Edwards acted for Lee. It appears from a statement drawn up by the seconds that the immediate occasion of the duel was that "General Lee had spoken of General Washington in the grossest and most opprobrious terms of personal abuse, which Colonel Laurens thought himself bound to resent, as well on account of the relation he bore to General Washington as from motives of personal friendship and respect for his character." Laurens was one of Washington's aides-de-camp. The duel took place on Christmas Eve, 1778, and was fought with pistols, each advancing and firing when he saw fit. Lee was slightly wounded in the right side at the first discharge. He demanded another exchange of shots, but the seconds intervened and decided that the affair should end where it was. Lee, while insisting upon his right to criticise Washington's military abilities, disavowed any intention of reflecting upon Washington's character as a man, and denied ever having spoken of him in terms of personal abuse. Hamilton and Edwards made a minute of the affair, in which they conclude: "Upon the whole, we think it a piece of justice to the two gentlemen to declare, that after they met, their conduct was strongly marked with all the politeness, generosity, coolness and firmness, that ought to characterize a transaction of this nature."

In this year Hamilton came of age, and there are strong evidences of his increasing usefulness to Washington. He was picked out for services requiring shrewdness and good judgment as well as intrepidity. He is a prominent figure in all of Washington's dealings with Congress and with other commanders, and always acquitted himself with credit. His prominence, of course, attracted the malice of the Tories. One of their prints in 1779 contained the report: "It is said little Hamilton, the poet and composer to the Lord Protector, Mr. Washington, is engaged upon a literary work which is intended to give posterity a true estimate of the present rebellion and its supporters, in case Clinton's light bobs should extirpate the whole race of rebels this campaign." An item published in 1780 says that "Mrs. Washington has a mottled tom-cat (which she calls in a complimentary way, 'Hamilton,') with thirteen yellow rings around his tail, and that his flaunting it suggested to the Congress the adoption of the same number of stripes for the rebel flag."

So long as communications were possible Hamilton tried to keep in touch with his friends at St. Croix by letters to Mr. Knox. There is no better explanation of Washington's strategy than Hamilton gave in a letter recounting the disasters of 1777. He prepared his West Indian friends for more bad news by admitting American inability to stand against British troops, but went on to say: "It may be asked, if, to avoid a general engagement, we give up objects of the first importance, what is to hinder the enemy from carrying every important point and ruining us? My answer is, that our hopes are not placed in any particular city or spot of ground, but in the preserving a good army, furnished with proper necessaries, to take advantage of favorable opportunities, and waste and defeat the enemy by piecemeal. Every new post they take, requires a new division of their forces, and enables us to strike with our united force against a part of theirs." This outlines the policy that was in the end successful.

CHAPTER VI

THE CONDUCT OF THE WAR

THE influences that shaped Hamilton's career and energized his activities as a statesman cannot be appreciated without taking into account the characteristics of the struggle as they were revealed in actual experience. The men who led the movement for armed resistance to British policy were well aware that this would cause a dissolution of public order that would bring in a train of miseries. But they thought that civil war, with all its risks, was preferable to the surrender of constitutional rights through submission to the jurisdiction of the British Parliament over the colonies in the matter of taxation. Nevertheless, they felt keenly and much deplored the turbulence and anarchy produced by the disorders of the times. It has been noted that Hamilton, while still at college, observed this tendency, analyzed its nature, and urged upon John Jay the necessity of stationing troops in New York to keep order. A diary kept by the Reverend Mr. Shewkirk, pastor of the Moravian Church, New York, has this entry, June 13, 1776: "Here in town very unhappy and shocking scenes were exhibited. On Monday night some men called Tories were carried and hauled about through the streets, with candles forced to be held by them, or pushed in their faces, and their heads burned; but on Wednesday, in the open day, the scene was by far worse; several, and among them gentlemen, were carried on rails; some stripped naked and dreadfully abused."

Hamilton's orderly mind detested such ruffianism, of which there were many instances. Alexander Graydon's *Memoirs* describes "the fashion of tarring, feathering, and carting" inflicted upon the Tories. One of the victims was Isaac Hunt, then a lawyer but subsequently a clergyman with a charge in Barbados. He became the father of Leigh Hunt, the English poet, essayist, and journalist. Graydon mentions that, when Doctor Kearsley, a prominent citizen of Philadelphia, was carted because of his Tory opinions, he "was seized at his own door by a party of the militia, and in the attempt to resist them received a wound in his hand from a bayonet." Militia of this class were the very kind whose liability to panic and precipitate retreat was the continual source of military disaster.

Graydon is a trustworthy witness. He was twenty-three when the Revolutionary War began, and on January 6, 1776, he was commissioned captain in a Pennsylvania regiment. He was well educated, a lawyer by profession, and he went into the war with just such patriotic motives as had actuated Hamilton, whom Graydon greatly admired. Graydon relates that when he joined the army in New

York it was characterized by "irregularity, want of discipline, bad arms, and defective equipment in all respects." Among the "miserably constituted bands from New England" the only force deserving respect was a Marblehead regiment under John Glover. Graydon was informed that "it was no unusual thing in the army before Boston, for a colonel to make drummers and fifers of his sons, thereby, not only being enabled to form a very snug, economical mess, but to aid also considerably the revenue to the family chest." Graydon, who had been much impressed with New England valor by the accounts that reached him of Bunker Hill, was puzzled to account for the poor quality of the New England troops, and particularly the absence of gentry among them. "There were some, indeed, in the higher ranks, and here and there a man of decent breeding, in the capacity of an aide-de-camp or a brigade major; but anything above the condition of a clown, in the regiments we came in contact with, was a rarity." But conditions were not much better in the militia from other provinces. Graydon relates that the colonel of his own regiment obtained leave of absence to visit his family and never returned. Graydon himself and some other officers were tempted to follow "his illaudable example," so disgusted were they with the jobbery of the Provincial Council, who "went on in the manufacture of majors and colonels, in utter disregard of the claims of the officers in service, and sometimes of the coarsest materials." At the time when Washington was with the remnant of his army at Morristown suffering from lack of men and supplies, Graydon notes that "captains, majors, and colonels had become 'good cheap' in the land; but unfortunately, those war functionaries were not found at the head of their men; they generally figured as bar-keepers, condescendingly serving out small measures of liquor to their less dignified customers."

It might be supposed that this account could be explained away as an explosion of spleen, but the case is put as strongly by other observers. When Baron de Kalb joined the army he was astonished to find that the blacksmith attached to his troop held a captain's commission. The Reverend Jacob Duché, chaplain of Congress, in a letter to Washington, October 16, 1777, remarked: "As to the army itself, what have you to expect from them? Have they not frequently abandoned even yourself in the hour of extremity? Have you, can you have, the least confidence in a set of undisciplined men and officers, many of whom have been taken from the lowest of the people, without principle and without courage? Take away those that surround your person, how few are there that you can ask to sit at your table!"

Washington's own opinion did not greatly differ from this, as many expressions in his letters attest.

Writing under date of February 10, 1776, of the army he commanded before Boston, he remarked: "To be plain, these people are not to be depended upon if exposed"; but he added: "I do not apply this only to these people. I suppose it to be the case with all raw and undisciplined troops." Writing soon after the engagements at Trenton and Princeton, the most creditable affairs of the New Jersey campaign, he said of the militia: "I am sure they never can be brought fairly up to an attack in any serious affair."

In a letter written in 1780 Hamilton gave this account of the condition of the army: "It is now a mob, rather than an army; without clothing, without pay, without provision, without morals, without discipline. We begin to hate the country for its neglect of us. The country begins to hate us for our oppressions of them."

The Chevalier de la Luzerne, who was sent to the United States by the French Government to view the situation, reported April 16, 1780: "It is difficult to form a just conception of the depredations which have been committed in the management of war supplies—forage, clothing, hospitals, tents, quarters, and transportation. About nine thousand men employed in this service, received enormous salaries and devoured the subsistence of the army, while it was tormented with hunger and the extremes of want."

The Congressional politicians had constantly in mind what happened to the English Parliament after they had allowed Oliver Cromwell to create a disciplined army. John Adams, the chairman of the War Board of Congress, was a timid man. When news came of the approach of the British to Philadelphia from the southwest he rode northeast as far as Trenton, in his panic-stricken rush to get as far away as possible, before directing his course to Lancaster, where Congress was to reassemble, making his way thither through Bethlehem—a route so circuitous that it more than doubled the length of his journey. But there was no risk so great to his mind as allowing a regular army to be formed. Adams's adherence to the principle of the casual levies for short terms was so deeply resented by Hamilton that it was a leading count of his famous indictment of Adams over twenty years later.

In addition to being an inefficient body, the Continental Congress was a corrupt and extravagant body. Officers' commissions were treated as a patronage fund in which members felt bound to secure equitable allotments. In addition to costly profusion there was favoritism so gross that Washington had sometimes to protest. The favor of a member of Congress might be a more potent source of advancement than brave and capable service in the field. The immediate cause of Arnold's treason was the neglect of his claims in favor of much less deserving officers who had political influence. In such respects, however, the Continental Congress was quite true to type. Government by an assembly has been everywhere and always corrupt, extravagant, and inefficient government. The only constitutional function that an assembly can properly discharge is to serve as a control over the government in behalf of the people, but the integrity of this function can be secured only by shutting it out from any participation in appointments to office or disbursement of public funds. Then and only then will it hold to strict accountability the administrative officers who do make appointments and disbursements. But this is representative government of the modern type, still rare in practice; in the eighteenth century it was unknown. Most of the assemblies that had existed in Europe had been abolished as intolerable impediments to efficient government. Those that still survived bore the feudal pattern of class interest and partitioned sovereignty, and even in England, where the representative type was eventually developed, it was still inchoate in form and unrecognized in its essential character. In its general characteristics the Continental Congress was like the Commonwealth Parliament that Cromwell turned out of doors; but suggestions made to Washington that he ought to do likewise were indignantly rejected by that loyal Virginian gentleman.

The Continental Congress was probably no more addicted to corruption than is usually the case with assemblies of its type, but there is evidence that rapid deterioration took place. It was referred to in the Reverend Jacob Duché's letter already mentioned. He said to Washington: "The most respectable characters have withdrawn themselves, and are succeeded by a great majority of illiberal and violent men. Your feelings must be greatly hurt by the representation from your native province. . . . As to those of my own province, some of them are so obscure that their very names never met my ears before, and others have only been distinguished for the weakness of their understandings and the violence of their tempers. . . . From the New England provinces can you find one that as a gentleman you could wish to associate with? unless the soft and mild address of Mr. Hancock can atone for his want of every other qualification necessary for the station he fills. Bankrupts, attorneys, and men of desperate futures are his colleagues."

This estimate of the character of Congress, made by the clergyman who was then acting as its chaplain, is corroborated by a letter written by Henry Laurens, who succeeded Hancock as president of Congress. A letter he wrote in the summer of 1778, in which he referred to "scenes of venality, peculation and fraud" in Congress, was intercepted by the British and published to discredit the American cause.

Although Congress was probably no more corrupt than the Commonwealth Parliament in England, yet, so far as there is material for comparison, it is to be inferred that it was much more fond of extravagant display. The Puritan composition of the Commonwealth Parliament kept down the showy vices. Congress seemed to revel in display. The men of whom it was originally composed included provincial magnates who lived in a lavish way themselves and regarded that as a proper incident of high station. The standard they set up was imitated by others at the public expense, in all branches of the civil government. An instructive document of the times is a bill for the entertainment given, December 1, 1778, in honor of the election of Joseph Reed as president of the Pennsylvania Council. The bill, contracted at a time when the army lacked food and clothing, amounted to £2,295 15s. It included such items as "116 large bowls of punch," "2 tubs of grog for artillery soldiers," "1 gallon spirits for bell ringers," "96 wine glasses broke," "5 decanters broke." [1] The festivities about Congress were never greater than during the darkest period of the American cause. Washington wrote that "party disputes and personal quarrels are the great business of the day, whilst the momentous concerns of an empire, a great and accumulating debt, ruined finances, depreciated money, and want of credit,

---

[1] The itemized account is given in A. S. Bolles's *Pennsylvania, Province and State*, vol. II, p. 45.

which in its consequences is the want of everything, are but secondary considerations and postponed from day to day and from week to week, as if our affairs wore the most promising aspect. . . . And yet an assembly, a concert, a dinner or a supper, will not only take men off from acting in this business, but even from thinking of it."

In his personal correspondence Hamilton sharply criticised the character of Congress. Writing to Governor Clinton, February 13, 1778, he said: "Many members of it are, no doubt, men in every respect fit for the trust, but this cannot be said of it as a body. Folly, caprice, a want of foresight, comprehension and dignity, comprise the general tenor of their action." Hamilton was so indignant with the behavior of a member of Congress that he twice assailed him in the public press, over the signature "Publius," which later he used for his *Federalist* articles. He prefaced his attacks by a letter to the printer of the New York *Journal*, in which he said that "when a man appointed to be the guardian of the State and the depositary of the happiness and morals of the people, forgetful of the solemn relation in which he stands, descends to the dishonest artifices of a mercantile projector, and sacrifices his conscience and his trust to pecuniary motives, there is no strain of abhorrence of which the human mind is capable, no punishment the vengeance of the people can inflict, which may not be applied to

him with justice." Two articles followed in which
the member of Congress was told that he had shown
that "America can already boast of at least one
public character as abandoned as any history of
past or present times can produce." The man
Hamilton thus censured was a signer of the Declaration of Independence, Samuel Chase of Maryland.
The particular charge against him was that, when
General Wadsworth, the commissary-general, was
arranging for purchases of flour, Chase delayed
action by the committee of Congress, meanwhile
forming "connections for monopolizing that article,
and raising the price upon the public more than one
hundred per cent." Hamilton denounced this proceeding as "an infamous traffic," and he characterized Chase as a man in whom love of money and
love of power predominated, and who was content
with the merit of possessing qualities useful only to
himself. The affair made a great stir at the time,
but the charge did not prevent Chase from arriving
at eminence in Maryland, and in 1796 he was appointed a justice of the Supreme Court of the United
States, from which office an ineffectual effort was
made to remove him by impeachment.

Hamilton's term of service as Washington's military secretary covered the period when the mal-
administration was at its worst. Drafts of the most
important reports made to Congress by Washington
on general conditions exist among the Hamilton

papers in his handwriting. Among those is the long report of January 28, 1778, on the reorganization of the army, addressed by Washington to the committee of Congress that visited the camp at Valley Forge; the report on the organization of the office of inspector-general, May 5, 1778, and also the actual plan as adopted by Congress, February 18, 1779; also, a number of reports on military discipline. He who prepares the reports of another person is in a position to influence that person's views and policy, and there is evidence that Hamilton wielded such influence. John Laurens, one of Washington's aides, was sent on a mission to France in 1781 to obtain aid in money and supplies. His instructions are all in the handwriting of Hamilton, with the exception of the four closing lines, which are in the handwriting of Washington. This document bears distinctly the marks of Hamilton's style and gives expression to his characteristic ideas on government. Hamilton's personal authorship is distinctly set forth in a comprehensive draft of military regulations which Hamilton proposed, "submitting to his Excellency the Commander-in-chief, to distinguish such as may be published under his own authority in General orders, and such as will require the sanction and authority of the Committee of Congress."

In a report to Congress on the military situation, August 20, 1780, Washington made a stern indict-

ment of the policy to which Congress had obsti-
nately adhered. This report, which defines issues
on which Congress has been at variance with expert
authority in every national crisis down to our own
times, bears the marks of Hamilton's composition in
every line. It declares that "to attempt to carry
on the war with militia against disciplined troops
would be to attempt what the common sense and
common experience of mankind will pronounce impracticable." The practice of short enlistments is
characterized as "pernicious beyond description,"
and a draft for three years or the length of the war
is declared to be the only effectual method. Then
followed this eloquent passage:

Had we formed a permanent army in the beginning,
which, by the continuance of the same men in service,
had been capable of discipline, we never should have had
to retreat with a handful of men across the Delaware in
1776, trembling for the fate of America, which nothing
but the infatuation of the enemy could have saved; we
should not have remained all the succeeding winter at
their mercy, with sometimes scarcely a sufficient body of
men to mount the ordinary guards, liable at every moment
to be dissipated, if they had only thought proper to march
against us; we should not have been under the necessity
of fighting at Brandywine, with an unequal number of
raw troops, and afterwards of seeing Philadelphia fall a
prey to a victorious army; we should not have been at
Valley Forge with less than half the force of the enemy,
destitute of everything, in a situation neither to resist nor

to retire; we should not have seen New York left with a handful of men, yet an overmatch for the main army of these States, while the principal part of their force was detached for the reduction of two of them; we should not have found ourselves this Spring so weak, as to be insulted by five thousand men, unable to protect our baggage and magazines, their security depending on a good countenance, and a want of enterprise in the enemy; we should not have been the greatest part of the war inferior to the enemy, indebted for our safety to their inactivity, enduring frequently the mortification of seeing inviting opportunities to ruin them pass unimproved for want of a force, which the country was completely able to afford; to see the country ravaged, our towns burnt, the inhabitants plundered, abused, murdered with impunity from the same cause.

Nor have the ill effects been confined to the military line. A great part of the embarrassments in the civil departments flow from the same source. The derangement of our finances is essentially to be ascribed to it. The expenses of the war, and the paper emissions have been greatly multiplied by it. We have had, a great part of the time, two sets of men to feed and pay, the discharged men going home and the levies coming in. . . . Our officers are reduced to the disagreeable necessity of performing the duties of drill sergeants to them, and with this mortifying reflection annexed to the business, that by the time they have taught those men the rudiments of a soldier's duty, their term of service will have expired, and the work is to recommence with an entire new set. The consumption of provision, arms, accoutrements, stores of every kind, has been doubled in spite of every precaution I could use, not only from the cause just mentioned, but from the carelessness and licentiousness incident to militia and irregular troops.   Our discipline also has been much injured, if not ruined, by such constant changes.   The frequent calls upon the militia have interrupted the cultivation of the land, and of course have lessened the quantity of its produce, occasioned a scarcity, and enhanced the prices.   In an army so unstable as ours, order and economy have been impracticable. . . .

There is every reason to believe the war has been protracted on this account.   Our opposition being less, made the successes of the enemy greater.   The fluctuation of the army kept alive their hopes, and at every period of the dissolution of a considerable part of it, they have flattered themselves with some decisive advantages.   Had we kept a permanent army on foot, the enemy could have had nothing to hope for, and would in all probability have listened to terms long since. . . .   It is an old maxim, that the surest way to make a good peace is to be well prepared for war.

It was while undergoing such experiences that Hamilton began to form the plans which he eventually applied to the organization of public authority.

CHAPTER VII

FIRST ESSAYS IN STATESMANSHIP

ABOUT the time that Hamilton became an aide to Washington, he was asked to correspond with the New York Convention through a committee, then composed of Gouverneur Morris, Robert Livingston, and William Allison. In a letter of March 20, 1777, he gave his understanding of the arrangement as being that, so far as his leisure would permit and his duty warrant, he should "communicate such pieces of intelligence as shall be received, and such comments upon them as shall appear necessary to convey a true idea of what is going on in the military line." That the Convention should have thought it important to establish such relations with a youth of twenty, might easily be construed as evidence of the deep impression already made by Hamilton's personality upon the public men with whom he was brought in contact; but a more probable opinion is that at the outset the arrangement was the expression of provincial solicitude, not to say jealousy, about transactions to which the State was a party and which yet lay beyond the bounds of State authority. The particularist spirit was then the strongest force in American politics, and, although yielding much to the military necessities of the situation, it did so reluctantly and with large reserve.

The result of this arrangement was a series of reports from Hamilton on the progress of the campaign and the prospects of the American cause, showing such clear vision and sound judgment that his reputation as a publicist, started by his early pamphlets, was confirmed, extended, and permanently established. General recognition of Hamilton's position among the leading men of New York dates from this period. The hospitality which Hamilton had received on arriving in New York was no more than was then readily extended to any visitor who had the dress and manners of polite society. Its significance of individual value was slight. But the position he speedily acquired after becoming the correspondent of the New York Convention was decidedly that of individual distinction. In a few months leading men were consulting him about the form of government to be adopted in New York. In May, 1777, Gouverneur Morris sent a pamphlet describing the scheme he proposed. In reply Hamilton remarked that while considering it "in the main as a wise and excellent system, I freely confess it appears to me to have some faults." There is no indication that Morris regarded this as a presumptuous attitude for a youth of twenty to take. Morris argued the case, defending the partitions of authority and system of checks he proposed on the usual ground of the caprice and instability of the mass of the people. Hamilton's comment is surprising in its discernment of the principles upon which democratic government may be and has been safely established. He observed: "That instability is inherent in the nature of popular governments I think very disputable; unstable democracy is an epithet frequently in the mouths of politicians, but I believe that from a strict examination of the matter—from the records of history, it will be found that the fluctuations of governments in which the popular principle has borne a considerable sway, have proceeded from its being compounded with other principles; and from its being made to operate in an improper channel. Compound governments, though they may be harmonious in the beginning, will introduce distinct interests, and these interests will clash, throw the State into convulsions, and produce a change or dissolution. When the deliberative or judicial powers are vested wholly or partly in the collective body of the people, you must expect error, confusion, and instability. But a representative democracy, where the right of election is well secured and regulated, and the exercise of the legislative, executive, and judiciary authorities is vested in select persons, chosen really and not nominally by the people, will, in my opinion, be most likely to be happy, regular and durable."

This judgment, now so abundantly vindicated by

the experience of Switzerland, Australia, New Zealand, Canada, and even little Barbados, with its negro electorate, under a simple form of representative democracy, as contrasted with the results of the compound government adopted by American States, displays a prescience that, for the period, is simply amazing. At that time the prevailing opinion in Europe was that absolutism had been the form of government most successful in preserving public order, whereas all other forms that had been tried had failed on that essential point. Although in England the actual form precluded absolutism, so acute and dispassionate a thinker as Hume held that "we shall at last, after many convulsions and civil wars, find repose in absolute monarchy, which it would have been happier for us to have established peaceably from the beginning." At a time when Hamilton was imbibing political ideas in his boyhood in the West Indies, Oliver Goldsmith was describing republics as places "where the laws govern the poor and the rich govern the laws," and was contending that every diminution of the power of the sovereign was "an infringement upon the real liberties of the subject." The concept of representative democracy, guarded against abuse of power, not by partition or limitation of authority but by exact accountability and full responsibility for every act of power, was quite unknown at the time Hamilton wrote. The plebeianizing of authority had begun in New England, through the town-meeting system which Congregationalism had extracted from mediæval parish arrangements, but nowhere was democracy in greater disrepute. John Adams's voluminous writings on politics are a continual dirge on the iniquity of democracy. Compound government, giving the people a slice of power but conferring the real control upon magisterial authority, was the most extreme concession thought to be practicable.

Hamilton's views had no effect upon the character of the State constitution adopted by New York in 1777. Indeed, his ideas had not then been put into systematic form, but were expressed merely in the way of dissent from the principles upon which the scheme of a State constitution was framed. However, the processes of his thought had already begun which eventually found practical expression in the organization of national authority. The ideas which he eventually put into practical effect, in his work as Secretary of the Treasury, were first stated in papers prepared while in winter quarters at Morristown in 1779–80. The first of these, the extant draft of which is undated, affords internal evidence that it was written about November, 1779. It is in the form of a letter, addressed to a member of Congress who is not mentioned by name. J. C. Hamilton, in his biography, says that it was sent "to Robert Morris, then a delegate from Pennsylvania to Congress," and this statement has been generally accepted by subsequent biographers. But Robert Morris was not at that time a member of Congress, his term having expired November 1, 1778. And if the letter was to Robert Morris, why was it sent anonymously? Hamilton was then on easy terms with Morris, but the letter says that, "though the writer has reasons which make him unwilling to be known, if a personal conference with him should be thought material he will endeavor to comply"; and that he may be communicated with by letter "directed to James Montague, Esquire, lodged in the Post Office at Morristown." It was not Hamilton's wont to be so shy, nor is there any other mark of such a feeling in his correspondence at this period.

It is at least a plausible conjecture that this letter was addressed to Major-General John Sullivan, then a member of Congress from New Hampshire. He commanded a division at Trenton, Brandywine, and Germantown, and in military rank Hamilton was much his inferior. This would account for the cautious approach made by Hamilton. Certain it is that Sullivan received such a deep impression of Hamilton's ability as a financier that he thought of having Hamilton appointed to the position of superintendent of finance, and wrote to Washington about it. If Hamilton's letter was to Sullivan and was followed by personal interviews, that would explain Sullivan's behavior, which otherwise seems unaccountable. The letter discussed the means of establishing a national bank, and it is the earliest known American project of that character. As it turned out, nothing came of Sullivan's proceedings. In February, 1781, he wrote to Washington: "I found the eyes of Congress turned upon Robert Morris as financier. I did not therefore nominate Colonel Hamilton, as I foresaw it would be a vain attempt."

Hamilton himself had strongly recommended Morris for that post, and when some difficulties occurred between Morris and Congress as to the extent of his authority Hamilton addressed to him the most earnest plea in favor of his retention of the office. "I know of no other in America," he said, "who unites so many advantages; and of course every impediment to your acceptance is to me a subject of chagrin. I flatter myself Congress will not preclude the public from your services by an obstinate refusal of reasonable conditions; and, as one deeply interested in the event, I am happy in believing you will not easily be discouraged from undertaking an office, by which you may render America, and the world, no less a service than the establishment of American independence! 'Tis by introducing order into our finances—by restoring public credit—not by gaining battles, that we are finally to gain our object."

This letter bears date of April 30, 1781, at which time Hamilton had not long turned twenty-four. Thus it appears that he had already adopted the economic criterion of political values, which was the guiding principle of his statesmanship. The letter does not merely urge Morris to face irksome responsibilities; it goes on to discuss the ways and means. "In expectation that all difficulties will be removed," he remarked, "I take the liberty to submit to you some ideas relative to the objects of your department." He proceeds at a length of over 14,000 words to offer what is, in fact, a systematic treatise on public finance, from the standpoint of American needs and interests, strongly recommending "the institution of a *National Bank*," for which he offers detailed plans digested into twenty articles, each of which is accompanied by explanatory remarks.

At that time Robert Morris was forty-seven years old. In twenty years of successful activity as a Philadelphia merchant he had gained a competence and was more desirous of taking his ease than of increasing his engagements. But his position and ability kept attracting public employment, and wherever he was management of financial arrangements seemed to drift naturally to him, not so much by express assignment as on the principle that the willing horse draws the load. Although he was elected Superintendent of Finance on February 20, 1781, he was loath to accept the troublesome office and Hamilton's advice and suggestions can hardly have failed to influence his decision. He did not shrink from responsibility, but, like every man of his calibre, he detested ignorant and incompetent interference. The idea with which the Congressional politicians started out was apparently that it would be the function of the superintendent to be a sort of managing clerk acting under a committee of Congress. Morris properly insisted that "the appointment of all persons who are to act in my office, under the same roof, or in immediate connection with me, should be made by myself," after agreement with Congress as to their number and their pay. He also was firm on the point that he should have an absolute power of dismissal. Congress, always more intent upon its patronage than anything else, was very reluctant to grant these reasonable demands, but at last grudgingly yielded, and on May 14 Morris formally accepted his appointment. In all these matters Hamilton's influence was steadily exerted in Morris's favor.

Hamilton's scheme of a national bank, as then drawn up, has been criticised by experts as containing some of the financial fallacies of the age. The treatise supplies internal evidence that it was based upon study of European models, and it is stamped with the ideas of the times. As Professor Sumner has justly observed: "It is the statesmanship of it that is grand; not the finance."

The quality of his statesmanship had already been more brilliantly revealed, in a letter of September 3, 1780, to James Duane, a New York member of Congress, who had requested Hamilton's opinion as to the way to correct the defects of the government. Hamilton criticised the organization and the behavior of Congress. He held that "the manner in which Congress was appointed would warrant, and the public good required, that they should have considered themselves as vested with full power *to preserve the republic from harm.*" By the phrase he italicized he avoided discussion of the origin and extent of the authority intentionally granted to Congress, consideration of which would have opened a subject interminable in its nature, as has since often been shown. He went to the heart of the matter by pointing out that Congress had in fact "done many of the highest acts of sovereignty, which were always cheerfully submitted to: the declaration of independence, the declaration of war, the levying of an army, creating a navy, emitting money, making alliances with foreign powers, appointing a dictator, etc." But Congress had been "timid and indecisive" in matters auxiliary and subordinate to the sovereignty they had actually assumed and exercised. The gist of Hamilton's remarks upon this point is that by failing to seize the taxing powers they had sunk into a state of helpless dependence on the States. "That power which holds the purse strings absolutely must rule." Confederation had had no practical result. "The particular States have no further attended to it than

as it suited their pretensions and convenience."
But, even were it respected, the Confederation was
inadequate. "It is neither fit for war or peace."
Hamilton then appealed to the lessons of history to
show that a government cannot maintain itself unless it can act directly upon its citizenship through
its own police power. "The idea of an uncontrollable sovereignty in each State over its internal police
will defeat the other powers given to Congress and
make our union feeble and precarious." It would
be even more so than the league of the Swiss can-
tons, which had been maintained through ties of
union due to special circumstances. "These ties
will not exist in America; a little time hence some of
the States will be powerful empires; and we are so
remote from other nations, that we shall have all
the leisure and opportunity we can wish to cut each
other's throats." The time came when this grim
anticipation was fulfilled, through the constitutional
defect that Hamilton instanced. It took a civil war
to destroy State pretensions of uncontrollable sovereignty.

In addition to being subject to defect of power,
Congress was addicted to misuse of power. "Congress have kept the power too much in their own
hands, and have meddled too much with details of
every sort. Congress is, properly, a deliberative
corps, and it forgets itself when it attempts to play
the executive." This observation, quite as applica-

ble to Congress now as when it was written, he explains by considerations even more cogent now than then: "It is impossible such a body, numerous as it is, and constantly fluctuating, can ever act with sufficient decision or with system. Two-thirds of the members, one-half the time, cannot know what has gone before them, or what connection the subject in hand has to what has been transacted on former occasions. The members who have been more permanent, will only give information that promotes the side they espouse in the present case, and will as often mislead as enlighten. The variety of business must distract, and the proneness of every assembly to debate must at all times delay." The remedy, he urged, was to create executive departments, each with one man at its head. "As these men will be, of course, at all times under the direction of Congress, we shall blend the advantages of a monarchy and a republic in our constitution." He points out that this would not lessen the importance of Congress. "They would have precisely the same rights and powers as heretofore, happily disencumbered of the detail. They would have to inspect the conduct of their ministers, deliberate upon their plans, originate others for the public good; only observing this rule—that they ought to consult their ministers, and get all the information and advice they could from them, before they entered into any new measures, or made changes in the old." The adoption of such a system, he held, "would give new life and energy to the operations of the government. Business would be conducted with dispatch, method and system. A million abuses now existing, would be corrected, and judicious plans would be formed and executed for the public good."

Government of this nature is yet to be introduced in the United States, and the characteristic defects of Congress when that body was originally formed have been perpetuated; but Hamilton's plan is an exact anticipation of what has been effected in the organization and procedure of the Congress of Switzerland, whose model was arrived at by correcting the defects of the American Constitution in just the way that Hamilton recommended, accomplishing just those results of economy and efficiency which he predicted. The most democratic country in the world has a constitution exactly such as Hamilton proposed for the United States. It is more than resemblance; it is identity, although arrived at independently by Swiss publicists, forming one of the most interesting parallels in history, and certainly the most complete.

Proceeding to a consideration of the steps to be taken to accomplish the needed improvements, Hamilton observed that the only practical alternative was either for Congress to resume and exercise sovereign authority or else to call a convention of the States to form a new constitution. The first plan he did not believe to be really available. It "will be thought too bold an expedient by the generality of Congress; and, indeed, their practice hitherto has so riveted the opinion of their want of power, that the success of this experiment may very well be doubted." The other mode, the convention plan, he thought was practicable, and he gave this account of the powers that should be granted to the general government: "Congress should have complete sovereignty in all that relates to war, peace, trade, finance; and to the management of foreign affairs; the right of declaring war; of raising armies, officering, paying them, directing their motions in every respect; of equipping fleets, and doing the same with them; of building fortifications, arsenals, magazines, etc., etc.; of making peace on such conditions as they think proper; of regulating trade, determining with what countries it shall be carried on, granting indulgences; laying prohibitions on all the articles of export or import; imposing duties; granting bounties and premiums for raising, exporting or importing, and applying to their own use the product of these duties—only giving credit to the States on which they are raised in the general account of revenues and expenses; instituting Admiralty, Courts, etc.; of coining money; establishing banks on such terms, and with such privileges as they think proper; appropriating funds, and doing whatever else relates to the operations of finance; transacting everything with foreign nations; making alliances, offensive and defensive, treaties of commerce, etc., etc."

On comparing this project with the scheme actually introduced by the adoption of the Constitution, a general resemblance will be noted, but some important differences will appear. The most important is that Hamilton reserved to the States a field of taxation which the Constitution opened concurrently to the national government, with the result that the field has been so extensively occupied as to crowd State authority out of it to an extent that leaves it little available for State use. The raising of money "by internal taxes," which Hamilton then thought ought to be reserved to State authority, is now so largely a federal function that the States have been practically deprived of the most commodious and lucrative sources of revenue in that field. State apportionment of credit for revenue raised from duties upon exports or imports, figured in Hamilton's scheme, and was probably meant to conciliate the particularist tendencies then so powerful. It did not find a place in the Constitution. Moreover, the Hamilton plan confers more power and dignity upon Congress than have been actually realized under the Constitution, but this has been due more to the character of political development under the Constitution than to the language of the Constitution itself. At present Congress by no means has complete control over the particulars mentioned by Hamilton; but the legal basis of power upon which Congress acts is as ample as was originally that of the British Parliament, and the actual inferiority of Congress is to be attributed to defects in the way in which its constitutional authority has been organized and applied. Its lack of direct contact with the administration—a circumstance not provided by the Constitution but by its own rules—is the principal cause of its inferiority.

The most remarkable feature of the Hamilton plan, and the most impressive evidence of the cool, dispassionate, enlightened character of his statesmanship, is the exalted station he sought to provide for Congress, at a time when Congress had become so corrupt and inefficient that the sharpest censures were passed upon its character. The usual tendency is to take power away where it has been abused, and provide new securities for public order by a new distribution of authority and by imposing new checks, limitations, and restraints. This process has been carried out in American State constitutions until they form as great a labyrinth of particular agency and coordinate powers as ever existed under the feudal system, to which in essence American politics are a reversion. That a young man only twenty-three years of age, acting in circumstances whose ordinary effect was to produce deep aversion, should have discerned that the true remedy for the misconduct of Congress lay in enlarging its powers and in augmenting its responsibilities, was an amazing exhibition of piercing insight, no parallel for which is to be found at that period except in the writings of Edmund Burke. Hamilton anticipated the means by which democracy has really been established, wherever that result has been actually attained. It has not yet been attained in the United States because those means have not yet been employed. The characteristic principle of feudalism—fractional sovereignty—still rules American politics, and responsible government is just beginning to appear as the proper goal of effort. As democratic principles of government advance in the United States, the more wonderful will it appear that in the darkest night there was a youthful statesman who had the vision of a day so remote that it has still to dawn in its perfect power and beauty.

CHAPTER VIII

ALLIANCE WITH A PATROON FAMILY

GRAYDON, in his *Memoirs*, gives a striking picture of the social position held by Hamilton. Graydon, who had been a prisoner of war for eight months in the hands of the British, sought the American camp, then at Morristown, as soon as he was released, and was entertained at Washington's quarters. "Here, for the first time," Graydon relates, "I had the pleasure of knowing Colonel Hamilton. He presided at the General's table, where we dined; and in a large company in which there were several ladies, among whom I recollect one or two of the Miss Livingstons and a Miss Brown, he acquitted himself with an ease, propriety and vivacity, which gave me the most favorable impression of his talents and accomplishments—talents, it is true, which did not indicate the solid abilities his subsequent career has unfolded, but which announced a brilliancy which might adorn the most polished circles of society."

The officers about Washington were of his own selection, and the contrast between the tone of manners at headquarters and that which was usually displayed by officers of the class who got their positions through Congressional patronage, was

such as ladies would be quick to recognize. The
character of many holders of commissions was such
as to give point to General Conway's query: "Did
Congress see you before they appointed you?" The
social distinction of the Washington circle was augmented in 1777 by the arrival of the Marquis de
Lafayette and other French officers. Hamilton's
familiar knowledge of French facilitated intimacies
that had an important bearing on the issues of the
war. At the time Lafayette joined the army Washington was under a cloud, and an intrigue to displace
him was under way. Lafayette wrote home that
Washington's "best friends, Greene, Hamilton and
Knox, were decried." Attempts were made to win
Lafayette to the side of the Congressional cabal, but
they did not move him. He wrote: "Attached to
the General, and still more to the cause, I did not
hesitate, but held to him whose ruin was anticipated."

This was really the turning-point of the Revolutionary struggle. It was saved by the French alliance after it had been ruined by the behavior of
Congress. The relations into which Hamilton easily
and naturally entered with the French officers, providing them with a source of clear and accurate information, exerted an influence of inestimable value
at this crisis. At the same time it identified Hamilton with coteries possessing the social brilliancy and
distinction always attractive to women, and pro-

vided for him friendships that were sometimes attended by embarrassments. To one lady, who had applied in behalf of friends who wanted to pass through the American lines, Hamilton softened his refusal by writing in a style of high-flown gallantry, concluding with the remark: "Trifling apart, there is nothing would give me greater pleasure than to have been able to serve Miss Livingston and her friends on this occasion, but circumstances really did not permit it."

In December, 1779, Hamilton wrote a letter to his intimate friend, John Laurens, in which, after some banter on Laurens's personal affairs he turns to his own, saying: "And now, my dear, as we are upon the subject of wife, I empower and command you to get me one in Carolina. Such a wife as I want will, I know, be difficult to be found, but if you succeed, it will be the stronger proof of your zeal and dexterity. Take her description—she must be young, handsome (I lay most stress upon a good shape), sensible (a little learning will do), well bred (but she must have an aversion to the word *ton*), chaste and tender (I am an enthusiast in my notions of fidelity and fondness), of some good nature, a great deal of generosity (she must neither love money nor scolding, for I dislike equally a termagant and an economist). In politics I am indifferent what side she may be of. I think I have arguments that will easily convert her to mine. As to religion a moderate stock will satisfy me.   She must believe in God and hate a saint."

In the succeeding portion of the letter Hamilton turns it all off as a joke.   "I am ready to ask myself what could have put it into my head to hazard this *jeu de folie*. Do I want a wife? No. I have plagues enough without desiring to add to the number that greatest of all. . . ."

At that time he had already met the lady who was to become his wife, although his relations with her had not then advanced beyond bare acquaintance.   When Hamilton was sent by Washington on a mission to General Gates in the autumn of 1777, he visited the Schuyler mansion at Albany, and among those to whom he was introduced was General Schuyler's second daughter, Elizabeth, then just turned twenty.   Colonel Tench Tilghman, who had had that honor some two years before, described her as "a brunette with the most good-natured, dark, lovely eyes that I ever saw, which threw a beam of good humor and benevolence over her entire countenance."   He remarked: "I was prepossessed in favor of this young lady the moment I saw her."   If Hamilton was similarly impressed on his first meeting, there is no record of it, and his letter of 1779 to Laurens does not suggest that his fancy had then been caught by any one.   The circumstances of Hamilton's visit in 1777 were such as to give anxious occupation to his thoughts.   Washington's authority as commander-in-chief was being undermined and Gates's attitude was disrespectful. It is quite possible that when he then visited General Schuyler to confer on the situation, the casual introduction he received to the daughter made no impression on him at the time. The young lady was, of course, differently circumstanced, and those bright eyes of hers could hardly have failed to note Hamilton's handsome appearance and polished manners.

Philip Schuyler, born in 1733, inherited a large estate from his father, and he was eminent and active in provincial affairs at the outbreak of the Revolution. Like Washington himself, Schuyler was a representative of the landed gentry whose adhesion to the Revolutionary movement gave to it influence and respectability without which it would probably have collapsed. He belonged to one of the great patroon families of New York, allied by ties of close kinship to the Van Cortlandts and the Van Rensselaers. When men of the lawyer-politician type obtained the ascendancy in Congress, Schuyler became a mark for their intrigues. He was the general in command of the forces collected to repel Burgoyne's invasion, and, like Washington at the same period, he had all he could do in maintaining the show of an armed force, lack of order, discipline, and equipment precluding any operation more important than an occasional foray. He behaved with fine magnanimity when Congress super-

seded him in favor of Gates, who arrived in time to
take credit for the battle of Saratoga, the fruit of
Schuyler's management.   At the time of Hamilton's
mission Congress was inclined to supersede Washington also, and did, in fact, pass an order prohibiting him from exercising any considerable authority
in the northern department without first consulting
General Gates and Governor Clinton.   Schuyler now
opportunely entered Congress as a delegate from
New York, and his presence in that body exerted a
strong influence toward the preservation of Washington's authority and toward improvement in the
behavior of Congress.

It was at this point that intimacy between Hamilton and the Schuyler family really began.   During
the winter and spring of 1779–80, when Washington's headquarters were at Morristown, General
Schuyler took a house there for his family.   Mrs.
Washington and the wives of several officers were
also living in Morristown, so that an agreeable
society was formed.   Hamilton was brought into
intimate relations with it as Washington's secretary,
and his wit, vivacity, and good-breeding inspired
liking and esteem.

Schuyler was very intimate with Washington.
They were men of the same class, nearly of the same
age, with like habits of thought and standards of
conduct.   Washington warmly sympathized with
Schuyler and deplored the shabby treatment he had

experienced from Congress. Schuyler was active
and influential in his support of Washington. His
position as one of the New York patroons made it
impossible for his enemies to divest him of political
importance. He had his own intelligence department, which included even agents in Canada, and
all his resources were at Washington's service. His
presence in Congress in 1780 was of inestimable
value to Washington, as Schuyler was able to secure
the appointment of a committee of three, with himself at the head, to effect changes and reforms in the
army much desired by Washington.

With. Schuyler himself Hamilton now began an
intimacy that lasted the rest of his life. Schuyler
was then forty-seven; Hamilton was twenty-three.
Schuyler's large experience in public affairs and intimate knowledge of all the personal springs of
action probably served as a valuable source of information to Hamilton. Elizabeth Schuyler was
with her father at Morristown, and Hamilton was
soon in love with her. They were both born in the
same year, but Hamilton was older by seven months.
It is an astonishing proof of the force of Hamilton's
vocation for statesmanship that at the very time he
was courting his sweetheart he produced the remarkable papers described in the preceding chapter. An
incident of that period preserved by tradition shows
that Hamilton was not wholly exempt from dis-
turbance by love's sweet fever. Once after spending

an evening with Miss Schuyler his thoughts were so full of her that on returning to his quarters in camp he could not remember the countersign, and was held back by the sentinel until a friend arrived who could give Hamilton the word.

Hamilton's passion for Elizabeth Schuyler was described by him in a letter to one of her sisters—probably Mrs. Angelica Church, written sometime during 1780. It is written in the high-flown style of the period, that seemed to go naturally in company with wigs, satin knee-breeches, lace ruffs, towering coiffure, trailing silk gowns, and stately manners, but which is much too pretentious for modern taste. Availing himself of a commission from Miss Schuyler to forward a letter to her sister, Hamilton wrote: "I venture to tell you in confidence, that by some odd contrivance or other your sister has found out the secret of interesting me in everything that concerns her; and though I have not the happiness of a personal acquaintance with you, I have had the good fortune to see several very pretty pictures of your person and mind which have inspired me with a more than common partiality for both."

He then offers it as proof of the good opinion he has formed that he may venture thus to introduce himself and even make her his confidant:

Phlegmatists may say I take too great a license at first setting out, and witlings may sneer and wonder how a man the least acquainted with the world should show so great facility in his confidence—to a lady. But the idea I have formed of your character places it in my estimation above the insipid maxims of the former or the ill-natured jibes of the latter.

I have already confessed the influence your sister has gained over me—yet notwithstanding this, I have some things of a very serious and heinous nature to lay to her charge.—She is most unmercifully handsome and so perverse that she has none of those pretty affectations which are the prerogatives of beauty. Her good sense is destitute of that happy mixture of vanity and ostentation which would make it conspicuous to the whole tribe of fools and foplings as well as to men of understanding so that as the matter now stands it is little known beyond the circle of these.—She has good nature, affability and vivacity unembellished with that charming frivolousness which is justly deemed one of the principal accomplishments of a *belle*. In short, she is so strange a creature, that she possesses all the beauties, virtues and graces of her sex without any of those amiable defects which from their general prevalence are esteemed by connoisseurs necessary shades in the character of a fine woman. The most determined adversaries of Hymen can find in her no pretext for their hostility, and there are several of my friends, philosophers, who railed at love as a weakness, men of the world who laughed at it as a phantasie, whom she has presumptuously and daringly compelled to acknowledge its power and surrender at discretion. I can the better assert the truth of this, as I am myself of the number. She has had the address to overset all the wise resolutions I had been framing for more than four years past, and from a rational sort of being and a professed contemner of Cupid has in a trice metamorphosed me into the veriest inamorato your perhaps . . .

Here there is a portion of the manuscript that is quite illegible, and, although what follows is plain enough, it is all in the same Grandisonian style, of which a sufficient sample has been given. It was quite the fashion then, and English literature affords many models of that sort of thing. The Marquis de Chastellux, who visited Washington's headquarters in this year, and published an account of his American travels, remarked upon the frequent toasting of sweethearts and the elaborate gallantries at formal dinners. It should be noted that Hamilton's employment of this style in writing to Mrs. Church had a defensive use. If nothing had come of the affair it might have been passed off as merely the language of compliment. This affected style was dropped forthwith as soon as Hamilton was accepted as Miss Schuyler's affianced, and his letters thereafter are simple, direct, sincere, manly, and tender, almost devoid of personal compliment except that highest sort which is implied by the character of the matter. The position now tacitly assigned to her is that of a woman of good sense and intelligence, whose interest in public affairs is as keen as Hamilton's own. Under date of September 6, 1780, Hamilton tells her of Gates's defeat in South Carolina, and of his flight, leaving "his troops to take care of themselves, and get out of the scrape as well as they could." After referring to the general dismay occasioned by this reverse, Hamilton's sanguine disposition crops out in the remark: "This misfortune affects me less than others, because it is not in my temper to repine at evils that are past, but to endeavor to draw good out of them, and because I think our safety depends on a total change of system, and this change of system will only be produced by misfortune."

Arnold's treason occurred during the period of Hamilton's courtship, and as soon as the news was received Hamilton was sent to Verplanck's Point to try to intercept Arnold; but on his arrival he found that Arnold, always rapid and energetic in his movements, had already made good his escape and was then safe on board the *Vulture*, an English sloop-of-war. Hamilton at once took measures for the protection of West Point, taking upon himself to issue instructions, concerning which he at once wrote to Washington: "I hope your Excellency will approve these steps, as there may be no time to be lost." On the same day, September 25, 1780, he wrote to Miss Schuyler, giving her an account of the affair which overflows with kindness and magnanimity with respect to Mrs. Arnold. He said:

I went in pursuit of him but was much too late; and could hardly regret the disappointment, when, on my return, I saw an amiable woman, frantic with distress for the loss of a husband she tenderly loved; a traitor to his country and to his fame; a disgrace to his connections: it was the most affecting scene I ever was witness to. . . .

All the sweetness of beauty, all the loveliness of inno-
cence, all the tenderness of a wife, and all the fondness
of a mother showed themselves in her appearance and
conduct. . . . This morning she is more composed. I
paid her a visit, and endeavored to soothe her by every
method in my power, though you may imagine she is not
easily to be consoled.

In his dealings with Major André, the unfortunate
British officer whose transactions with Arnold
brought him into the American lines and who was
hanged as a spy, Hamilton displayed military se-
verity coupled with refined and chivalrous personal
consideration. Writing to Miss Schuyler on October
2, 1780, he said:

Poor André suffers to-day. Everything that is amiable in virtue, in fortitude, in delicate sentiment, pleads
for him; but hard-hearted policy calls for a sacrifice. He
must die.—I send you my account of Arnold's affair; and
to justify myself to your sentiments, I must inform you
that I urged a compliance with André's request to be
shot; and I do not think it would have had an ill effect;
but some people are only sensible to motives of policy,
and sometimes from a narrow disposition, mistake it.
When André's tale comes to be told, and present resentment is over, the refusing him the privilege of choosing
the manner of his death will be branded with too much
obstinacy.

It was proposed to me to suggest to him the idea of an
exchange for Arnold; but I knew I should have forfeited
his esteem by doing it, and therefore declined it. As a

man of honor, he could but reject it, and I would not for the world have proposed to him a thing which must have placed me in the unamiable light of supposing him capable of meanness, or of not feeling myself the impropriety of the measure. I confess to you I had the weakness to value the esteem of a dying man, because I reverenced his merit.

The account of Arnold's affair to which he refers was probably the same as that which he sent to his friend, Colonel John Laurens, the same month. It is written with great literary skill, and the account it gives of the execution of André is deeply affecting from the simplicity and completeness with which it narrates the incidents. Hamilton's comments upon André's personal characteristics and behavior are marked throughout by generosity and high-mindedness.

Mingled with these letters between a statesman and a gentlewoman properly interested in public affairs by her social station, were, of course, other letters in which there was the ardent outpouring of a lover's heart. Among the few letters of this other type that have been preserved is one that is undated but which from its allusions to events may be safely assigned to October, 1780. In it Hamilton wrote:

I have told you and I told you truly that I love you too much. You engross my thoughts too entirely to allow me to think of anything else. You not only employ my mind all day, but you intrude on my sleep. I meet you in every dream and when I wake I cannot close my eyes again for ruminating on your sweetness. 'Tis a pretty story indeed that I am to be thus monopolized by a little *nut brown maid* like you, and from a soldier metamorphosed into a puny lover. I believe in my soul you are an enchantress; but I have tried in vain, if not to break, at least to weaken the charm, and you maintain your empire in spite of all my efforts, and after every new one I make to withdraw myself from my allegiance, my partial heart still returns and clings to you with increased attachment. To drop figures, my lovely girl, you become dearer to me every moment.

From other portions of this letter it appears that they were arranging for their marriage. He speaks of the difficulties he is having in getting his leave from headquarters, owing to the absence of other members of Washington's staff, but he declares: "I will not be delayed beyond November." He brings up the question of dress. "You will laugh at me for consulting you about such a trifle, but I want to know whether you would prefer my receiving the nuptial benediction in my uniform or in a different habit. It will be just as you please, so consult your whim and what you think most consistent with propriety."

Of course, like all lovers with power to turn a phrase, Hamilton wrote verses to his sweetheart. Some experiments in that line are also reported of him in his student days, but the little known of them suggests he was too much the exact thinker to soar freely in flights of poetic fancy. Naturally, his efforts were liked by his sweetheart. She lived to be ninety-seven, and when she died, in a tiny bag hanging from her neck were found these verses written by Hamilton:

ANSWER TO THE INQUIRY WHY I SIGHED

"Before no mortal ever knew
A love like mine so tender—true—
Completely wretched—you away
And but half blessed e'en while you stay.

"If present love [illegible] face
Deny you to my fond embrace
No joy unmixed my bosom warms
But when my angel's in my arms."

The exact date of Hamilton's marriage has not been preserved, but it is supposed to have taken place in December, 1780. If so, it must have been early in that month. Under date of December 9 he wrote to General Washington from Albany on army business there, and in ending his letter remarked: "Mrs. Hamilton presents her respectful compliments to Mrs. Washington and yourself. After the holidays we shall be at headquarters." Remembering Hamilton's declaration that he would "not be delayed beyond November," and considering the determination with which he pursued his objects, it seems a permissible conjecture that the marriage really took place in the latter part of November, and this supposition tallies very well with the tenor of the letter of December 9. If the wedding had just taken place, it seems unlikely that Hamilton would already be so occupied with army business at Albany as that letter indicates.

At any rate, it is certain that the wedding was celebrated in the Schuyler family mansion at Albany, a stately building of yellow brick, with everything upon an ample scale. The main hall, entered through the handsome colonial doorway, was sixty feet long. The drawing-room, in which presumably the wedding took place, was spacious and ornate, with deep window-seats and broad mantels handsomely carved. General Schuyler had given cordial approval to Hamilton's suit, and, although details are lacking, there can be no doubt that the wedding was a fine affair. It is known that McHenry, of Washington's staff, was at the wedding, for verses he wrote on the occasion have been preserved. In them the bridegroom figures as "dear Ham," and in thus trimming the name to suit the metre the versifier made it a rather grotesque companion to the classic gods and nymphs he introduced.

Hamilton's honeymoon was necessarily brief, and shortly thereafter he was again at work. His elaborate memorandum upon the establishment of a national bank, sent to Robert Morris, must have been drafted within a few months after his marriage. Devotion to public affairs was the ruling passion of his life, but for the rest of his life he now had a helpmate the stanchness of whose devotion could bear any test, even such as came from folly and wickedness in Hamilton himself.   Her nature is exactly characterized by Robert Louis Stevenson's lines:

"Honor, anger, valor, fire;
A love that life could never tire,
Death quench or evil stir,
The mighty Master
Gave to her."

CHAPTER IX

A BREACH WITH WASHINGTON

Shortly after his marriage Hamilton had a tiff with Washington that was really a small affair in itself, but he made so much of it that nothing would satisfy him short of leaving Washington's staff. The following is his own account of it, in a letter of February 18, 1781, to General Schuyler:

I am no longer a member of the General's family. This information will surprise you, and the manner of the change will surprise you more. Two days ago, the General and I passed each other on the stairs. He told me he wanted to speak to me. I answered that I would wait upon him immediately. I went below and delivered to Mr. Tilghman a letter to be sent to the commissary, containing an order of a pressing and interesting nature.

Returning to the General, I was stopped on the way by the Marquis de La Fayette, and we conversed together about a minute on a matter of business. He can testify how impatient I was to get back, and that I left him in a manner which, but for our intimacy, would have been more than abrupt. Instead of finding the General, as is usual, in his room, I met him at the head of the stairs, where, accosting me in an angry tone, "Colonel Hamilton," said he, "you have kept me waiting at the head of

114

the stairs these ten minutes. I must tell you, sir, you treat me with disrespect." I replied, without petulancy, but with decision: "I am not conscious of it, sir; but since you have thought it necessary to tell me so, we part." "Very well, sir," said he, "if it be your choice," or something to this effect, and we separated. I sincerely believe my absence, which gave so much umbrage, did not last two minutes.

In less than an hour after, Tilghman came to me in the General's name, assuring me of his great confidence in my abilities, integrity, usefulness, etc., and of his desire, in a candid conversation, to heal a difference which could not have happened but in a moment of passion. I requested Mr. Tilghman to tell him—1st. That I had taken my resolution in a manner not to be revoked. 2nd. That, as a conversation could serve no other purpose than to produce explanations, mutually disagreeable, though I certainly would not refuse an interview if he desired it, yet I would be happy if he would permit me to decline it. 3d. That, though determined to leave the family, the same principles which had kept me so long in it would continue to direct my conduct towards him when out of it. 4th. That, however, I did not wish to distress him, or the public business, by quitting him before he could derive other assistance by the return of some of the gentlemen who were absent. 5th. And that, in the meantime, it depended on him to let our behavior to each other be the same as if nothing had happened. He consented to decline the conversation, and thanked me for my offer of continuing my aid in the manner I had mentioned.

I have given you so particular a detail of our difference from the desire I have to justify myself in your opinion. Perhaps you may think I was precipitate in rejecting the overture made by the General to an accommodation. I assure you, my dear sir, it was not the effect of resentment; it was the deliberate result of maxims I had long formed for the government of my own conduct.

I always disliked the office of an aide-de-camp as having in it a kind of personal dependence. I refused to serve in this capacity with two major-generals at an early period of the war. Infected, however, with the enthusiasm of the times, an idea of the General's character which experience taught me to be unfounded, overcame my scruples, and induced me to *accept his invitation* to enter into his family. It was not long before I discovered he was neither remarkable for delicacy nor good temper, which revived my former aversion to the station in which I was acting, and it has been increasing ever since. It has been often with great difficulty that I have prevailed upon myself not to renounce it; but while, from motives of public utility, I was doing violence to my feelings, I was always determined, if there should ever happen a breach between us, never to consent to an accommodation. I was persuaded that when once that nice barrier, which marked the boundaries of what we owed to each other, should be thrown down, it might be propped again, but could never be restored.

I resolved, whenever it should happen, not to be in the wrong. I was convinced the concessions the General might make would be dictated by his interest, and that his self-love would never forgive me for what it would regard as a humiliation.

I believe you know the place I held in the General's confidence and counsels, which will make it the more extraordinary to you to learn that for three years past I have felt no friendship for him and have professed none. The truth is, our dispositions are the opposites of each other, and the pride of my temper would not suffer me to profess what I did not feel. Indeed, when advances of this kind have been made to me on his part, they were received in a manner that showed at least that I had no desire to court them, and that I desired to stand rather upon a footing of military confidence than of private attachment.

You are too good a judge of human nature not to be sensible how this conduct in me must have operated on a man to whom all the world is offering incense. With this key you will easily unlock the present mystery.

At the end of the war I may say many things to you concerning which I shall impose upon myself till then an inviolable silence.

The General is a very honest man. His competitors have slender abilities, and less integrity. His popularity has often been essential to the safety of America, and is still of great importance to it. These considerations have influenced my past conduct respecting him, and will influence my future. I think it is necessary he should be supported.

His estimation in your mind, whatever may be its amount, I am persuaded has been formed on principles which a circumstance like this cannot materially affect; but if I thought it could diminish your friendship for him, I should almost forego the motives that urge me to justify myself to you. I wish what I have said to make no other impression than to satisfy you I have not been in the wrong. It is also said in confidence, as a public knowledge of the breach would, in many ways, have an ill effect. It will probably be the policy of both sides to conceal it, and cover the separation with some plausible pretext. I am importuned by such of my friends as are privy to the affair, to listen to a reconciliation; but my resolution is unalterable.

Allowances for the pomposity and conceit of this letter should be made on account of the youth of the writer and the temper in which it was written. He had turned twenty-four only a little over a month before; he wrote while still under the excitement of the breach, and while in a rage that was intensified by the formal restraints put upon it. And he was writing to a father-in-law of only a few months' standing, in whose eyes he naturally desired to exhibit his behavior in a dignified aspect. On his own showing, Washington did everything possible to expiate an offense committed in a moment of irritation not unwarranted by the circumstances. A few words of explanation would have set the matter right at once. That Hamilton was so deeply hurt shows that he had got into the state in which a slight wound festers. The disparaging remarks he made about Washington are such as are usually consequent upon such a falling out between intimates. Nothing is more common on the part of clever juniors than such an attitude toward elders with whose dignity they are too familiar to be impressed by it, while they are still too inexperienced to appreciate it.

Hamilton was not mistaken in thinking that it would take strong argument to convince General Schuyler of the propriety of the step he had taken. Hamilton's letter reached the general at night, and the next day he made a reply which is a model of kindness and tact. He began: "I confess the contents surprised and afflicted me—not that I discover any impropriety in your conduct in the affair in question, for of that, I persuade myself, you are incapable; but it may be attended with consequences prejudicial to my country, which I love, which I affectionately love."

The letter then goes on to appeal to Hamilton's patriotism not to abandon a post in which his services were so important. After putting adroitly and forcibly the argument from this standpoint, he concluded with this touching appeal to Hamilton's good feeling:

It is evident, my dear sir, that the General conceived himself the aggressor, and that he quickly repented of the insult. . . . It falls to the lot of few men to pass through life without one of those unguarded moments which wound the feelings of a friend. Let us then impute them to the frailties of human nature, and with Sterne's recording angel, drop a tear, and blot it out of the page of life. I do not mean to reprehend the maxims you have formed for your conduct. They are laudable, and though generally approved, yet times and circumstances sometimes render a deviation necessary and justifiable. This necessity now exists in the distresses of your country. Make the sacrifice. The greater it is, the more glorious to you. Your services are wanted. They are wanted in that particular station which you have already filled so beneficially to the public, and with such extensive reputation.

If any argument or appeal would have moved Hamilton, no more effective approach could have been made than that which Schuyler used. If there had been nothing more in the case than wounded pride, Schuyler's efforts would certainly have succeeded, but, as Hamilton now felt assured that he could serve public interests more effectually in other ways, appeals to his patriotism only served to confirm his resolution. Lafayette, whose casual detention of Hamilton was the immediate cause of Washington's annoyance, also exerted himself to effect a reconciliation, but he found, to his regret, "each disposed to believe the other was not sorry for the separation."

In resigning his position as aide-de-camp Hamilton had no intention of leaving the army. "I cannot think of quitting the army during the war," he wrote to Schuyler. His first preference was for the artillery, the branch of the army to which he had formerly belonged, but in returning to it he would have gone to the bottom of the list in his rank. As he believed that the war was drawing to a close, and a command in the infantry would leave him time for study during the winter, he decided in favor of an infantry position. By virtue of his staff position he was entitled to a commission as lieutenant-colonel, dating from March 1, 1777, and this he now obtained, but it did not carry with it any regimental connection, and he made formal application to General Washington for an appointment. The general felt somewhat embarrassed by the application, as he had had trouble from appointments of the kind desired by Hamilton. In his reply, which bears the same date as Hamilton's application, he referred to cases in which the giving of commands to outsiders had been deeply resented by the officers of the line. "To add to the discontent of the officers of those lines, by the further appointment of an officer of your rank . . . would, I am certain, involve me in a difficulty of a very disagreeable and delicate nature, and might, perhaps, lead to consequences more serious than it is easy to imagine." Washington undoubtedly felt keenly his inability to gratify Hamilton, particularly in view of the recent breach in their relations. He concluded his letter with the remark: "My principal concern arises from an apprehension that you will impute my refusal of your request to other motives than those I have expressed, but I beg you to be assured, I am only influenced by the reasons which I have mentioned."

Hamilton wrote again, urging that his case differed from the case of those appointments which had been resented as favors to outsiders, as he had entered the army in the line, held a regular commission, and had simply been detached for staff duty, so that he was now only seeking a restoration to his original sphere. In closing he declared: "I assure your Excellency, that I am too well persuaded of your can-

dor, to attribute your refusal to any other cause
than an apprehension of inconveniences that may
attend the appointment."

Nothing came of Hamilton's application until
July, when he again wrote to Washington, and with
the letter returned his commission. Washington
sent one of his aides, Colonel Tilghman, to induce
Hamilton to retain his commission, promising an
appointment to active command at the first opportunity. Events soon assumed such shape that Hamilton was able to obtain the military employment
he desired. When the campaign of 1781 opened, it
had been Washington's intention to lay siege to the
British position at New York, and military arrangements to that end went on until the middle of
August. The British commander-in-chief, Sir Henry
Clinton, planned a counter-stroke by way of the
Chesapeake Bay, and Lord Cornwallis, who was
then operating in Virginia, was instructed to establish a base either at Williamsburg or Yorktown,
whence by water conveyance he could strike at Bal-
timore, or Philadelphia, to destroy stores and resources upon which Washington would be depending. The plan was not a bad one, provided control
of the sea remained in British hands. On August 15
advices reached Washington that Count de Grasse,
who commanded the French fleet in the West Indies,
would sail for the Chesapeake, thus cutting Cornwallis's communications and isolating his position.

Washington promptly decided to take advantage of the opportunity thus presented, and he made arrangements for transferring his army to Yorktown, and Hamilton was appointed to the command of a regiment of light infantry which formed part of Lafayette's corps.

Hamilton's letters to his wife at this period are full of the great love that accompanies a high sense of honor. He wrote:

A part of the army, my dear girl, is going to Virginia, and I must, of necessity, be separated at a much greater distance from my beloved wife. I cannot announce the fatal necessity, without feeling everything that a fond husband can feel. I am unhappy; I am unhappy beyond expression. I am unhappy, because I am to be so remote from you; because I am to hear from you less frequently than I am accustomed to do. I am miserable, because I know you will be so; I am wretched at the idea of flying so far from you, without a single hour's interview, to tell you all my pains and all my love. But I cannot ask permission to visit you. It might be thought improper to leave my corps at such a time and upon such an occasion. I must go without seeing you—I must go without embracing you; alas! I must go.

Hamilton's command embarked for Yorktown at Head of Elk on September 7. On the day before he wrote:

I would give the world to be able to tell you all I feel and all I wish, but consult your own heart and you will know mine. What a world will soon be between us! To support the idea, all my fortitude is insufficient. What must be the case with you, who have the most female of female hearts? I sink at the perspective of your distress and I look to heaven to be your guardian and supporter. Circumstances that have just come to my knowledge assure me that our operations will be expeditious, as well as our success certain. Early in November, as I promised you, we shall certainly meet. Cheer yourself with this idea, and with the assurance of never more being separated. Every day confirms me in the intention of renouncing public life and devoting myself wholly to you. Let others waste their time and their tranquillity in a vain pursuit of honor and glory; be it my object to be happy in a quiet retreat with my better angel.

On October 16 he gave his wife this brief account of a gallant military exploit:

Two nights ago, my Eliza, my duty and my honor obliged me to take a step in which your happiness was too much risked. I commanded an attack upon one of the enemy's redoubts; we carried it in an instant and with little loss. You will see the particulars in the Philadelphia papers. There will be, certainly, nothing more of this kind; all the rest will be by approach; and if there should be another occasion, it will not fall to my turn to execute it.

Hamilton thus briefly and modestly dismissed what was a brilliant military exploit, the details of which illustrate the sensitive quality of his honor as well as his dauntless courage. The position occupied by Cornwallis at Yorktown was most readily assailable from the southwest against his left wing, to protect which fortifications had been thrown up, with redoubts at commanding points. The American siege was begun by establishing a parallel fortification on which batteries were posted. With the French aid, the besiegers had a preponderance of guns and in a few days an advance upon the first line of the British fortifications was deemed practicable. In making the arrangements for the assault Hamilton was passed over. Accounts of the affair differ, that given in J. C. Hamilton's biography of his father being to the effect that Washington gave the command to Colonel Barber from a supposed precedence due to his rank and service. General Henry Lee, in his *Memoirs*, states that Lafayette gave the command of the van to his own aide-de-camp, Lieutenant-Colonel Gimat. Hamilton protested on the ground that the time fixed for the assault came within his tour of duty. Lafayette excused himself on the ground that the arrangements had been approved by Washington and were no longer open to change. Lee's account proceeds:

Hamilton . . . left the marquis, announcing his determination to appeal to headquarters. This he accordingly did, in a spirited and manly letter. Washington, incapable of injustice, sent for the marquis, and inquiring into the fact, found that the tour of duty belonging to Hamilton had been given to Gimat. He instantly directed the marquis to reinstate Hamilton, who consequently was put at the head of the van.

As Lee took part in the siege of Yorktown, and he expressly says that he obtained the particulars from Hamilton himself, his account should be regarded as the authentic version of the affair.

It was one of Hamilton's characteristics all through life that his interest was in getting things done, not in celebrating the doing of them. He always looked forward. The only account Hamilton himself left of the assault is his official report, which abounds with complimentary references to the behavior of officers and men, but does not mention his own behavior. The assault took place as soon as it had become dark on the evening of October 14, 1781. Lee says: "Hamilton, with his own and Gimat's corps of light infantry, rushed forward with impetuosity. Pulling up the abatis and knocking down the palisades, he forced his way into the redoubt." In Leake's biography of General John Lamb, who was at the siege of Yorktown, this account is given: "La Fayette's forlorn hope was led by Colonel Hamilton, and the redoubt was carried, with great gallantry at the point of the bayonet. The palisades and abatis were scaled, and Hamilton, placing one foot on the shoulder of a soldier who knelt for that purpose, sprang upon the parapet, and was the first man within the wall. The French attack was also successful, but the work was not so soon carried, and was attended with greater loss, owing to the troops being under a heavy fire, until the sappers opened a passage; a loss which ours avoided by the promptness of the escalade."

This latter account of Hamilton's leadership is the more probable one. It tallies with all the circumstances set forth in his official report. Hamilton was in command, and the force was composed of his battalion, a battalion under Lieutenant-Colonel Gimat, a detachment under Lieutenant-Colonel Laurens, and a detachment of sappers and miners under Captain Gilleland. The approach was probably as stealthy as possible. The attack was made at night and Hamilton's report expressly states that the troops advanced "with unloaded arms." The British line on which Hamilton moved was probably carried with a rush, and so small was his stature that he could hardly have reached the parapet without a lift from a soldier. The rapidity of Hamilton's assault explains the slight loss sustained by his battalion. No one was killed and only four of the soldiers were wounded. Gimat's battalion, which waited until the sappers breached the abatis, experienced severe loss. Gimat himself received a musket-ball in his foot and retired from the field. Two of his captains were wounded, a sergeant was killed and another sergeant wounded. Seven of his rank and file were killed and fifteen were wounded.

Altogether, nine were killed and thirty-one were wounded on the American side; on the British side the killed and wounded did not exceed eight. The facts indicate that the British were rather taken by surprise and that the position was not tenaciously held. The truth was that the British were hopelessly entrapped and they knew it. Washington moved his batteries up to the captured line and the British position then became untenable. On the 19th Cornwallis surrendered and the garrison marched out as prisoners of war. This event was practically the close of the Revolutionary War, so that Hamilton gained his laurels as a field commander in what turned out to be the decisive action. In commenting upon it Washington wrote: "Few cases have exhibited greater proofs of intrepidity, coolness and firmness, than were shown on this occasion."

CHAPTER X

THE START TOWARD NATIONAL UNION

With the close of the Yorktown campaign Hamilton felt free to go on with his plans for establishing himself in civil life. He went to Albany, where his wife was staying in her father's home, and remained there until the birth of his first child, Philip, January 22, 1782. That event naturally sharpened Hamilton's desire for a settled occupation in which he could provide for his family. Writing to his friend, Colonel Meade, of Washington's staff, the following March, to congratulate him on the birth of a daughter, Hamilton remarked: "I can well conceive your happiness on that occasion, by that which I feel on a similar one. Indeed, the sensations of a tender father of the child of a beloved mother, can only be conceived by those who have experienced them." Farther on he tells Meade: "You cannot imagine how entirely domestic I am growing. I lose all taste for the pursuits of ambition. I sigh for nothing but the company of my wife and my baby. The ties of duty alone, or imagined duty, keep me from renouncing public life altogether. It is, however, probable I may not any longer be engaged in it."

This letter was written from Philadelphia, whither Hamilton had gone to arrange for preserving his military rank so long as the war might continue. General Washington was in Philadelphia to consult with Congress, then sitting in that city. Hamilton's views were set forth in two letters to Washington, March 1, 1782, one of which was written with a view to having it shown to members of Congress so that they should understand his position exactly. In it he renounced "all claim to the compensations attached to my military station during the war or afterwards." But he also declared: "I am unwilling to put it out of my power to renew my exertions in the common cause in the line in which I have hitherto acted." He therefore desired to retain his rank, saying, "I shall be at all times ready to obey the call of the public in any capacity, civil or military (consistent with what I owe to myself), in which there may be a prospect of my contributing to the final attainment of the object for which I embarked in the service."

Returning to Albany, Hamilton studied hard to fit himself for legal practice. He rented a house and invited his college chum, Robert Troup, to live with him. In less than five months he was admitted to the bar. That fact, standing alone, might as well imply lax requirement as unusual ability; but other circumstances leave no doubt of the solid preparation he was able to make in so short a time.

It should be considered that his mind had been addressed to law by all his studies.   His deficiency was
in the technique of the profession, and in supplying
that lack he availed himself of a principle well
known to every student, which is that no information is so fully seized and so tightly held as that
which is collected and arranged for a special purpose.   With Troup at hand to answer his inquiries
and direct his research, he composed a manual on
the practice of law, which, Troup relates, "served as
an instructive grammar to future students, and
became the groundwork of subsequent enlarged
practical treatises."   J. C. Hamilton, writing about
seventy years later, remarked: "There are gentlemen now living who copied this manual as their
guide, one of which is in existence."   It was an
astonishing feat for him to perform at the age of
twenty-five, while still a novice, but he was made
quite capable of it by his extraordinary powers of
mental application and orderly analysis.

Hamilton's letters at this time declare strong intention to keep out of politics and stick to the law.
His most intimate friends were urgent in counselling
him to do that very thing, and cease neglecting his
own interests to engage in public service from which
he could expect neither reward nor gratitude.   Two
of his former companions on Washington's staff,
Harrison and Meade, left the army about this time,
feeling that they had no right to be neglecting their

own interests any longer, and they both pressed the same view upon Hamilton. In August, 1782, another army friend, Doctor McHenry, wrote:

It appears to me, Hamilton, to be no longer necessary or a duty, for you and I to go on to sacrifice the small remnant of time that is left us. We have already immolated largely on the altar of liberty. At present, our country neither wants our services in the field or the cabinet, so it is incumbent upon us to be useful in another line. . . . You have a wife and an increasing offspring to urge you forward. . . .

In this letter, which was long, rambling, and gossipy, McHenry gave this warning anecdote:

Hamilton, there are two lawyers in this town [Baltimore], one of which has served the public in the General Assembly for three years with reputation, and to the neglect of his practice. The other has done nothing but attend to his profession, by which he has acquired a handsome competency. Now the people have taken it into their heads to displace the lawyer which has served them till he became poor, in order to put in his stead the lawyer who has served himself & become rich. . . . What is the moral of all this, my dear friend, but that it is high time for you and I to set about in good earnest, doing something for ourselves.

Hamilton's answer to this has not been preserved, but he wrote to Lafayette, November 3, 1782:

I have been employed for the last ten months in rocking the cradle and studying the art of *fleecing* my neighbors. . . . I am going to throw away a few months more in public life, and then retire a simple citizen and good *paterfamilias*. . . . You see the disposition I am in. You are condemned to run the race of ambition all your life. I am already tired of the career, and dare to leave it.

There can be no doubt that Hamilton was quite sincere in what he said. Affectation was not one of his faults. But in this letter, as in other revelations of the state of his mind, distaste for the money-grubbing side of legal practice is manifested, and his interest in public affairs was too strong to be stifled. Busy as he was in the summer of 1782, he could not forbear making his protest against an act that he regarded as barbarous, although in a way he seemed to be going against General Washington himself. A loyalist had been killed by his guard while attempting to escape. In retaliation a band of loyalists hanged Captain Huddy, of the American army, captured by them in New Jersey. On his body was found the label: "Up goes Huddy for Philip White." Washington convened a council of officers, who unanimously decided that either Lippincott, the captain of the loyalist band, should be executed as a murderer, or else an officer of equal rank among the British prisoners should suffer in his stead. Washington approved the decision, and wrote to Sir Henry Clinton, "to save the innocent, I demand the guilty." But Clinton refused to surrender Lippincott, and Washington gave orders that one of the British captains should be selected to suffer in his stead. The lot fell on Captain Asgill, a youth of nineteen.

Hamilton wrote to General Knox: "As this appears to me clearly an ill-timed proceeding, and if persisted in will be derogatory to the national character, I cannot forbear communicating to you my ideas upon the subject. A sacrifice of this sort is entirely repugnant to the genius of the age we live in, and is without example in modern history, nor can it fail to be considered in Europe as wanton and unnecessary. . . . So solemn and deliberate a sacrifice of the innocent for the guilty must be condemned on the present received notions of humanity, and encourage an opinion that we are in a certain degree in a state of barbarism." The letter argues the case at length, and makes the strong point that the British commander had taken steps to prevent any repetition of the Huddy affair, "and, therefore, the only justifying motive of retaliation, the preventing of a repetition of cruelty, ceases." As to the point that General Washington could not now recede from the position he had taken, he declared: "Inconsistency in this case would be better than consistency. But pretexts may be found and will be readily admitted in favor of humanity."

Washington, from his own feelings, was quite desirous of finding a pretext, and he delayed proceedings in that hope. He laid the matter before Congress, on the ground that "it is a great national con-

cern, upon which an individual ought not to decide."
But Congress took no action, refusing to move even
after Washington had written to Duane, a member
from New York, begging to be relieved from his
"cruel situation." Eventually French influence intervened, and Congress was very susceptible to that,
since France was the source of its supplies of real
money. Lady Asgill, the mother of the young officer, wrote such a moving letter that Louis XVI and
his Queen took an active interest in the case, and
their representations, communicated to Washington,
were laid by him before Congress, with the result
that a resolution was passed directing that Captain
Asgill be set at liberty.

At the time Hamilton intervened in this affair he
was a federal office-holder, as a temporary employment reluctantly accepted at a time when he was
busy with his legal studies. Among the improvements in administration he had recommended while
still on Washington's staff was the appointment of
a "Continental Superintendent" in each State to
attend to federal requisitions. In the autumn of
1781 Congress created the office, and on May 2,
1782, Robert Morris appointed Hamilton to it for
the State of New York, his compensation to be one-
fourth of one per cent on his collections. As New
York's quota for the year had been fixed at $373,598,
a commission amounting to $934 was allowed, but
the prospect of collections was such that the com-

mission would scarcely exceed $500. Hamilton at first declined the office, observing: "Time is so precious to me, that I could not put myself in the way of interruptions unless for an object of consequence to the public or myself." Morris would not be refused. He said that the pay would be fixed by the quota irrespective of the collections, and while this "will not be equal to what your own abilities will gain in the profession of law," he particularly desired Hamilton's acceptance. But Hamilton still had scruples. "As the matter now stands, there seems to be little for a Continental receiver to do." If he did no more than to receive money handed to him his official duty would be discharged. Said Hamilton: "There is only one way in which I can imagine a prospect of being materially useful; that is, in seconding your application to the State. In popular assemblies much may sometimes be brought about by personal discussions, by entering into details and combating objections as they rise. If it should, at any time, be thought advisable by you to empower me to act in this capacity, I shall be happy to do everything that depends upon me to effectuate your views."

This was just what Morris wanted, and on July 2 he wrote: "It gives me singular pleasure, to find that you yourself have pointed out the principal objects of your appointment." He enlarged upon the point, urging Hamilton to address "all the abilities with which Heaven has blessed you to induce the legislature to take proper action." Hamilton replied that he would do what he could, but that little could be accomplished until there was a deep change in the whole system of government. "To effect this, mountains of prejudice and particular interest are to be levelled."

The series of reports Hamilton now transmitted to Morris give an instructive survey of the complicated defects of the situation. He gave an account of the State's financial situation, pointing out how it had been weakened by the fact that five out of the fourteen counties were still in the hands of the enemy. Deprived of foreign trade, internal traffic was carried on upon the most disadvantageous terms. These untoward circumstances were aggravated by mismanagement. He instanced what has always been the great bane of American legislation when he observed: "The inquiry constantly is what will *please*, not what will *benefit* the people. In such a government there can be nothing but temporary expenditure, fickleness and folly."

Hamilton estimated that early in the war nearly one-half the people sided with Great Britain, and probably a third still had their secret wishes on that side. "The remainder sigh for peace, murmur at taxes, clamor at their rulers, change one incapable man for another more incapable, and, I fear, if left to themselves, would, too many of them, be willing to purchase peace at any price." He did not regard this situation as peculiar to New York. "However disagreeable the reflection, I have too much reason to believe that the true picture of other States would be, in proportion to their circumstances, equally unpromising. All my inquiries and all that appears induce this opinion."

No wonder Hamilton indorsed this letter as "*Private*"; it was not published in its entirety until 1885. It displays the actual conditions under which the movement for national union began. In his letter to Duane, September 3, 1780, Hamilton had been the first to propose a constitutional convention. Now he was able to start the movement. In carrying out his plans he was greatly aided by the fact that General Schuyler was then a member of the State Senate. Hamilton's first step was to address a letter to Governor Clinton, notifying him of his appointment, stating that it was "a part of his duty, to explain to the legislature from time to time, the views of the Superintendent of Finance, in pursuance of the orders of Congress," and asking the honor of a conference with a committee of the two houses. Clinton laid the matter before the legislature and conferences were held in which Hamilton virtually acted in the capacity of a chancellor of the exchequer, explaining and recommending projects of taxation. While not able to secure the adoption of all his plans, he had considerable success, and incidentally he launched the project of a new constitution. Although that result was not to be attained for five years yet, the definite sequence of events begins at this time.

On July 19, 1782, the Senate, on motion of General Schuyler, resolved itself into a committee of the whole, "to take into consideration the state of the Union," and the Assembly at once followed suit. The next day an important set of resolutions was reported. They declared "that the situation of these States is in a peculiar manner critical, and affords the strongest reason to apprehend, from a continuance of the present constitution of the Continental government, a subdivision of the public credit, and consequences highly dangerous to the safety and independence of these States."

After a series of preambles dealing with particular features of the situation, there followed a resolution declaring that the desired ends can never be attained through the deliberations of the States individually, "but that it is essential to the common welfare, that there should be as soon as possible a conference of the whole on this subject, and that it would be advisable for this purpose to propose to Congress to recommend, and to each State to adopt, the measure of assembling a general convention of the States, specially authorized to revise and amend the Confederation, reserving a right to the respective legislatures to ratify their determinations."

The resolutions were passed by the Senate and were immediately sent to the Assembly, which concurred by unanimous vote on Sunday, July 21. The next day the governor was requested to transmit a copy to Congress and to each of the States. These resolutions came from Hamilton's pen. Writing to Morris on July 22, Hamilton remarked: "I think this a very eligible step, though I doubt of the concurrence of the other States; but I am certain without it, they will never be brought to cooperate in any reasonable or effectual plan."

Besides adopting Hamilton's resolutions, which, however, appeared before it simply as a report from one of its own committees, the legislature on the next day elected him as a State delegate to the Continental Congress, to succeed General Schuyler, who withdrew in his favor. Hamilton's indebtedness to Schuyler's influence shows plainly enough in these transactions.

A letter to his intimate friend John Laurens, under date of August 15, shows that Hamilton's election to Congress turned his thoughts strongly again to public activities. After telling Laurens that peace negotiations were under way, he continued:

Peace made, my dear friend, a new scene opens. The object then will be to make our independence a blessing. To do this we must secure our Union on solid foundations —a herculean task,—and to effect which, mountains of prejudice must be levelled. It requires all the virtue and all the abilities of the country. Quit your sword, my friend; put on the toga. Come to Congress. We know each other's sentiments; our views are the same. We have fought side by side to make America free; let us hand in hand struggle to make her happy.

Laurens probably never received this letter, for, with the slow carriage of the mails at that time, it could hardly have reached him in his South Carolina camp by August 27, on which day he was killed. He was ill in bed when word came of the approach of a party of the enemy, and he arose at once to direct his troops. The affair turned out to be a mere skirmish, but in it Laurens was mortally wounded. Hamilton felt the loss deeply. Writing to Lafayette, he said: "You know how truly I loved him, and will judge how much I regret him." Writing to General Greene, he said: "The world will feel the loss of a man who has left few like him behind." It was, indeed, an abrupt ending of a career of brilliant promise. Born in the same year as Hamilton, John Laurens became one of Washington's aides at the outbreak of the Revolution. He performed a service of inestimable value as a commissioner to France in 1781, when his polished manners and engaging personality greatly facilitated the arrangements by which France contributed money and supplies for the Yorktown campaign. His death was regarded by Hamilton as a great loss to the movement for a national union, which soon began to take shape, and which was mainly carried on by the younger set among the American leaders, in which Laurens had been a distinguished figure.

CHAPTER XI

THE CRUMBLING OF THE CONFEDERATION

WHEN Hamilton entered Congress in November, 1782, the federal government was in the last stage of decrepitude. So long as its issues of paper money would circulate, Congress lived high and spent profusely. The amount issued in 1775 was $6,000,000; in 1776, $19,000,000; in 1777, $13,000,000; in 1778, $63,000,000; in 1779, $140,000,000. Toward the end of 1779 Congress tried to support the credit of its emissions by an address pledging faithful redemption of them, declaring that "a bankrupt, faithless republic would be a novelty in the political world, and appear among respectable nations like a common prostitute among chaste and respectable matrons." The clique of lawyer-politicians that then ran Congress could always produce fine language, but they could eat their words with equal professional facility. In little more than three months later they enacted a sweeping measure of repudiation, by a complicated scheme which accomplished that result while avoiding the proper name for it. By the act of March 18, 1780, forty dollars in Continental currency were rated as equivalent to only one dollar in coin, in payments made by the States

143

to the general government. Bills thus turned in
were to be destroyed, but a new issue was authorized, to be redeemed in specie within six years,
meanwhile bearing interest at five per cent. These
bills were to be issued by the States with the guarantee of the United States, and each State was to
retain six-tenths of the issue signed by it, the remainder to be at the disposition of the United States,
credited to the States respectively on their assessed
quotas. The act provided that the States should
establish sinking-funds, and apparently all that
legal ingenuity could do was done to make the
people think the new bills had real value, although
the old had none.

In effect, the scheme was a substitution of the
credit of the States for the lost credit of the United
States. The States could levy taxes and hence had
the means of meeting their obligations; the United
States could not levy taxes and was dependent upon
loans or upon assessments, to which the States could
respond as they pleased. The act of 1780 was too
dependent upon State co-operation to provide much
revenue, and what bills were issued under its provisions soon began to sink in value. In the spring
of 1781 State notes were officially rated as 3 to 1 in
specie and Continental notes at 175 to 1. Continental notes were actually rated at 525 to 1 before
they went out of circulation altogether. In May,
1781, men marched through the streets of Philadel-

phia with cockades in their hats made of twists of paper money, and a dog, led in the procession, was tarred and plastered over with paper money.

The Yorktown campaign was made possible by the creation of the treasury department, managed by Robert Morris, and by the money and supplies which France then became willing to send. But Congress had been very reluctant to let go its own custody of the treasury and yielded only because there was no longer any way of getting money through its own devices. While willing to let Morris borrow money wherever he could get it, the members could not be depended on to support any scheme of taxation. He took office with the expectation that the States would allow Congress to levy five per cent upon imports. Virginia at once assented, but later rescinded its action, and according to a statement in one of Madison's letters this change of attitude was due to influence exerted by Arthur Lee, a member of Congress. Massachusetts and Rhode Island remonstrated against the impost. In general, the attitude of New England was strongly against any taxing authority other than that of each State in its own area. Samuel Adams was opposed to the very existence of a national treasury department and made gloomy prognostications as to its effect on the liberties of the people.

This, then, was the national situation when Hamilton entered Congress: an empty treasury, no taxing power, no credit, no resources save those obtained by borrowing or begging. Although the theory of the existing union was that the cost of the general government would be met by assessments upon the States, each State might judge for itself of the fairness of its quota and act accordingly. The best record for 1782 was made by Rhode Island, which paid about one-fourth of its quota; Pennsylvania came next, with over a fifth paid; next, Massachusetts, with about an eighth; then Virginia, about a twelfth, with the excuse of war ravages for delinquency; New York and Maryland, each about a twentieth; New Hampshire, about a one hundred and twenty-first part; North Carolina, Delaware, and Georgia nothing at all. South Carolina was the only State credited with full payment of its quota, and that was because it was credited with supplies to the troops serving there.

Congressional financiering gave great opportunity to rogues. The *Pennsylvania Packet* of April 17, 1779, published a letter from a young lady stating that her trustee had taken advantage of the legal-tender acts to pay her the principal of her inheritance in depreciated currency. Transactions of that character were going on all the time. Merchants and farmers could protect themselves to some extent by refusing to make sales except for goods of real value. The troops were, however, helpless victims. A memorial of Virginia officers in November, 1781, stated that the depreciation of the currency in which they were paid was such that the actual value of what they received was then $3⅓ a month for a colonel, $1.66 for a captain, and 20 cents for a private. In the same month Robert Morris wrote that the government was no longer able to buy anything with its paper money.[1]

Upon this scene of distress, confusion, and disorder, Hamilton entered alert, energetic, clearsighted, and resourceful. The correspondence of the public men of the period shows that the general attitude of mind was that of grim endurance, in the hope that Great Britain would tire of the struggle, and then the different States might again manage their own affairs as before the war. The sorry plight of the general government was therefore a matter of only temporary concern, and meanwhile it would not be a matter of vital importance, if France should continue her aid. Early in his congressional term Hamilton wrote a long letter to the Vicomte de Noailles, who had returned to France, giving him an account of the military and political situation, in which he admitted that "the capital successes we have had, have served rather to increase the hopes than the exertions of the particular States." Things were "in a mending way" through

---

[1] The most complete account of the financial situation during the Confederation period is contained in W. G. Sumner's *The Financier and the Finances of the American Revolution*.

Robert Morris's banking arrangements, "but upon the whole, however, if the war continues another year, it will be necessary that Congress should again recur to the generosity of France for pecuniary assistance."

Hamilton sent a letter of like tenor, but more familiar in style, to Lafayette, who also was then back in France. Said Hamilton: "These States are in no humor for continuing exertions; if the war lasts it must be carried on by external succors. I make no apology for the inertness of this country. I detest it, but since it exists I am sorry to see other resources diminish." This was an allusion to the withdrawal of the French troops.

While doing what he could to induce France to continue its aid, Hamilton was well aware that this was asking that country to tax its people for the support of a country that was unwilling to tax its own people for its own support. Morris was trying hard to carry the five per cent impost. It was his belief that its prospects hinged on the consent of Rhode Island, which in the days before railroads occupied a position of peculiar advantage with respect to New England commerce. Under date of November 30, 1782, the Speaker of the Rhode Island Assembly wrote to Congress stating the reasons of that State for refusing. They were to the effect that the impost scheme would allow Congress to introduce officers into the State, unknown to and unaccountable to the State, and would permit Congress to collect money from the commerce of the State, for the expenditure of which Congress would not be accountable to the State. The argument put Congress in the same position formerly assigned to the British Parliament, as a body making unconstitutional pretensions.

The answer of Congress to these objections was written by Hamilton. It pointed out that the position taken by Rhode Island "would defeat all the provisions of the Confederation, all the purposes of the Union. The truth is that no Federal Constitution can exist without powers that, in their exercise, affect the internal police of the component members." The reply went on to show how impossible it would be to obtain foreign loans unless Congress was in a position to offer security. "We must pledge an ascertained fund; simple and productive in its nature, general in its principle, and at the disposal of a single will. There can be little confidence in a security under the constant revisal of thirteen different deliberations. It must, once for all, be defined and established on the faith of the States solemnly pledged to each other, and not revocable by any without a breach of the general compact."

All this is an assertion of national authority against a claim of State sovereignty. But Hamilton was not content with merely making the point. He proceeded to emphasize it. Rhode Island contended that it was necessary for each State to keep all collection of revenue within its own borders in its own hands, to protect itself against the possibility of exorbitant demands by Congress. Hamilton made the square reply that this was a point on which the States "have no constitutional liberty to judge. Such a refusal would be an exertion of power; not of right." He went on to show that the very idea of a general government implied that the security of the public was through representation in Congress, and not through the interposition of State authority. After this sharp assertion of principle, the document made an appeal to interest by pointing out the immediate benefits that would accrue from the measure.

Although Hamilton was able to present a case that was logically complete it was practically defective, as he was keenly aware. Congress could say ought, but could not say must. It could exert influence, but it could not wield power; and, as Washington pithily observed, "influence is not government." What influence Congress had possessed had declined because of its record of waste, extravagance, and mismanagement; and, moreover, it was impaired by the fact that the members themselves were apt to regard Congress as a diplomatic assembly in which they looked after the particular interests of their own States, rather than as a national legislature. This tendency was prominently displayed by an incident in connection with the Rhode Island negotiation. A Boston newspaper published a statement —promptly copied by Rhode Island papers—that there was no longer any need for an impost since a foreign loan had been arranged. This was true to the extent that a loan was being negotiated in Holland, but it was quite untrue that it was enough to enable Congress to meet its engagements. It was rumored that a member of Congress was the source of this report and an investigation was voted, whereupon David Howell declared himself to be the author. He was a Princeton graduate, serving his first term in Congress, of which he was a member from 1782 to 1785. In 1790 he became professor of law in Brown University. When a man of his standing could pursue such a course, it shows how strong particularist tendencies were at that period. In fact, Hamilton's assertion of national ideals met with little genuine support in Congress. In debate, about this time, Hamilton observed that one reason why the government should have its own revenue collected by its own agents was that "as the energy of the federal government was evidently short of the degree necessary for pervading and uniting the States, it was expedient to introduce the influence of officers deriving their emoluments from, and, consequently, interested in supporting, the power of Congress." Madison relates that the members "smiled at the disclosure." Madison's record is,

then, evidence that, at a time when Congress was inclined to acquiesce in conditions of dependence on
State aid, Hamilton grasped the problem in its entirety as being the creation of national authority,
and he insisted upon honest statement of it. His
reference to the mode of collection was no slip of
the tongue. A little later, February 12, 1783, he
moved the following, in which the marks of emphasis
are his own:

Resolved, That it is the opinion of Congress that complete JUSTICE cannot be done to the creditors of the
United States, nor the restoration of PUBLIC CREDIT
be effected, nor the future exigencies of the war provided
for, but by the establishment of permanent and adequate
funds to operate generally throughout the United States,
to be collected by Congress.

John Rutledge, of South Carolina, with a view to
softening the opposition, moved that the impost
should be applied only to the support of the army.
Hamilton at once dissented. He "would never
assent to such a partial administration of justice,"
and, moreover, "it was impolitic to divide the interests of the civil and military creditors, whose
joint efforts in the states would be necessary to pre-
vail on them to adopt a general revenue." It
plainly appears from this that Hamilton had firmly
grasped the principle that the true constitution of a
country is the actual distribution of political force,

and to understand his statesmanship this should be
kept in mind.

Washington's attitude was of such central importance that his correspondence at this period reflects
all the political currents of the times.   The most
impetuous was that issuing from the army, where
the feeling was strong that unless they looked out
for themselves the politicians would bilk them.   In
communications received by Washington there was
much in the way of deploring and trusting and hop-
ing, but nothing that exhibits plan or direction until
Hamilton entered, which was not until February 7,
1783.   The rupture that had occurred when Hamilton resigned his military secretaryship had meanwhile stopped their intimacy.   But Hamilton could
not proceed with his plans without Washington's
co-operation, and this he now endeavored to secure.
"Flattering myself," he wrote, "that your knowledge of me will induce you to receive the observations I make as dictated by a regard to the public
good, I take the liberty to suggest to you my ideas
on some matters of delicacy and importance."   After
this deferential approach, he made a plain statement of the actual situation, showing that "there
has scarcely been a period of the Revolution which
called more for wisdom and decision in Congress.
Unfortunately for us, we are a body not governed
by reason or foresight but by circumstances."   He
pointed out that the attitude of the army was a

prime factor in the situation. "The claims of the army, urged with moderation but with firmness, may operate on those weak minds which are influenced by their apprehensions more than by their judgments. . . . But the difficulty will be to keep *a complaining and suffering army* within the bounds of moderation." Hamilton then gave Washington some advice as to his own behavior. "It is of moment to the public tranquillity that your Excellency should preserve the confidence of the army, without losing that of the people. This will enable you in case of extremity to guide the torrent, and to bring order, perhaps even good, out of confusion." He suggested that it would "be advisable not to discountenance their endeavors to procure redress, but rather, by the intervention of confidential and prudent persons, to *take the direction of them*." Washington's attention was then called to the fact that there was an idea in the army that he was not "espousing its interests with sufficient warmth."

The phrase which Hamilton emphasized is the point to which the letter is addressed. It was a tactful instruction to Washington from one much his junior. Washington was then but a fortnight short of fifty-one, and he was already world-famous; Hamilton had just turned twenty-six, and he was barely started in his profession as a lawyer. Washington, than whom no man known to history had more magnanimity, not merely took Hamilton's suggestions in good part but at once entered into confidential relations. He laid aside the cautious reserve which characterizes his replies to all other correspondents, and opened his heart to Hamilton about his troubles. He remarked: "The predicament, in which I stand as a citizen and as a soldier, is as critical and delicate as can well be conceived." He declared that for several months his behavior had been in accord with the suggestions now made by Hamilton, and he had not much fear now that army sentiment would exceed "the bounds of reason and moderation."

As a matter of fact, it required all the influence that Washington could exert to prevent an outbreak, but enough money was scraped up by Morris to give the troops a payment on account, sufficient to induce them to accept the proposed furlough, as it was called, although it was really a disbandment. Keeping in close and frequent correspondence with Washington, Hamilton took a leading part in all these proceedings. He was chairman of the committee of three appointed by Congress to deal with the situation created by the mutiny of certain troops at Philadelphia and at Lancaster, and he was prompt and vigorous in his measures. He wrote a *Vindication of Congress*, in which he pointed out that the system was more at fault than those who labored under it. "On the one hand they are blamed for not doing what they have no means of doing; on the other, their attempts are branded with the imputation of a spirit of encroachment and a lust of power." He urged that "in these circumstances, it is the duty of all those who have the welfare of the community at heart to unite their efforts to direct the attention of the people to the true source of the public disorders—the want of an EFFICIENT GENERAL GOVERNMENT."

This was Hamilton's main object during his congressional career, but when it became manifest that nothing more could then be done in that direction his longing to be with his family became irrepressible. Under date of July 22, 1783, he wrote to his wife that he would soon start for home.

I am strongly urged to stay a few days for the ratification of the treaty; at all events, however, I will not be long absent. I give you joy of the happy conclusion of this important work in which your country has been engaged. Now in a very short time we shall be happily settled in New York. . . . Kiss my boy a thousand times.

After he got back to Albany he gathered up some loose ends of his congressional work. In one of his letters to Washington, in the spring of 1783, Hamilton had observed:

It now only remains to make solid establishments within, to perpetuate our Union, to prevent our being a ball in the hands of European powers, bandied against each other at their pleasure; in fine, to make our independence truly a blessing. . . . I will add that your excellency's exertions are as essential to accomplish this end as they have been to establish independence. I will upon a future occasion open myself upon this subject.

Writing from Albany, September 30, he recalled this promise, and went on to explain:

At the time I was in hopes Congress might have been induced to take a decisive ground; to inform their constituents of the imperfections of the present system, and of the impossibility of conducting the public affairs with honor to themselves and advantage to the community, with powers so disproportionate to their responsibility; and having done this, in a full and forcible manner, to adjourn the moment the definitive treaty was ratified. In retiring at the same juncture, I wished you, in a solemn manner, to declare to the people your intended retreat from public concerns, your opinion of the present government, and of the absolute necessity of a change.

Before I left Congress I despaired of the first, and your circular letter to the States had anticipated the last. I trust it will not be without effect, though I am persuaded it would have had more, combined with what I have mentioned. At all events, without compliment, Sir, it will do you honor with the sensible and well-meaning; and ultimately, it is to be hoped, with the people at large, when the present epidemic frenzy has subsided.

This letter makes an interesting disclosure of the reach of Hamilton's political strategy and also of its wariness. The resolutions he prepared for Congress were found among his papers, indorsed, "Intended to be submitted to Congress in seventeen hundred and eighty-three, but abandoned for want of support." The document is a complete analysis of the defects of government, digested under twelve heads, concluding with a call for a constitutional convention. But Hamilton correctly judged that the time was not propitious for the national movement, and that it would be necessary to delay matters until the teachings of experience had begun to produce effect. Meanwhile he made a gallant fight against the spread of the "epidemic frenzy" in the politics of his own State.

CHAPTER XII

LAW PRACTICE

IT can scarcely be called to mind too frequently that while Hamilton was lavishly spending his powers for the public good, he was a poor man with the bread-and-butter problem always before him. In May, 1783, he wrote to Governor Clinton that it would be very injurious to him to remain in Congress much longer, and that, "having no future views in public life, I owe it to myself without delay to enter upon the care of my private concerns in earnest."

New York was evacuated by the British in November, 1783, and soon after Hamilton settled there to practise his profession, opening his office at No. 58 Wall Street. Claims arising out of transactions during the war produced a great crop of cases. In those days there was no specialization and Hamilton took both civil and criminal cases, so that at one time he might be in the mayor's court and again in the highest court in the State. He was at one time counsel for the defendant in a rape case, and he also figured in assault and murder cases. The rapidity with which he gained distinction at the bar is attested by the fact that so early as 1784 he began to receive applications for admission of law students to his office. Such students paid a fee of $150, and were rated as clerks. Hamilton's office books note in his own handwriting that one such fee was returned because the pupil "did not continue his clerkship." That of itself did not require a refund, but Hamilton always displayed a generous consideration for people's circumstances. In 1796, when he was at the height of his professional renown, a client offered him $1,000 as a general retainer, without any case then pending. The letter bears Hamilton's indorsement, "Returned as being more than is proper."

It appears from his office records that for many years his office fee was only £1 10s., and that was his usual charge for drawing a petition or giving legal advice in an ordinary case. He charged £5 a day for trying a case in court. It appears that he was not above taking a contingent fee, for the receipt of $100 is noted with the remark, "if successful an additional hundred." Although he was associated in many cases with his friend, Robert Troup, Hamilton took as his law partner Balthazar De Heart, a circumstance readily accounted for by the fact that De Heart appears to have been what is now known as a managing clerk. The arrangement really meant that Hamilton desired individual freedom of action as a lawyer.

Among Hamilton's early cases is one that is deservedly famous, both from the massiveness and solidity of his argument in support of national authority, and also as displaying his dauntless courage in confronting a furious popular opposition. By the treaty of peace with England it was provided that there should be no more confiscations or prosecutions on account of the side taken in the war, and that no person should thereby "suffer any future loss or damage, either in his person, liberty, or property." Among the vindictive measures passed by the New York Whigs against the loyalists was the act of March 17, 1783, providing that loyalists who had occupied Whig property by British authority, might be sued for trespass and held liable for arrears of rent. This was dead against the treaty stipulations and was known to be so when enacted. The effect of the treaty in restricting State action was pointed out by the American commissioners, in transmitting a copy from Paris, December 14, 1782, and they had distinctly asserted that in their opinion Congress was supreme in this matter. It fell to Hamilton to be the first to maintain this principle in practice and secure for it judicial sanction.

Although the issue involved the whole question of national sovereignty, the particular case in which it was raised was as disadvantageous as could be for the purpose of securing a thoughtful and just decision—the plaintiff a widow, the defendant a firm of brewers who had carried on their business as British subjects. In 1778 they had rented a brewery and malt house on Maiden Lane, at a rent of £150 per annum, which they paid to a person designated by the British commander. They had to make considerable outlay in fitting the property for use, and were still carrying on the business when in November, 1783, the city again passed under American control. They were quite ready to pay the rent to any person who could legally receipt for it, and at once complied with an order from the American commander to pay current dues to the son of Mrs. Elizabeth Rutgers, the former owner, who had now returned to claim her property. But she wanted the back rent also, which they had already paid elsewhere by British authority, and she entered suit under the trespass act.

The issue, although deep, was narrow. It was simply whether a treaty obligation contracted by federal authority could override the laws of the State of New York. The widow had State law and popular sentiment on her side. There were then no federal courts, and, indeed no federal government except the weak and ailing one carried on by the Continental Congress. The suit was brought before a local tribunal, the mayor's court. And yet such was the force of Hamilton's reasoning that he convinced the court and obtained a judgment in his favor. Such ability in a man of twenty-seven, who had been practising law less than two years, seems almost supernatural; and, indeed, it does not become intelligible until the circumstances are attentively considered.

The only record that remains of Hamilton's argument is the skeleton he used, covering nineteen pages of closely written foolscap. Notwithstanding its length, it contains merely bare notes of the points he intended to make, such as

A. Introduction.
>Question concerns National faith—character—safety—Confederation.

B. Serious because wrong judgment good cause of war.

C. Present case somewhat new—*law of reason Public good*—ubi lex tacet judex loquitur.

D. Question embraces the whole law of nations.

and so on through the letters of the alphabet until with *T* he finished his analysis. But all this was introductory. Then followed a series of propositions, such as

>Judges of each State must of necessity be judges of the United States.

>And the law of each State must adopt the laws of Congress.

>Though in relation to its own Citizens local laws might govern, yet in relation to foreigners those of United States must prevail.

Under the subhead "Principles" he enters into an extended examination of the law of nations. Another section is devoted to "Rules of Construction of Statutes." Evidently he prepared his argument with the utmost thoroughness and care, so as to explore the whole field of law touched by the case.

It now seems odd that the mayor's court should have been the forum for such an argument, but not so in those times. The mayor, recorder, sheriff, coroner, and town clerk were all at that time appointed by the governor of the State. James Duane, who was appointed mayor, February 7, 1784, was a man of wealth and high social position. During the war he had had terms of service in the New York Provincial Congress, in the Continental Congress, and in the State Senate. Eventually, under Washington's administration, he became the first United States judge of the district of New York. The recorder, the chief judicial officer, was Richard Varick, who had been Washington's private secretary during the latter part of the war. It therefore appears that the mayor's court was then so officered that any question of public obligation could count upon appreciative consideration. The case turned on the question whether or not the authority under which the defendants had acted could be pleaded against the claim. By the law of the State that plea was inadmissible. The real point which the court had to decide was whether the treaty overruled the State inhibition, and its judgment went straight to that point. The court declared:

> Our Union, as has been properly observed, is known, and legalized in our Constitution, and adopted as a fundamental law in the first act of our legislature. The federal compact hath vested Congress with full and exclusive powers to make peace and war. This treaty they have made and ratified, and rendered its obligation perpetual; and we are clearly of opinion, that no State in this union can alter or abridge, in a single point, the federal articles or the treaty.

Such a decision at such a time was a brave act. Local sentiment was strongly in favor of proscribing all who had been on the Tory side during the war. General Lamb and others who had been active "Sons of Liberty," the organization to which Hamilton had attached himself while a college student, were now determined to push Whig triumph to the uttermost, despite the treaty. A mass meeting was held at which an address was adopted exhorting the people "to elect men who would spurn any proposition that had a tendency to curtail the privileges of the people, and who would protect them from judicial tyranny." In fact, in the first election after the peace the party of vengeance swept the polls. General Lamb and other active partisans were elected members of the Assembly, in which their influence was so supreme that resolutions were passed calling upon the Governor and Council "to appoint such persons as will govern themselves by the known law of the land." The Assembly by a vote of 32 to 9 passed a bill declaring a "certain description of persons without the protection of the laws of this State"; and the Senate, without material amendment, passed it by a vote of 10 to 6. A like wave of rancor swept other States. In Virginia the House of Delegates declared that any return of confiscated property was wholly inadmissible, and that "laws made by any independent State of this Union" should not be "subject to the adjudication of any power or powers on earth." In New Jersey meetings were held urging non-compliance with the treaty of peace. In Massachusetts a committee of the legislature, of which Samuel Adams was chairman, reported that no person who had borne arms against the United States, or lent money to the enemy to carry on the war, should ever be permitted to return to the State. A spirit of proscription, resembling in its malignity that which characterized a victorious faction in the civil wars of Greece and Rome, was abroad in America.

Hamilton's action in pleading treaty obligations in behalf of clients, against State law, might have secured some indulgence as a performance of professional duty, although even then it was a hazardous proceeding in the existing state of sentiment. Later on, after he had led the way, lawyers generally employed that argument, among them Giles of

Virginia, who eventually became Hamilton's most active congressional foe. But Hamilton not only stemmed the tide at its flood, but he carried the issue from the court into the public forum. While the legislature was passing disfranchisement acts and prescribing test oaths, Hamilton wrote an appeal "to the Considerate Citizens of New York, on the Politics of the Times, in Consequence of the Peace." This letter, signed "Phocion," is more impassioned in its style than was usual with him, and was done in a rush, for he concluded with an apology for "the hasty and incorrect manner." The letter was a sharp rebuke to the violent counsels then prevailing, with some pointed advice that it was a mistake to think that spite and malevolence could now have their way without risk. "Suppose," he asked, "Great Britain should be induced to refuse a further compliance with the treaty, in consequence of a breach of it on our part; what situation should we be in? Can we renew the war to compel a compliance? We know and all the world knows, it is out of our power." Nor could other powers be expected to come to America's aid as before. "They will not think themselves bound to undertake an unjust war, to regain to us rights which we have forfeited by a childish levity, and a wanton contempt of public faith. We should then have sacrificed important interests to the little, vindictive, selfish, mean passions of a few."

Most of the leading men in the War of the Revolution felt about the matter just as Hamilton did, but he was the only man who dared to come out and say so. The peculiar heroism of his statesmanship is his utter fearlessness of unpopularity. Public men are apt to shrink from that, and face it only when brought to bay; but Hamilton seems never to have hesitated to brave it whenever a political issue appeared to him to involve the honor of his country. That is not a trait by which American politicians get ahead, and it worked against Hamilton's personal success in public life. His achievements were all accomplished by sheer force of intellect; his career owed nothing to popular favor.

Hamilton's letter attracted so much attention that the party of proscription felt that some justification of their policy was desirable, and this was supplied by Isaac Ledyard, a State politician of some prominence, writing over the signature of "Mentor." His letter adopted a judicial tone, and by applying rigorous strict-construction principles to the language of the treaty, concluded that it was still within the power of the States to exclude such as would be undesirable citizens. Hamilton's reply is a more solid performance than his first letter. He made a detailed analysis of the subject, and he entered into an inquiry into the nature of constitutional authority and the true principles of government. In conclusion, he made a powerful appeal to patriotic feeling. "Those who are at present entrusted with power, in all these infant republics, hold the most sacred deposit that ever was confided to human hands. 'Tis with governments as with individuals; first impressions and early habits give a lasting bias to the temper and character. Our governments, hitherto, have no habits. How important to the happiness, not of America alone, but of mankind, that they should acquire good ones!" He referred to the influence which America would exert upon the world as a republican example. Would it be such as to show the efficacy of self-government or its impracticability? If instead of exhibiting justice, moderation, liberality, the public counsels are guided by passion and prejudice, then, with the greatest advantages for promoting it that ever a people had, we shall have betrayed the cause of liberty.

Hamilton's letters were printed and circulated in other States and were republished in London. Besides the reply of "Mentor," articles by "Gustavus," "Anti-Phocionite," and others appeared, but Hamilton's superiority in any pamphlet war was so overwhelming that there was some talk of forcing upon him a succession of duels, until he was done for. The only existing authority for this statement is J. C. Hamilton's biography, which relates that Ledyard heard of the plot and broke it up by his indignant protest; furthermore, that Hamilton shook hands with Ledyard and thanked him for saving his life. Isaac Q. Leake's memoir of General John Lamb, a well-documented work, questions the accuracy of the account so far as Ledyard is concerned, but gives precise details of a challenge sent to Hamilton by Colonel Eleazer Oswald, subsequently withdrawn, as "the affair was adjusted honorably to both parties." It is at least clear that Hamilton took serious risks in braving local sentiment as he did, but such considerations never daunted him at any time in any way.

All sorts of professional business now flowed to Hamilton. In 1784 he organized the Bank of New York. From a letter of March 10, to his brother-in-law, John Barker Church, it appears that Hamilton went into this enterprise to counteract a land-bank scheme which was being urged upon the legislature as "the true philosopher's stone that was to turn all their rocks and trees into gold." Alarmed by this project, New York merchants started a subscription for a money bank, and on their application Hamilton prepared its constitution and by-laws.

This was but an item of his numerous professional activities. His gains by them did not dull his perception of the fact that much of the legal practice of the times was due to bad government. He remarked to a correspondent that "legislative folly had afforded so plentiful a harvest that he had scarcely a moment to spare from the substantial business of reaping."

There is plenty of evidence to show that Hamilton had taken a leading rank at the New York bar, and all he needed to do to make his fortune was to keep out of politics; but this he could not do.

CHAPTER XIII

THE NATIONAL MOVEMENT

THE four years that elapsed between the end of the war and the meeting of the constitutional convention of 1787 was a period of increasing anarchy. The only organ of national authority was the Continental Congress, and that was profoundly distrusted. Whatever funds it could get hold of were disbursed through its own committees, which were not subject to much accountability. The payment of members was supposed to come from the States that sent them, and it varied from time to time and from place to place, according to the disposition of the State authorities and the personal popularity of a member. The Massachusetts delegates were allowed £10 a day and expenses. An account of Elbridge Gerry is on record which shows that from January 5, 1776, to July 5, 1780, he was allowed for his time and expenses £40,502 6s. and 2d., which is at the rate of over $44,000 a year. On the face of it this is a larger sum than was charged by Washington for his expenses for eight years as commander-in-chief, but nominal amounts were so different from real values that exact comparison is impossible.

The household of the president of the Continental

Congress was maintained by that body as a public institution. No fixed allowance was made, but Congress by resolution directed that "a convenient, furnished dwelling house be hired, and a table, carriage and servants provided at the public expense." The committee on the treasury appointed a steward and supervised his accounts. The president was expected to keep open house. General Washington wrote that "the table was always crowded, and with mixed company, and the president considered in no better light than as a *maitre d'hotel.*"

The profusion which always surrounded Congress was one of the sources of army discontent. In 1780 Congress raised the pay of its principal clerks to $8,000 a year; of the auditor-general to $12,000; of the secretary of Congress to $14,000. All these sums are subject to large discount, from the depreciation of the currency; but the army suffered in the same way, and meanwhile could not get arrears of pay due them. In a letter to Hamilton, April 22, 1783, Washington said: "Let me assure you that it would not be more difficult to still the raging billows in a tempestuous gale, than to convince the officers of this army of the justice or policy of paying men in civil office full wages, when they cannot obtain a sixtieth part of their dues."

The members of Congress voted as States and were alert to see that in the distribution of patronage each State got its share, which, of course, tended to multiply offices. Robert Morris introduced economies which incurred for him bitter enmities. Madison wrote to Jefferson, September 20, 1783: "The department of finance is an object of almost daily attack, and will be reduced to its crisis on the final resignation of Mr. Morris, which will take place in a few months." In November Morris wrote to Jay that the members of Congress, instead of supporting him as they had promised to do, were trying to frustrate his plans so as to ruin him personally. Early in 1783 he offered his resignation, but was persuaded to stay long enough to arrange a settlement with the army. Then he insisted on getting out and he retired on November 1, 1784. Congress then returned to its old methods and put the treasury in the hands of a board of three commissioners, one of them being Arthur Lee, who had been the tireless enemy of Morris's administration.

The States were loath to impose taxes and collect money for such an irresponsible body as Congress, and were apt to turn sulky when lectured about their behavior. In March, 1783, General Greene wrote a letter to the South Carolina Legislature, urging that something should be done for the public credit and for the support of the army. In this he did no more than he had often done during the war, with the approval of the legislature, but now it treated his action as an offense to its dignity, and resented it by repealing its former consent to the

five-per-cent impost.   The circular letter of June 8,
1783, which Washington addressed to the governors
of all the States urging compliance with the demand
of Congress for the power to levy taxes, wholly
failed to move the States, and from a letter of Randolph to Madison it appears that there was a general
murmur "against what is called the unsolicited ob-
trusion of his advice."

In fact, distrust of the Continental Congress never
could be overcome, although that body did what it
could to remove opposition by promises of amendment and by reducing its demands.   In its efforts
to conciliate the States, Congress agreed to become
a migratory body.   There was jealousy over the
sectional advantage which it was held that Pennsylvania derived from the meeting of Congress in Philadelphia.   In 1783, after Congress had left Philadelphia for Princeton, there were numerous debates
on the subject of a federal city, and it was resolved
that there should be two national capitals, one on
the Delaware and the other on the Potomac, to be
used alternately by Congress; but until suitable
buildings should be erected Congress should sit in
Trenton and at Annapolis by turns.   But nothing
that Congress could do could persuade the States
to provide Congress with sources of revenue under
its own administration.   All that years of coaxing
and pleading could effect was the cession of all the
western lands to the United States, which from the

State point of view was a handsome provision of assets with which in time Congress should be able to meet its liabilities.

Meanwhile the national government was bankrupt and its prospects seemed hopeless. For a long time everything indicated that the Confederation would run the usual career of dissolution, such as had been followed by every Confederation known to history up to that time, and that was the general expectation among thoughtful observers. Those who labored to keep the States together sustained their hopes by the belief that the people would learn by experience the need of a general government, and meanwhile they used every possible means to direct the course of events. Their efforts were powerfully aided by increasing evidence of the weakness and incompetence of State authority. Distrust of the Continental Congress was now associated with distrust of the State legislatures, and the effect was to produce a desire for authority superior to both. Thoughts turning in that direction rested comfortably upon the stanch figure of George Washington, in whose prudence and integrity there was universal confidence.

Conditions did not become ripe for action until 1786, when, in addition to their other troubles, the States were in a snarl about commercial regulations. Such important waters as Long Island Sound, New York Bay, the Delaware, the Chesapeake, were not any of them under the jurisdiction of a single State, and regulations adopted by one State were affected by the action of neighboring States. The whole subject of interstate relations received a large addition of interest when schemes of internal navigation became a general topic of discussion. No subject was more popular, as it contained many elements appealing to the imagination—business opportunity, means of transportation, commercial expansion, development of natural resources, the advance of America in wealth and population. Joel Barlow, the Connecticut poet, whose masterpiece, the *Vision of Columbus*, made its appearance in March, 1787, told in it how

"Canals, long-winding, ope a watery flight,
   And distant streams and seas and lakes unite.
   From fair Albania, toward the setting sun,
   Back through the midland, lengthening channels run,
   Meet the fair lakes, their beauteous towns that lave,
   And Hudson join to broad Ohio's wave."

This poetic vision was eventually realized by the construction of the Erie Canal. A project of like character gave the nationally minded statesmen the leverage they needed to lift their scheme into the field of practical politics. In 1784, upon Washington's recommendation, Virginia became interested in plans for a waterway between the Chesapeake and the West. This matter gave added importance to pending commercial negotiations between Maryland and Virginia. Commissioners from both States were appointed to meet in Alexandria, in March, 1785. Washington invited them to Mount Vernon, and there they reached an agreement for joint action by the two States. The discussion which ensued brought out so clearly the need of general action that in January, 1786, the Virginia Legislature appointed commissioners "to meet such as might be appointed by the other States of the Union" to consider the whole subject of commercial regulations.

These commercial negotiations gave Hamilton the handle for which he had been waiting. By 1785 the excesses of the dominant faction in New York had provoked such a strong reaction that in the elections that year many changes took place in the composition of the legislature. Of the nine members of the delegation from New York City, seven failed of reelection, among them Aaron Burr. The new members included some of Hamilton's closest friends. One of them, Robert Troup, has related that "Hamilton had no idea that the legislature could be prevailed on to adopt the system as recommended by Congress, neither had he any partiality for a commercial convention, otherwise than as a stepping-stone to a general convention, to form a general constitution. In pursuance of his plan, the late Mr. Duer, the late Colonel Malcolm, and myself, were sent to the state legislature as part of the city delegation, and we were to make every possible effort to accomplish Hamilton's objects."

The mercantile interests of New York were deeply aggrieved by the impotence of national authority. The expanding commerce of the nation was without any sort of public guardianship. On May 19, 1785, the ship *Empress*, the first American vessel to visit China, returned to the port of New York, the event arousing great enthusiasm. But in that same year came doleful accounts of the way Algerine corsairs preyed upon American commerce, capturing vessels and enslaving the crews. Mercantile advocacy of some regular provision for the support of the national government became so urgent that the dominant faction was impressed with the need of conciliatory measures. Although the congressional scheme was rejected, there was great profession of willingness to allow federal taxation under State control, and it was decided to make a favorable response to the Virginia call for a commercial convention. As such a convention had no power to bind, and whatsoever recommendations it might make could have no legal effect save such as the State legislature might choose to allow, the matter did not seem to be of sufficient importance to become a bone of contention, and hence Hamilton's friends were able to have his name included in the list of delegates, six in number.

The convention met in Annapolis, in September, 1786. Of the New York delegates only two attended, Hamilton and the attorney-general, Egbert Benson. Only five States were represented, and the affair looked like a failure, but it was known that in the case of some States absence did not imply want of sympathy with the announced purpose of the convention. Although the convention met in the Maryland capital, Maryland was not represented through fear that the effect might be to weaken the powers of Congress. South Carolina sent no delegates, but she had already defined her position on the question by instructing her delegates in Congress to vote for the national regulation of commerce for fifteen years. New Hampshire, Rhode Island, and Massachusetts appointed delegates but they did not attend. Hamilton saw in the situation the means of impressing the public mind with the impossibility of a commercial settlement without a political settlement. He framed an address, which was unanimously adopted by the convention, recommending the appointment of commissioners to a convention to meet in Philadelphia in May, 1787, "to take into consideration the situation of the United States, to devise such further provisions as shall appear to them necessary to render the Constitution of the Federal Government *adequate to the exigencies of the Union*, and to report such an act for that purpose to the United States in Congress assembled as, when agreed to by them and afterwards confirmed by the Legislature of every State, will effectually provide for the same."

Of all the various pleas that Hamilton made for the meeting of a constitutional convention, the Annapolis address is vaguest in its terms. According to Madison, this was due to the insistence of Randolph, of Virginia, to whose advice Hamilton deferred, since Virginia's active support of the movement was all-important. Otto, the French minister, in a dispatch to his government, gave an exact account of what was done. He remarked: "By proposing a new organization of the general government, all minds would have been revolted; circumstances ruinous to the commerce of America have happily arisen to furnish the reformers with a pretext for introducing innovations."

On returning from Annapolis Hamilton went energetically to work to bring New York into line with the movement. On the face of it, the situation looked hopeless. Governor Clinton, a man of the Ulster breed, who possessed to the fullest extent the inflexible character which goes with that breed, was opposed to anything that would abate State supremacy, and he was now assured of that solid support to his position which is supplied by large vested interests identified with it. The State had created a tariff system of its own: custom-houses had been established; collectors, surveyors, gaugers, weighers, and tidewaiters had been appointed. Thus there was a phalanx of active politicians committed by their class interest against any transfer of commercial control to the Federal Government and, as usual when a class interest is imperilled, they invoked the spirit of liberty with ardent zeal. An argument energetically pressed in the pamphlet controversies of the period was that republicanism had never flourished except in small states, and the creation of "a mighty Continental legislature" would be the doom of American liberty. A writer who signed himself "Sydney" made rather a plausible argument from English history, to the effect that a despotic oligarchy would be erected if Congress were allowed to levy taxes through its own agents.

Hamilton threw himself into the fray, and in the election of 1786 he came forward personally as a candidate for the legislature. His ticket won at the polls in New York City through the warm support of the business community, but up-State sentiment was still strongly antifederal, and Governor Clinton was supported by a compact majority in both branches of the legislature. Hamilton had but a small following on any test of party strength, but he was able to accomplish his main purpose, that of engaging the State in the national movement. He was able to do this by sheer dexterity of management, in which he displayed that fine statesmanship which extracts success from untoward circumstances.

To view the developments in their right relation it is important to bear in mind that Hamilton did not approve the scheme which Congress was urging.

While a member of Congress Hamilton had opposed
that scheme and voted against it, standing out in
opposition to his own colleagues from New York.
In a letter to Governor Clinton at the time he justified his action on the ground that he could never
consent to "attempts which must either fail in the
execution or be productive of evil," and that he
"would rather incur the negative inconveniences of
delay than the positive mischiefs of injudicious expedients."   This scheme was adopted by Congress,
April 18, 1783, with the idea of wheedling the States
into providing it with a definite source of revenue.
By it the five-per-cent impost previously urged was
abandoned, and instead of it there was proposed a
schedule of specific duties on spirits, tea, coffee,
sugar, and molasses, not to be continued longer than
twenty-five years, the proceeds to be applied to no
other purpose than the discharge of the interest or
principal of the debts contracted on the faith of the
United States for supporting the war, the collectors
to be appointed by the States within which their
duties were to be exercised, but "amenable to and
removable by" Congress; and Congress was to render an annual account to the States of the proceeds
of each of the specified articles.   In Hamilton's judgment this scheme fell immensely short of what the
situation demanded, but it was the only national
proposal then pending, and so he pressed it upon
the attention of the legislature.   It is, however,

clear from what is now known of all the circumstances that what this really meant was simply a turn of the screw.

In addition to handling an adverse State legislature, Hamilton had also to handle an adverse Congress. After leaving Philadelphia in 1783 Congress had held a session at Princeton, one at Annapolis, and one at Trenton; but, tiring of a migratory life, it settled down in New York City in 1785, and that continued to be the place of meeting until after the adoption of the new Constitution. In 1786 Congress issued a statement declaring that it could not recommend any other scheme than the one proposed in 1783, and regretting that Maryland, Georgia, Rhode Island, and New York still refused to assent to a system "so long since and so repeatedly presented for their adoption." The attitude of New York was regarded by Congress as the decisive factor, and by sitting in New York City the members hoped to influence the action of the State legislature which also met there. In 1786 the legislature yielded sufficiently to pass an act giving Congress the proceeds of the duties but reserving to the State "the sole power of levying and collecting" them. This was a great disappointment to Congress, as meanwhile other States had concurred and it now seemed that only New York stood in the way of the success of the plan. Congress therefore adopted resolutions declaring that the New York enactment was not a compliance with the plan proposed by Congress and urging Governor Clinton to reconvene the legislature to consider the subject again; but Clinton was immovable.

When news came of the action of the Annapolis convention Congress was much disturbed by it, regarding it as still another hindrance to the adoption of the pending scheme. The call for a convention to revise the Articles of Confederation was denounced as illegal, that being the proper function of Congress. This view was adopted by leading men in a number of States. There was no prospect of inducing Congress to concur in the call for the Philadelphia convention until the members were convinced that there was no hope that the New York Legislature could be persuaded to accept their financial scheme.

The skill with which Hamilton managed the diverse elements of this complicated situation so as to produce the result he desired finely displays his political genius. The particulars deserve full consideration, the more so since a confused account of what occurred has passed into history. While other periods in his career were more brilliant, at no time was there such a rich and varied exhibition of his statesmanship as in this wonderful year of 1787.

CHAPTER XIV

THE WONDERFUL YEAR

THE session of 1787 of the New York Legislature lasted from January 12 to April 21. During most of this period Congress was in session almost alongside. Members could therefore inform themselves directly of what was going on in State politics, and many of them were listeners to Hamilton's speeches. At that time colonial practice was still retained by the legislature. Its proceedings began with a speech from the governor to which an answer was voted by each house. This arrangement allowed any question to be made an issue forthwith if such was the desire.

Hamilton was appointed a member of the committee to prepare the answer of the Assembly, and he reported a draft which simply declared that "the several important matters mentioned in your Excellency's speech, and communicated in the papers that accompany it, shall, in the course of the session, engage our serious attention." The Speaker, Richard Varick, moved an amendment expressing "approbation of your Excellency's conduct in not convening the legislature at an earlier period." This brought on an animated debate, in which feelings excited by the struggle over the federal impost received strong expression. Varick offered to withdraw his motion, but objection was made. All this took place in committee of the whole, and it was finally decided that the committee should rise and report. During this stage of the controversy Hamilton kept out of it, remarking that "he would reserve himself on this subject until it came again before them, when he hoped to be enabled to offer such arguments as would strike with conviction the candid part of the House." The matter then went over until January 19, when General Malcolm moved a further amendment noting the fact that the federal-revenue act, passed at the last session, had not been considered by Congress "as a compliance with their act of April, 1783," and declaring that "although our inclination, as well as the persuasion that it is the sentiment of our constituents, will dispose us on all occasions to manifest the most respectful attention to the recommendations" of Congress, yet, in view of the expense and inconvenience which an extra session would have imposed, "we are of opinion that your Excellency was justifiable in forbearing to convene the legislature until the time appointed by law."

It would be a mistake to think that these amendments were offered in a spirit of hostility to Hamilton. Both Varick and Malcolm were members of the city delegation and were among Hamilton's per-

sonal friends. Both were men of independent character and individual judgment, who formed and
acted upon their own views. Varick had been
General Schuyler's military secretary early in the
war, eventually becoming recording secretary to
General Washington. He was Mayor Duane's judicial colleague in the city court, when that tribunal
adopted Hamilton's views of the supremacy of a
national treaty over State law. In 1786 he was appointed with Samuel Jones to revise the State laws,
which work has preserved his memory in the legal
profession, while in general civic life he is remem-
bered as a founder and president of the American
Bible Society. Malcolm entered the war as colonel
of a local regiment of infantry at the same time
Hamilton entered as artillery captain. The relations of Hamilton with both were so intimate that
it is scarcely possible that he did not know just
what they intended to do.

Not until after Malcolm's amendment was offered
did Hamilton take part in the debate. He began
by remarking:

I have seen with regret the progress of this business,
and it was my earnest wish to have avoided this present
discussion. I saw with regret the first application of
Congress to the governor, because it was easy to see that
it involved a delicate dilemma: Either the governor, from
consideration of inconvenience, might refuse to call the
Assembly, which would derogate from the respect due to

Congress; or he might call them, and by being brought together at an unreasonable period before the time -appointed by law for the purpose, they would meet with reluctance. . . .

Hence it was that he had thought wise to omit any mention of the subject in the reply of the House to the governor's speech. "I thought," he said, "we might safely be silent without any implication of censure on the governor. It was neither in my mind to condemn nor approve. I was only desirous of avoiding an interference in a constitutional question, which belonged entirely to the province of the executive authority of the State, and about which I knew there would be a difference of opinion, even in this house. I submit it to the house, whether this was not a prudent course, and whether it is not to be lamented that the proposed amendment forces the discussion upon us. Constitutional questions are always delicate; they should never be touched but from necessity."

But since, in spite of his efforts, the matter had been brought forward and the House committed to an examination of the subject, it should be viewed in its full extent. He proceeded to depict in grave and impartial language the miseries of the situation and the impossibility of satisfactory action of any kind in such circumstances. On the pending question he was, of course, defeated. Matters had gone so far that the Clinton men insisted upon distinct approbation of the governor's decision. Malcolm's amendment was voted down, although Varick voted for it. Malcolm in his turn voted for Varick's amendment, which was carried by a vote of 36 to 9. Hamilton voted against both amendments, but he had made it clear that he did so in no spirit of antagonism, but for reasons which deeply impressed the House and influenced its subsequent action.

Although the Clinton men carried their point, that made them the more desirous that their action should not be taken to mean that they acted in any spirit of opposition to the Continental Congress or to federal authority. As to that, they were entirely sincere. Popular history has not done justice to Governor Clinton's motives. On October 14, 1783, he wrote to Washington: "I am fully persuaded, unless the powers of the National Council are enlarged, and that body better supported than it is at present, all their measures will discover such feebleness and want of energy, as will stain us with disgrace, and expose us to the worst of evils." If his subsequent behavior now seems to have been inconsistent with such professions, it never wore that appearance to him, for he steadily exerted his influence in favor of State support to the authority of the Confederation. He was not opposed to granting to Congress the sources of revenue it demanded. The point on which he insisted was that the agency should be wholly State agency; that a foreign set of

tax-collectors should not be intruded within the
sphere of the State, to impair its jurisdiction within
its own area and possibly to clash with its authority.   As he viewed the case, that was the very issue
over which the War of Independence had been
fought.   If the States should now waive their independence in favor of the Continental Congress, why
should they not have done so in favor of the British
Parliament, whose demands were, in fact, small in
amount in comparison with those now being pressed?
Such views were very generally held among the elder
statesmen, the men who had been leaders of American resistance at a time when Hamilton was a child.
Clinton's attitude in New York was no other than
that of Samuel Adams in Massachusetts and Patrick
Henry in Virginia.

On one point the Clinton men were entirely
correct, namely, that grant of authority to the Federal Government to operate within the States by its
own agents would be incompatible with State sovereignty.   Hamilton admitted this with a frankness
which the Congressional politicians regarded as injudicious.   Their line was to contend that the grant
was so carefully limited that there could be no actual
impairment of State sovereignty.   The line of the
Clinton men was to profess entire willingness to
comply with the wishes of Congress, provided the
sovereignty of the State was respected.   It was, of
course, known both to the members of Congress

and to the Clinton men that Hamilton had been opposed to the Congressional scheme, but that did not prejudice its chances now because the ground of his opposition was that it did not go far enough, and this would naturally suggest to the Clinton men the expediency of acceding to the Congressional demand and thus ending a troublesome agitation. But their leaders were too sincerely attached to the principle of State sovereignty to yield on that point. At the same time the Congressmen could not but feel that Hamilton had made the strongest possible presentation of their case. The most cogent argument they could now offer was that if New York still insisted upon its modification of the Congressional scheme the concurrence of the other States would go for nothing, and the whole weary business of getting assent to the plan would have to begin over again. Hamilton pressed that consideration with great force. "The immediate consequences of accepting our grant," he told the Assembly, "would be a relinquishment of the grants of other States. They must take up the matter anew, and do the work over again to accommodate it to our standard. In order to anchor our State, would it have been wise to set twelve, or at least eleven, others afloat?"

Incidentally he portrayed with great power the miserable situation into which the country was drifting. All factions felt that anxiety, however obstinate their attachment to their particular principles. No attempt was made to reply to Hamilton's argument, but acceptance of the Congressional plan of impost was defeated by a vote of 36 to 21. The decision was rendered in such silence that among the New York Federalists it became a saying that "the impost was strangled by a band of mutes." The silence was a recognition of the extreme seriousness of the situation, and that was just what Hamilton aimed to produce. The effect was to convince the members of Congress that everything had been done that could be done to get New York to accept their plan, and they were now quite ready to favor the movement for a federal convention. At the same time the Clinton men were now keen to show that in doing what they had done they meant no disrespect to the Continental Congress, and were ready to make concessions so long as the principle of State sovereignty was not violated.

Hamilton promptly availed himself of this favorable situation, and now events moved rapidly. The impost was defeated on February 15. On the 17th Hamilton offered a resolution instructing the New York delegates to move in Congress for its recommendation to the States to send representatives to a convention to revise the Articles of Confederation. The resolution was promptly adopted by the Assembly, but action was delayed in the Senate for one day, and concurrence was then barely obtained, there being a majority of just one vote. On the

21st the matter was taken up in Congress, and a resolution was adopted recommending the States to send delegates to the Philadelphia convention, but while adopting the suggestions of the Annapolis address as to place and time the purpose was somewhat differently stated. According to the Annapolis address, drafted by Hamilton, the purpose was "to render the constitution of the Federal Government *adequate to the exigencies of the Union.*" According to the Congressional resolution, it was "for the sole and express purpose of revising the Articles of Confederation." On the 26th, on Hamilton's motion, the New York Assembly adopted a resolution for the appointment of five delegates to the Philadelphia convention; but the Senate reduced the number to three, and in joint convention Yates, Hamilton, and Lansing were elected by ballot. Both from his personal eminence and from the fact that he was the mover of the resolution, Hamilton could not have been omitted from the list of delegates, but care was taken to hobble him by giving him two rigid State-sovereignty men as his colleagues. The arrangement was so disagreeable to Hamilton that toward the end of the session he made an attempt to have two additional commissioners chosen, so as to make the number five, as he had originally planned, but on that point he was defeated. Nevertheless, he had attained his main object, through his ability to use as his instruments

a hostile State legislature and a reluctant Congress.
Up to that time the success of the movement for a
convention had been very doubtful. The example
and influence of Virginia had in a short time caused
the appointment of delegates by five other States;
but then the movement seemed to be exhausted.
It was the adhesion of New York and the sanction
of Congress that made the business go. All the
remaining States now sent delegates, except Rhode
Island; but that did not matter much, as its reputation was then such that it was nicknamed "Rogues'
Island."

In addition to his successful pilotage of the convention movement, Hamilton accomplished much
important legislation during this memorable session.
The proscriptive legislation he had assailed in his
Phocion letters was now wiped off the statute books.
In urging the repeal of all acts inconsistent with the
treaty of peace, he reiterated his old contention that
the judges were bound to apply the treaty, no matter what State law might direct. He said: "Their
powers will be the same, whether this law was passed
or not," but he held that "it would be impolitic to
leave them to the dilemma, either of infringing the
treaty to enforce the particular laws of the State,
or to explain away the laws of the State to give
effect to the treaty." This was strong doctrine to
address to an assembly devoted to State sovereignty.
And so also, in another important matter, he took

a line so apt to irritate State pride that no politician would have ventured upon it who determined his principles by their popularity.   Hamilton advocated recognition of the State of Vermont, although it had been formed in territory claimed by New York. The speech in which he presented his views is a fine exhibition of the breadth of Hamilton's statesman-ship.   The matter had been previously discussed in the spirit of a conveyancer, with reference to ancient grants and titles.   Discarding such considerations, Hamilton took up the fundamental objects of gov-ernment, and from these he drew cogent reasons against any attempt to coerce the people of Ver-mont.   The entire frankness with which Hamilton declared his principles, at any stage of the tide of popular sentiment, is very striking.   Anything like dissimulation was foreign to his nature throughout his entire career up to its closing years, when there was a decline that will be noted in its place.   All his achievements were due to his intellectual power, without aid from any of the arts of cajolery.

It has been remarked that Hamilton did not take as prominent a part in the Philadelphia convention as might have been expected, and it is certainly the case that he did not figure among its leaders, to the extent that might have been expected from his pre-vious activity.   In Jefferson's papers is preserved a record of some table-talk in which George Mason, a Virginia delegate, related that "Yates and Lansing never voted in a single instance with Hamilton, who was so much mortified at it that he went home." The notion that Hamilton was snuffed out by Yates and Lansing shows that Mason did not understand the situation. Nothing could daunt Hamilton, and he could not have been surprised or mortified that Yates and Lansing opposed him; that is just what they had been put there to do. It would be absurd to think that such a familiar situation had bereft Hamilton of the activity, shrewdness, dexterity, and practical power of which he had just before made such a signal display.

The true explanation of Hamilton's periods of absence from the convention is very simple—he had to make his living. He was not situated like the plantation statesmen, whose business affairs could be looked after by their overseers while they were away; his income depended upon his personal efforts. At the time the convention met he had three children, the youngest just a year old; another child was born the following spring. To provide for this growing family he had no resource save his professional practice. Hamilton was always disposed to go to greater lengths of personal sacrifice in the public service than his family and his friends approved; but the public motive could not operate strongly in the case of the convention, for it soon appeared that where his efforts were most needed was in his own State and not in the convention. As soon as it became plain that the convention intended to discard the Articles of Confederation, Lansing and Yates withdrew. The differences which broke out in the convention related chiefly to the demands of the small States, which feared that in a national system the large States would override them unless they were allowed special security. The adjustment of this matter was the main problem the convention had to solve, and in this New York had no interest apart from Virginia and Massachusetts, which in the convention, as in the Continental Congress, were in the habit of working together. The legend that has grown up, to the effect that radical differences existed as to principles, is a throw-back from a later period, when party divisions had taken place in the conduct of the government. In 1787 the model all had in mind was the English constitutional system. Nobody then thought that there was any important difference between Madison and Hamilton in their political principles. They were then working in close accord. Hamilton felt at liberty to be occasional in his attendance, although he went as often as his professional engagements would allow. He took part in organizing the convention, May 27, and remained until June 29. He appears to have been again in Philadelphia on July 13, and he took part in convention proceedings on August 13 and for some days later, leaving in time to reach New York on August 20. He reappeared in the convention on September 6, and stayed on to the final session, which took place on the 17th.

Meanwhile there was much in the New York situation to require his attention. Lansing and Yates withdrew from the convention on July 5, justifying their action in a letter to Governor Clinton, which was in effect a campaign document on the State-sovereignty side. On the 21st Hamilton made a brief reply in a New York newspaper, in which he criticised Clinton's antagonism to the convention, writing on the assumption that Clinton had inspired the withdrawal of Lansing and Yates. Hamilton was at once accused of having made a wanton attack upon the governor of the State. He made a sharp reply, asserting his right to unmask "the pernicious intrigue of a man high in office to preserve power and emolument to himself, at the expense of the Union, the peace and the happiness of America." As for the grounds on which he criticised the governor's course, he declared his readiness "to bring forward to public view the sources of his information, and the proofs of his charge," should the governor deny having "made use of the expressions imputed to him."

Clinton apparently took the position that it was beneath his dignity to notice this challenge. But an association of Federal Republicans was formed, with General John Lamb at its head, to defend the principle of State sovereignty. The opposition to the new Constitution was so well prepared for action that on the very day, September 24, that a copy reached New York for publication, a letter attacking the proposed system of government appeared in the New York *Journal*, the organ of the State administration. It was signed "Cato," but it was well known that Clinton himself was the author. In allusion to this signature, Hamilton replied over the signature of "Cæsar," by which he meant to suggest that sheer obstinacy of the Cato type played into the hands of demagogy of the Cæsar type. The allusion was too far-fetched to be understanded of the people, and it exposed Hamilton to rejoinders in which he was put on the defensive. Hamilton had no turn for humor or satire. The few examples found in his writings are the only instances in which his pen suffered from awkwardness. His "Cæsar" articles were a false move, of which his adversaries took prompt advantage. Clinton, as "Cato," continued to address the public with effect, and his attacks on the new Constitution were strongly reinforced by a series of able articles by "Brutus," which signature was known to be that used by Robert Yates, judge of the State supreme court and one of the delegates who had withdrawn from the Philadelphia convention.

At this time not only was Hamilton getting rather the worst of it in the argument, but his pride was stung by some of the personal slurs put into circulation. He wrote to Washington that "among many contemptible artifices practiced by them they have had recourse to an insinuation that I *palmed* myself upon you, and that you *dismissed* me from your family. This I confess hurts my feelings." This had reference to the way Hamilton had thrown up his position as Washington's military secretary during the war, an affair in which he displayed boyish vanity and which now came back to plague him. Washington, with characteristic magnanimity, at once wrote a letter declaring "that both charges are entirely unfounded."

Before Washington's reply was received Hamilton had regained his poise. A trait of character displayed throughout his whole career was that no shock of circumstances could stun his mind or paralyze its activities. His spirits then rose, his mind was then clearest in its vision, and his powers attained their greatest efficiency. He now took action which put his opponents on the defensive and kept them there. He stripped them of their title of Federal Republican so completely that they themselves had to accept the name and place of Antifederalists to which he assigned them. This huge change was accomplished by *The Federalist*, the first number of which appeared on October 27, in the *Independent Journal*, over the pen-name of "Publius." At one stroke Hamilton lifted the controversy from the smoky atmosphere of passion into the clear light of reason. "It seems," he said, "to have been reserved to the people of this country, by their conduct and example, to decide the important question, whether societies of men are really capable or not of establishing good government from reflection and choice, or whether they are forever destined to depend for their political constitutions on accident and force." He went on: "If there be any truth in the remark, the crisis at which we are arrived may with propriety be regarded as the era in which that decision is to be made; and a wrong election of the part we shall act may, in this view, deserve to be considered as the general misfortune of mankind."

This was certainly putting the matter on a very high and broad plane, which he went on to survey with appropriate dignity of style. Upon these noble premises he announced his intention, "in a series of papers, to discuss the following interesting particulars":

The utility of the UNION to your political prosperity —The insufficiency of the present Confederation to preserve that Union—The necessity of a government at least equally energetic with the one proposed, to the attainment of this object—The conformity of the proposed Constitution to the true principles of republican government—Its analogy to your own State constitution—and lastly, The additional security which its adoption will afford to the preservation of that species of government, to liberty, and to property.

This large project, carried out in the midst of electioneering activities, in addition to engagements arising from law practice, was, in fact, more than fulfilled by the actual performance. The task was completed in eighty-five letters appearing in the space of seven months. These casual essays, rapidly produced for immediate service, alone among all the voluminous writings of the period, have survived to become a political classic. It is related by his son that Hamilton wrote the memorable first number in the cabin of a sloop while returning to New York from Albany, where he had been attending to cases before the State supreme court. The labor of carrying on the series amidst his other engagements was so burdensome that he asked help from his friends, and both Jay and Madison contributed, but the great majority of the articles were by Hamilton. Their power secured immediate attention, and so great was the public interest that even the New York *Journal*, the organ of the State administration, reprinted a number. The regular publication was made alternately in the *Independent Journal* and in the *Daily Advertiser*, and portions were frequently copied by journals in other States.

In New York City the Federalists swept all before them, but elsewhere Clinton's control of the situation was unbroken. When the convention met in June, 1788, to pass upon the question of adoption, Governor Clinton was chosen to preside, and it was then computed that out of the fifty-seven delegates the Federalists could count assuredly upon only eleven. The debates lasted for three weeks, Hamilton taking an active and prominent part. His opponents found it easier to say that he was dishing up *The Federalist* again than to reply to his arguments. The Antifederalists were in an awkward situation. Their leaders could not hold that the existing system of general government was satisfactory, and yet there was no practical alternative to acceptance of the new Constitution. While they delayed action by New York, enough States had ratified the Constitution to put it into effect, and eventually they gave way. On July 26 ratification was carried by 30 yeas to 27 nays.

Governor Clinton wrote to General Lamb that Hamilton had threatened that in case of defeat the southern end of the State would adopt the Constitution as an independent State, leaving the interior counties without any outlet to the sea for their commerce. It is certain that in New York City support of the new Constitution was overwhelmingly strong. Three days before the final action of the convention a grand popular demonstration took place. The plans had been made and the arrangements supervised by Major Pierre L'Enfant, a French engineer, who during the war had been an aide of Baron Steuben. A man of fine taste, an enduring memorial of which is the way in which he laid out the city of Washington, he arranged the Federalist procession with a splendor of effect that can never be surpassed, now that machinery has taken over so many of the old handicrafts. The blacksmiths began and completed an anchor on their stage during the march, under a banner inscribed:

"Forge me strong, finish me neat,
I soon shall moor a Federal fleet."

The sail-makers, too, exercised their craft, with the motto:

"Fit me well, and rig me neat,
And join me to the Federal fleet."

The stone-masons displayed a temple supported by thirteen pillars, three of which were significantly shown as unfinished, and above them the motto:

"The foundation is firm, the materials are good,
Each pillar's cemented with patriots' blood."

All trades, degrees, professions, and interests were represented in the procession, but the chief feature was a full-rigged ship, the *Hamilton*, fully manned, armed, and equipped.

CHAPTER XV

A BREACH IN THE CONSTITUTIONAL SCHEME

THE adoption of the Constitution by the requisite number of States barely insured a trial of the new scheme of government; whether it would make good was very doubtful. It satisfied nobody, and was accepted by its best friends simply on the principle that half a loaf is better than no bread. Its enemies were active and determined. Patrick Henry, of Virginia, expressed their general sentiment when he said that he would "seize the first moment for shaking off the yoke in a constitutional way." The original idea of the Antifederalist leaders had been to work through the Continental Congress. It was probably only in the way of precaution that Hamilton again became a member of that body in February, 1788, but its proceedings turned out to be quite unimportant. In the autumn of 1788 a few members attended; gradually they fell off and the Congress finally came to an end without adjournment or any formal action.

The method now adopted by the Antifederalists was to agitate for the meeting of another convention to revise the work of the Philadelphia convention. Patrick Henry's influence carried a resolution to that effect through the Virginia Assembly by a vote of more than two to one. In New York the opponents of the new Constitution revived the old association of "Federal Republicans" under the leadership of General John Lamb, and an address to the several States was issued in favor of electing delegates to another convention. Governor Clinton called a special session of the legislature, and in his message asserted that the Constitution had been ratified "on the express confidence, that the exercise of the different powers would be suspended until it should undergo a revision by a general convention of the States." No positive action was taken by the legislature, but New York took no part in the Presidential election, the appointment of electors being defeated by obstinate disagreement between the Senate and the Assembly.

While the opponents of the Constitution were planning to overthrow it, its adherents were disturbed by reports that Washington was unwilling to serve as President. Hamilton regarded this as a vital matter, and he entered into a correspondence with Washington, remarkable for its candor and urgency. Washington wrote: "It is my great and sole desire to live and die in peace and retirement on my own farm." Hamilton's rejoinder was virtually that he had no right to give himself that indulgence. "In a matter so essential to the well-being of society as the prosperity of a newly-instituted government, a citizen of so much consequence as yourself to its success has no option but to lend his services if called for.   Permit me to say, it would be inglorious, in such a situation, not to hazard the glory, however great, which he might have previously acquired."   Hamilton went on to point out that Washington had committed himself by recommending the new Constitution for adoption, so he would not escape blame if it should turn out to be a failure, which it would be without his aid.   Washington took all this in good part, telling Hamilton he was "particularly glad that you have dealt thus freely and like a friend."   It was not in Washington's nature to refuse to do his duty, and Hamilton applied just the kind of pressure to which he would yield, but he thought it hard that after eight years of campaigning he should not be allowed to retire.   He was entirely sincere in declaring: "If I should be prevailed upon to accept it, the acceptance would be attended with more diffidence and reluctance than I ever experienced before in my life."   Hamilton would not allow him any loophole; his acceptance was indispensable; circumstances left no option.   "It is no compliment to say, that no other man can sufficiently unite the public opinion, or can give the requisite weight to the office, in the commencement of the government."

The same logic by which Hamilton engaged Washington to public service also engaged himself should

Washington summon him, which he did at the outset of his administration. While passing through
Philadelphia, Washington saw Robert Morris and
inquired whether he would be willing to resume
charge of the Treasury Department. Morris declined, but strongly recommended Hamilton, and
soon after reaching New York Washington offered
Hamilton the post. In accepting it Hamilton went
against the advice of some of his best friends. Gouverneur Morris warned him against taking a position
in which he would have to bear calumny and persecution. "Of that," Hamilton replied, "I am aware;
but I am convinced it is the situation in which I can
do most good." Robert Troup, who was Hamilton's
closest friend at the New York bar, was asked by
him to wind up his law business. "I remonstrated
with him," wrote Troup, in a letter giving an account of the incident; "he admitted that his acceptance would be likely to injure his family, but said
there was a strong impression on his mind that in
the financial department he could essentially promote the welfare of the country; and this impression,
united with Washington's request, forbade his refusal of the appointment."

As it turned out, the Antifederalists were not
strong enough to overthrow the Constitution, but
they were able to give it a twist that defeated the
main feature of the original design, which was to
complete and establish the executive authority that

had been already introduced, and at the same time erect barriers against Congressional invasion of executive functions. The miserable results of administration of public services by committees and boards appointed by the Continental Congress had forced the creation of executive departments, and it was the practice for the heads of those departments to go before the Congress with plans and recommendations, like a business manager appearing before a board of directors. In accepting the office of Secretary of the Treasury, Hamilton expected to have the same facilities of access to Congress as Robert Morris had possessed. The act creating the Treasury Department was drawn on the same lines as the resolution of February 7, 1781, creating the office of Superintendent of Finance, and like it gave authority "to digest and report plans." An attack was made in Congress on this clause, which resulted in action excluding the Secretary of the Treasury from the floor and condemning him to work in the lobby. This alteration of the constitutional scheme has had and is having profound consequences. To it must be ascribed the singular degradation that has taken place in the position of the House of Representatives, and, indeed, the whole constitutional scheme was turned awry by it, which fact must be allowed for in reading *The Federalist*. It may seem that its estimates of relative power and importance in the various organs of authority are sadly out of true reckoning, but it should be considered that the procedure then in mind differed from that actually introduced.

It is a remarkable fact that this change was due more to James Madison than any one else, and it was the first manifestation of a variance that soon developed into open hostility. Up to that time Hamilton and Madison had been working in friendly accord. Hamilton had no idea that there was any important difference in their views on public policy. He was delighted when Madison was elected to the House, and counted upon his aid. In 1792 Hamilton wrote to a friend:

When I accepted the office I now hold, it was under full persuasion, that from similarity of thinking, conspiring with personal good-will, I should have the firm support of Mr. Madison in the general course of my administration. Aware of the intrinsic difficulties of the situation, and of the powers of Mr. Madison, I do not believe I should have accepted under a different supposition.

In the First Congress Madison occupied a position of singular influence. In addition to his high rank as a leader in the movement for a new constitution he was regarded as the possessor of Washington's confidence and as an exponent of the policy of the Administration. At Washington's request Madison drafted for him his replies to the addresses of the House and the Senate at the opening of the session.

He took the leading part in carrying a series of amendments to the Constitution to remove some of the objections that had been urged against it. This action was very efficacious in allaying hostility to the new Constitution, and thereafter many who had been its opponents now aimed at getting control of the new government and shaping procedure under the Constitution. When opposition to the government formed on this new line, Madison himself joined it. Hamilton was slow in recognizing this change of attitude, and he gave Madison his confidence while Madison was making plans for his defeat.

The first evidence of Madison's opposition came during the struggle over the organization of the government, but even then, although perplexed by it, Hamilton failed to comprehend its significance. When the business of creating the executive departments was taken in hand, there was at the outset a sharp contention over the question whether the heads of departments should be removable by the President. On such issues the Antifederalists as such had no distinct policy, but there was so much uneasiness, suspicion, and anxiety that it was easy to stir up opposition on any issue that might be raised. The situation was favorable to the activities of an experienced politician who was attached to the kind of government originally carried on by the Continental Congress, and who was bent upon rein-

stating it, so far as possible, under the new Constitution. Elbridge Gerry was a member of the Continental Congress from 1776 to 1785. As a delegate
to the Philadelphia convention he had opposed the
main features of the new Const tution, and he was
among those who refused to sign the report recommending it to the States for adoption. In the debate on the removal power he introduced a style of
argument that has flourished in Congress ever since
—the use of slur and innuendo against people not
present to defend themselves. He dwelt upon the
possibility that the President might be influenced by
other than public motives if allowed to remove from
office in his own discretion. "Perhaps the officer is
not good-natured enough; he makes an ungraceful
bow, or does it left leg foremost; this is most unbe-
coming in a great officer at the President's levee.
Now, because he is so unfortunate as not to be so
good a dancer as he is a worthy officer, he must be
removed." Madison met this onslaught by the sensible argument that the President could not be held
to responsibility unless he could control his sub-
ordinates, and carried the house with him by a
decisive majority.

What Gerry was really after was to obtain for
Congress the same direct custody of public funds
that the Continental Congress had formerly possessed and had reluctantly surrendered when Robert
Morris was made Superintendent of Finance. When

Morris resigned in disgust in 1784, Congress put the treasury in the hands of three commissioners appointed and supervised by it. Gerry now labored hard to perpetuate this arrangement, arguing that to allow one man to hold an office of such power might be too great a trial to any one's integrity and would at least give continual reason to suspect misconduct, thus repelling popular confidence in the new government. On this issue Gerry met a crushing defeat, for it was notorious that the board system of treasury management had been accompanied by confusion, extravagance, and dishonesty. Gerry was overwhelmed by instances given by members from their personal knowledge. Wadsworth, of Connecticut, described the disorder that existed in the records of the treasury board at that very time, making it impossible to check their accounts, and he declared that they had handled the finances in such a way as to double the national debt.

When they were defeated in the attempt to perpetuate the board system, it became the object of the Antifederalists to reduce the authority of the Secretary of the Treasury. Page, of Virginia, attacked the authority to "digest and report plans" as an attempt to give the administration undue influence over the House. Page himself was a new figure in the national field, although he had been active and prominent in his own State. The opponents of the new government at once fell in line with him, and did everything they could to excite suspicion and alarm as to the purposes of the national leaders. Gerry declared: "If the doctrine of having prime and great ministers of state was once well established, he did not doubt but that we should soon see them distinguished by a green or red ribbon, or other insignia of court favor and patronage."

The debate on the merits of the case went heavily against the antis. It was pointed out that the true way to keep the secretary from exercising undue influence over the House was to confront him with his responsibilities in the presence of the House, exposed to its inquiry and to its criticism. Fisher Ames observed that merely to call for information would not be advantageous to the House. "It will be no mark of inattention or neglect, if he take time to consider the questions you propound; but if you make it his duty to furnish you plans and he neglect to perform it, his conduct or capacity is virtually impeached." Sedgwick, with prophetic vision, declared: "Make your officer responsible, and the presumption is that plans and information are properly digested; but if he can secrete himself behind the curtain, he might create a noxious influence, and not be answerable for the information he gives."

Argument of this tenor was carrying the House with it, and doubtless the clause would have been adopted in its original form, had not Madison altered the whole situation by favoring a compromise, to be effected by changing the word "report" into "prepare," so that the secretary should have authority to "digest and prepare plans" but should no longer have authority to report them to the House, as had been Robert Morris's practice. Madison did not say that there was anything wrong about that practice; he said he did not believe that the danger apprehended by some really existed, but he admitted that "there is a small possibility, though it is but small, that an officer may derive a weight from this circumstance, and have some degree of influence upon the deliberations of the legislature." The position which Madison then occupied made his advice decisive, and the change of phrase was agreed to without a division.

In considering the nature of the influences which brought about this profound alteration of the constitutional scheme, it should be noted that it was favored by a school of political thought according to which the principle of the separation of powers as laid down by Montesquieu in his *Spirit of the Laws* required not only that the executive, legislative, and judicial branches of government should be separately constituted, but that furthermore they should be entirely disconnected. The only logical formulation of this doctrne in eighteenth-century constitution-making is contained in the French constitution of 1791, which makes it the exclusive function of the national legislative assembly "to propose and enact the laws; the King can only invite the legislative body to take the matter under consideration." Very different is the language of the American Constitution as to the functions of the President. "He shall, from time to time, give to the Congress information of the state of the Union, and recommend to their consideration such measures as he shall judge necessary and expedient." This power of executive recommendation was that which had been developed under the Confederation by the creation of executive departments, which system the Constitution was expected by Hamilton to confirm. One of the points made by the opponents of the new Constitution was that it violated the principles of constitutional government as stated by Montesquieu. Logically, it is only fair to say that the point was well taken. The truth is that the framers of the Constitution were not animated by doctrinaire notions of government but by the need of practical measures to arrest the drift to anarchy and to establish national authority. The model they had in mind was the English constitution, and for theoretical exposition of it they looked to Blackstone's *Commentaries* and not to Montesquieu's *Spirit of the Laws*. Nor is there any evidence that doctrinaire opinion of the Montesquieu type formed any considerable element of Antifederalist opinion. The force which that possessed was derived from the prejudices and interests of local politics. Its favorite citation from Montesquieu was his dictum that "it is natural to a republic to have only a small territory; otherwise it cannot long subsist." To this argument, which was urged by Clinton, Hamilton made a strong reply in No. 9 of *The Federalist*, on "The Union as a Safeguard against Domestic Disturbances." It may be added that this particular doctrine of Montesquieu was strongly condemned by Jefferson in 1801, when he bluntly characterized it as "a falsehood."

If Madison accepted Montesquieu's doctrine of the separation of the powers, his action in shutting out the Administration from direct access to Congress with legislative proposals was logical and consistent. But as a matter of fact he did not accept that doctrine. To refute it was one of the tasks he assumed in his contributions to *The Federalist*. In Nos. 47 and 48 he examined at length the constitutional significance to be properly allowed to the doctrine of the separation of the powers. With a logical evasiveness rather characteristic of his mentality he did not attempt to state or analyze Montesquieu's own formulation of his doctrine, but, after mentioning that Montesquieu derived the doctrine from his study of the British constitution, he remarked then: "Let us recur to the source from which the maxim was drawn." He then proceeded to give an account of the British constitution, which is really Blackstone's and not Montesquieu's, and in that way figured out that the principle of separation "does not require that the legislative, executive, and judiciary departments should be wholly unconnected with each other." On the contrary, he argued that, "unless these departments be so far connected and blended as to give each a constitutional control over the others, the degree of separation which the maxim requires, as essential to a free government, can never in practice be duly maintained." Truer words were never written, as the whole course of American politics abundantly attests.

Why, then, did Madison violate his own principles, to bring about an arrangement that in effect threw the new Congress back into the dirty ruts of the Continental Congress? This is a question that has bothered his biographers. Gaillard Hunt's masterly *Life of James Madison* candidly admits that "Madison at this period of his career often found himself in a position foreign to his former political habits," and that his course was steered by calculations of expediency rather than by principle. The truth of the matter appears to be that Madison was more notable for keenness of intelligence than strength of character. Fisher Ames, in his private correspondence at this period, while speaking with great respect of Madison's abilities, noted that he was very timid on any point affecting Virginia politics, "whose murmurs, if louder than a whisper, make **Mr.**

Madison's heart quake." Hamilton had as great, and probably greater, antagonism to encounter in New York politics, but nothing could make his heart quake. His way of meeting opposition was to confront it and overthrow it by superior force of argument. Madison betook himself to tactics and cajolery. Examination of his correspondence and of his course in Congress at this period leaves no doubt that his main consideration was to please the home districts. With this purpose in view, the question of the site of the national capital took the lead over everything else in Madison's mind. As a member of the Continental Congress he had tried hard to defeat the selection of New York as a meeting-place, and as a member of the new Congress he was bent upon getting away from New York as soon as possible. His politics now pivoted upon that issue. Senator Maclay's diary notes that on the very day General St. Clair came out against the Potomac site Madison made a motion to reduce St. Clair's salary as governor of the Western Territory, although previously he had favored a larger amount.

A man playing this sort of politics would be naturally unwilling to let so able and forceful a speaker as Hamilton reach the floor of the House if he could prevent it. Probably he did not act in a spirit of hostility to Hamilton as a man or as an officer, but to Hamilton as a New York politician. He pointed out that the way was left open for the Secretary of the Treasury to appear before the House whenever it should see fit to call him, and there are indications that Hamilton believed that considerations of convenience would tend to maintain the practice that had been developed in the Confederation period with manifest benefit to the character of the government. His own sanguine temperament probably helped to mislead him in his estimate of the situation. At any rate he was so completely in the dark as to Madison's intentions that he assumed that the confidential intimacy that had continued throughout years of struggle for the new Constitution was still unbroken and that Madison still adhered to the principles he then professed. On the cardinal principle of Hamilton's financial policy, the assumption by the national government of the debts contracted by the States during the war, Hamilton had no doubt whatever of Madison's support, for as a member of the Continental Congress Madison had strongly advocated assumption and during the sittings of the constitutional convention had again declared himself in favor of it. Hamilton seems to have had no suspicion that the violent opposition to assumption that had developed in Virginia had swung Madison into line with it, and Madison seems to have been careful not to disclose his change of

views. On October 12, 1789, Hamilton wrote to
Madison:

I don't know how it was, but I took it for granted that
you had left town earlier than I did; else I should have
found an opportunity, after your adjournment, to con-
verse with you on the subjects committed to me by the
House of Representatives. It is certainly important that
a plan as complete and as unexceptionable as possible
should be matured by the next meeting of Congress; and
for this purpose it could not but be useful that there
should be a comparison and concentration of ideas, of
those whose duty leads them to a contemplation of the
subject. As I lost the opportunity of a personal communication, may I ask of your friendship, to put to paper
and send me your thoughts on such objects as may have
occurred to you, for an addition to our revenue, and also
as to any modifications of the public debt, which could
be made consistent with good faith—the interest of the
public and of the creditors.

Madison's reply to this has not been preserved.
It must have been indefinite, for Hamilton seems still
to have counted upon Madison's support; but when
his plan was actually presented to Congress, Hamilton was chagrined and mortified to find that Madison was flatly opposed to every feature of it.

CHAPTER XVI

HAMILTON'S RECOMMENDATIONS DEFEATED

ALTHOUGH Hamilton took an active part in the arrangements for setting up the new government, he did not take office until near the close of the first session. In the creative enactments the Treasury Department came last, but Washington waited until the list was complete before making any of his cabinet appointments, and Hamilton was the first to be commissioned—September 2, 1789. Then followed Henry Knox, as Secretary of War and of the Navy, September 12; Thomas Jefferson, Secretary of State; and Edmund Randolph, Attorney-General, September 26. Jefferson, who was then in France, did not assume the duties of his office until March 21, 1790. Besides these cabinet officers there was a postmaster-general, but he was then considered a purely business functionary who was not consulted upon matters of general policy. The office was not raised to cabinet rank until 1829.

Shortly after Hamilton took office the House resolved that "an adequate provision for the support of the public credit" should be made, and the Secretary of the Treasury was directed "to prepare a plan for that purpose and to report the same to the House at its next meeting." The House soon after adjourned until January, 1790. Meanwhile Hamilton was to organize his office, digest and formulate his plans, all of which he did with a thoroughness that made his arrangements solid and durable. Doubtless his old commercial experience and his recent banking experience were now of great value to him. The confusion and disorder in which he found the Treasury Department were forthwith removed and a system of accounts was introduced that provided clearness and accuracy of statement. It soon had to undergo a hostile and exacting scrutiny, but it passed unscathed through every test, and it has remained as the permanent basis of treasury methods.

It may be doubted whether in all the world's history any statesman save Alexander Hamilton has had to cope with so great a task with such small resources as he could command when he framed his plans to lift the nation out of bankruptcy and establish the public credit. Default in interest upon the foreign loans had gone on for years, and public opinion—demoralized by paper emissions and periodical scaling of obligations—had become indifferent to the situation. The domestic debt was enormous in amount and was so much beyond the value received for it that the feeling was wide-spread that there was little equity in the claims of holders. In every State there was an alert opposition, strong both in the reputation of its leaders and in the volume of popular support, ready to jump upon any proposal running counter to the vulgar prejudices and distorted standards of the times.   The membership of Congress naturally tended to reflect the clash of opinion going on throughout the country, and the risks of this situation were aggravated by the presence and activity of experienced politicians intent on forming and directing faction spirit for personal ends.

The man who had to face this situation had no estate to secure his independence, and he had a growing family to support.   The circumstances of his career supplied his enemies with material in support of their habitual contention that he was a social interloper and a political adventurer.   In this respect, perhaps, he was not much worse off than Edmund Burke, in England, at the same period, but Burke could depend upon the stanch support of the rich and influential Rockingham Whig connection, which the Schuyler influence in New York politics could but poorly replace, for at best it was only a provincial and not a national influence.   It may be doubted whether Hamilton had the unhesitating support of the Administration of which he was a part, in the period during which his financial policy was developed.   Washington's correspondence and his behavior indicate that at this time he was on terms of greater intimacy with Madison than with

Hamilton. According to Jefferson, Washington was originally more inclined to confide in him and in Madison than in Hamilton, and what evidence there is rather supports this view. It is certainly the case that so late as 1793, long after Madison had become Hamilton's open enemy, Washington proposed giving Madison the State Department on Jefferson's retirement but was told that he would not accept it. There are indications that the relations between Washington and Hamilton were not then very cordial. It was easy for a man of Washington's magnanimity to overlook the youthful vanity and irritability with which Hamilton had behaved to him in the past, but his knowledge of Hamilton's touchiness doubtless affected Washington's relations with him. Add to all these disabling circumstances the fact that Hamilton was not allowed to explain and defend his plans in the presence of the body that was to pass judgment upon them, and then could any statesman be worse situated for accomplishing designs intended for nothing less than creating a nation?

When Congress again met the first day was consumed by the opening exercises. On the next day a letter from Hamilton was read in the House stating that he had prepared a plan in response to the resolution of the previous session and was ready to report the same to the House when they should be pleased to receive it. This announcement at once renewed the issue that had been fought over in the previous session. Gerry was on his feet at once with a motion that the report should be made in writing. This brought forth some earnest appeals that the Secretary be allowed the means of making a full communication of his ideas. Boudinot, of New Jersey, "hoped that the Secretary of the Treasury might be permitted to make his report in person, in order to answer such inquiries as the members might be disposed to make, for it was a justifiable surmise that gentlemen would not be able to comprehend so intricate a subject without oral illustrations." Benson, of New York, contended that since the resolution of Congress had directed the Secretary to make a report, it was left to his discretion to "make it in the manner for which he is prepared." Gerry, who was as adroit as he was unscrupulous, turned this argument to the advantage of his side by arguing that the first step was to get from the Secretary the report called for by the resolution. That done, then it might be in order "to give him the right to lay before them his explanations, if he thinks explanations necessary." Acceptance of this view was facilitated by a feeling in the House that it might be well to have a detailed written statement for studious examination. Hence Ames, of Massachusetts, who had formerly strongly championed the personal appearance of the Secretary, now desired that the Secretary's communications be first put in writing, since "in this shape they would obtain a degree of permanency favorable to the responsibility of the officer, while, at the same time, they would be less liable to be misunderstood." The result of the discussion was that the motion calling for a written report was adopted without a division; but the intimation that the Secretary might be allowed a hearing later on was never acted upon. Having served its purpose it was dropped, and the Secretary was never accorded an opportunity to make explanations or reply to objections.

It would seem that Hamilton had originally prepared for an oral address, in which case—as we know from his papers—it was his practice to make only a skeleton brief of the points of his argument. This brief he had now to expand into a written statement, and five days elapsed before it was laid before the House. The body of the report contains over 20,000 words of terse argument, and it was accompanied by schedules of greater total length. Doubtless the schedules were in readiness at the time Hamilton made his offer of personal appearance. The short time he took to put his views in writing is one of the many instances of the extraordinary facility with which he used his pen. This facility was founded upon his habit of thorough analysis of his subject before attempting any presentation of his views. His power of mental concentration was so great as to make him for the time oblivious to his surroundings. A letter from General Schuyler to his daughter, Mrs. Hamilton, gives an amusing instance of this, at the very time Hamilton was framing his financial plans. Writing in October, 1789, Schuyler tells how a gentleman was seen walking about, "apparently in deep contemplation, and his lips moving as rapidly as if he was in conversation with some person," and how a shopkeeper who did not know who he was refused to change a bill for him for fear of being involved in the affairs of a person who seemed to be not quite right mentally. "Pray, ask my Hamilton," wrote Schuyler, "if he can't guess who the gentleman was."

The incident related by Schuyler was exceptional. Hamilton's ordinary practice was to retire to his study, where he would be served with coffee, and then he would put his mind on his task with steady application. When his opinion had been formed by deep study, expression of it then proceeded in a rapid and orderly manner. He wrote carefully, forming every letter distinctly, so that his manuscript is always easily legible, and it is remarkably free from corrections. The clearness of his style came from the clearness of his thought, and not from any process of literary elaboration. So it was that his report of January 9, 1790, upon the public credit, whose clearness, brilliancy, and power now strike with admiration every one who reads it, was probably written as rapidly as pen could move over paper.

Broad as is the range of this report and lofty its aims, the policy it embodies is plain and simple—the exact and punctual fulfilment of obligations. "States, like individuals, who observe their engagements are respected and trusted; while the reverse is the fate of those who pursue an opposite conduct." Such a complicated variety of mischiefs proceed from neglect of the maxims that uphold public credit that "on their due observance at the present juncture, materially depends . . . the individual and aggregate prosperity of the citizens of the United States; their relief from the embarrassments they now experience; their character as a people; the cause of good government."

With a high confidence that was triumphantly vindicated by the results of his measures, but which at the time there was little in the actual situation to justify, Hamilton declared:

The most enlightened friends of good government are those whose expectations are the highest. To justify and preserve their confidence; to promote the increasing respectability of the American name; to answer the calls of justice; to restore landed property to its due value; to furnish new resources, both to agriculture and commerce; to cement more closely the union of the States; to add to their security against foreign attack; to establish public order on the basis of an upright and liberal policy;—these are the great and invaluable ends to be secured by a proper and adequate provision, at the present period, for the support of public credit.

Proceeding to details of policy, he remarked that "the Secretary has too much deference for the opinions of every part of the community, not to have observed one, which has more than once made its appearance in the public prints, and which is occasionally to be met with in conversation. It involves this question: 'Whether a discrimination ought not to be made between original holders of public securities, and present possessors by purchase.'" He then put the case in favor of discrimination as strongly as possible. "In favor of this scheme, it is alleged that it would be unreasonable to pay twenty shillings in the pound to one who had not given more for it than three or four. And it is added, that it would be hard to aggravate the misfortune of the first owner, who probably through necessity, parted with his property at so great a loss, by obliging him to contribute to the profit of the person who had speculated on his distresses."

The most rabid advocate of discrimination could not have stated his case with more vigor. Hamilton then stated his own position with equal positiveness. "The Secretary, after the most mature reflection on the force of this argument, is induced to reject the doctrine it contains, as equally unjust and impolitic; as highly injurious, even to the original holders of public securities; as ruinous to public credit." He proceeded to show in detail why this was so, supporting his reasoning with particular illustrations. He urged that any attempt at discrimination would be replete with absurd as well as inequitable consequences. "That the case of those who parted with their securities from necessity is a hard one, cannot be denied. But whatever complaint of injury, or claim of redress they may have, respects the Government solely. They have not only nothing to object to the persons who relieved their necessities, by giving them the current price of their property, but they are even under an implied condition to contribute to the reimbursement of those persons. They knew that by the terms of the contract with themselves, the public were bound to pay those to whom they should convey their title the sums stipulated to be paid to them; and that, as citizens of the United States, they were to bear their proportion of the contribution for that purpose. This, by the act of assignment, they tacitly engaged to do; and, if they had an option, they could not, with integrity or good faith, refuse to do it, without the consent of those to whom they sold." He pointed out that the purchaser "ought to reap the benefit of his hazard—a hazard which was far from inconsiderable, and which, perhaps, turned on little less than a revolution in government." And it was not necessarily the case that all original holders sold through necessity. Some might have done so to raise money for profitable investment, and were better off than they would be if they had retained their securities for eventual redemption. How should these different classes be discriminated from each other? Discrimination, once admitted, "would operate a diminution of the value of stock in the hands of the first as well as of every other holder," as without security of transfer no one could tell exactly what there was to buy or sell, and this uncertainty would be destructive of the availability of public stocks for purposes of commercial accommodation and currency supply.

It is a marked instance of Hamilton's habit of getting down to fundamental principles in framing a case that he examined at length the equities of the situation before citing the solemn pledges of Congress to redeem the public obligations at their face value without any attempt to discriminate between different classes of creditors. These pledges alone should have sufficed to settle the matter without further discussion, but it soon appeared that regard for public faith was so weak in Congress that there was real need for the argument that it pays to be honest.

Another matter to which Hamilton gave detailed consideration was assumption by the nation of the debts contracted by the States during the war. Inasmuch as the debts had been contracted for the common cause of independence it properly followed that they should form a common charge upon the national resources, but so strong were particularist tendencies that this view was not readily accepted, and in this matter, too, Hamilton felt constrained to press considerations of particular advantage even from the narrow view of State interest. "If all the public creditors," he observed, "receive their dues from one source, distributed with an equal hand, their interest will be the same. And having the same interests, they will unite in the support of the fiscal arrangements of the Government—as these, too, can be made with more convenience where there is no competition. These circumstances combined, will ensure to the revenue laws a more ready and satisfactory execution. If, on the contrary, there are distinct provisions, there will be distinct interests, drawing different ways. That union and concert of views among the creditors, which in every Government is of great importance to their security, and to that of public credit, will not only not exist, but will be likely to give place to mutual jealousy and opposition. And from this cause, the operation of the systems which may be adopted, both by the particular States and by the Union, with relation to their respective debts, will be in danger of being counteracted."

Here we have, as it were in a nutshell, an explanation of the fact that the American Constitution actually marched, despite the fatal tendency of written constitutions to remain mere inert paper schemes. The actual constitution of a country is always the actual distribution of political power. The American Constitution succeeded because Hamilton's management accomplished such a distribution of power as to secure for the Union such a general attachment of interests as to counteract particularist tendencies.

Hamilton computed the amount of the foreign debt to be, principal and arrears, $11,710,378.62; the domestic debt, including that of the States, over $42,000,000—a total of over $54,000,000, with an annual interest charge of $4,587,445, apparently an intolerable burden for a thinly populated country exhausted by seven years of war. Nevertheless, Hamilton refused to admit that "such a provision would exceed the abilities of the country," but he was "clearly of the opinion that to make it would require the extension of taxation to a degree and to objects which the true interest of the public creditors forbids." He therefore favored a composition, in which there should be strict adherence to the principle "that no change in the rights of its creditors ought to be attempted without their voluntary consent; and that this consent ought to be voluntary in fact as well as in name. . . . Every proposal of a change ought to be in the shape of an appeal to their reason and to their interest, not to their necessities." He then went into details of a funding loan, in which various options were offered to the creditors, including land grants in part payment and conversion in whole or in part into annuities, several

kinds of which were offered. There was an intricacy
in his plans which might not have been a hindrance
to them could he have been present to reply to
questions and explain details, but which in the actual
circumstances was a clog, and eventually the scheme
had to be simplified to bring it within reach of Congressional understanding. He submitted estimates
how the various plans of composition would work
out in practice, and he concluded that an annual
revenue of $2,239,163.09 would enable the Govern-
ment to meet its interest obligations. To provide
this amount, as well as the sum necessary to defray
the current expenses of the Government, he submitted in particular detail a scheme of taxation
applying mainly to wines, distilled spirits, teas, and
coffee.

Although when now examined under the instructions of history, Hamilton's plans make a deep impression of grand statesmanship, many members of
the Congress to which they were submitted regarded
them as wild and visionary. Senator Maclay, of
Pennsylvania, in his private diary—whose publication in our own times casts many instructive side-
lights upon the situation with which Hamilton had
to deal—characterized the whole scheme as "a
monument of political absurdity." In his opinion
Hamilton had "a very boyish, giddy manner, and
Scotch-Irish people could well call him a 'skite.'"
Hamilton's supporters figure in the diary as his

"gladiators" and as "a corrupt squadron." Jackson, of Georgia, regarded it as sufficient evidence of the folly of Hamilton's proposals that to adopt them would create a funded debt, the inevitable effect of which would be national decay. He pointed to England as "a melancholy instance of the ruin attending such engagements." If it were asked how otherwise the public indebtedness could be provided for, the answer was ready—by repudiation, in whole or in part. Livermore, of New Hampshire, admitted that the foreign debt should be acknowledged, but the domestic debt was not a fair obligation, since it was "for depreciated paper, or services done at exorbitant rates, or for goods and provisions supplied at more than their real worth, by those who received all the benefits arising from our change of condition." Page, of Virginia, argued that "our citizens were deeply interested, and, I believe, if they were never to get a farthing for what is owing to them for their services, they would be well paid; they have gained what they aimed at; they have secured their liberties and their laws." When such argument was confronted with the solemn pledges of the Continental Congress that the obligations contracted would be discharged at their face value, it was explained by Livermore that this was merely for effect—that it was "done on a principle of policy, in order to prevent the rapid depreciation which was taking place," and that those who would now take advantage of the circumstance were not animated by a spirit of patriotism but were merely a set of speculators.

Repudiation did not obtain support enough to make it really formidable, and the only dangerous attempt to impair the obligation of contracts took the form of a movement in favor of discrimination. It received the powerful championship of Madison, who in his efforts to adjust his behavior to the political situation in his State, appears now to have discarded the principles he used to profess. In a series of elaborate speeches he argued that present holders should be allowed only the highest market price previously recorded, the residue to go to the original holders. He stuck to this in the face of statements of its impracticability which he made no attempt to refute. Boudinot, of New Jersey, pointed out that great quantities of certificates of indebtedness had been originally issued to government clerks who distributed them among those who furnished supplies to the government, or who performed services entitling them to pay. He mentioned that he himself appeared on the record as original holder in cases wherein he had really acted for his neighbors, to relieve them of the trouble of personal appearance. Madison's proposal would therefore invest him with a legal title to property which actually belonged to others. Madison answered that "all that he wished was that the claims of the original holders, not less than those of the actual holders, should be fairly examined and justly decided," and there he rested, avoiding particulars. He was, however, somewhat embarrassed by a home thrust from Benson, of New York, who put the question whether if Madison had sold a certificate he would now claim part of the value he had transferred. "I ask," said Benson, "whether he would take advantage of the law against me." Madison would not give a direct answer, but said that everything would depend upon the cirumstances of any particular case, and that circumstances were conceivable in which the most tender conscience need not refrain from taking the benefit of what the Government had determined.

The debate on Madison's proposal of discrimination occupied eleven days, during which it steadily lost ground, and when the issue came to a vote it was defeated in the House by the crushing vote of thirty-six to thirteen. The struggle now shifted to the assumption of State debts. The character of the debate shows how much the discussion suffered from the lack of the presence of the Secretary to state his case and define the issue. There is little evidence that the argument made in his report received any real consideration. The debate dragged along, including much that was fictitious or irrelevant, and it is plain that the usual point of view was merely that of local interest. Members would figure how much their States would have to pay as their share of the debt, and upon that consideration alone would reach conclusions as to how the States individually stood to win or lose by the transaction, as if they were so many different countries and not members of the same nation. Livermore, of New Hampshire, a State which had the luck to lie outside the field of actual warfare, declared: "I conceive that the debt of South Carolina, or Massachusetts, or an individual, has nothing to do with our deliberations. If they have involved themselves in debt, it is their misfortune, and they must extricate themselves as well as they can." Stone, of Maryland, another State that lay outside the track of war, admonished the war-debt States that they should "nobly bear the burthens" of debts which had been contracted in military efforts that were for the advantage of all the States. Such selfish particularism received the strong championship of Madison, who had on this issue made a complete change of front in deference to the opposition to assumption which had been developed in Virginia, on the supposition that it meant a heavy bill for that large State to pay on account of other States. The combination against assumption was too strong for its advocates to overcome, and on

April 12, 1790, the bill was defeated outright in the House, thirty-one to twenty-one. It was a deadly blow to Hamilton's plans, as the assumption of the State debts by the nation was an essential feature of his plans for establishing national union.

CHAPTER XVII

A FATEFUL BARGAIN

THE defeat of the Assumption Bill did not discourage Hamilton. It was only one more of the many rebuffs and disappointments he had met with in his years of effort to establish national authority. He had recently dealt with a more difficult situation in the New York Convention than that which now confronted him in Congress, and he now energetically applied himself to that situation, using pressure of interest to move those who could not be stirred by reason. His own literary remains furnish no details of his activity at this period, and such glimpses as one gets of it in the records are afforded mainly through notice of it taken by his opponents.

It is plain that the leverage which Hamilton now brought to bear was the intense interest felt in Congress over the site of the national capital. With many members that appears to have been a consideration above everything else in importance. It became the prominent topic in Madison's correspondence as soon as the Constitution was adopted. Legislative bargaining about it started as soon as Congress met. On April 26, 1789, before Washington had been installed in office, Maclay noted a meeting "to concert some measures for the removal of Congress." Thereafter notices of attempted bargains frequently appear in his diary, and after the defeat of the Assumption Bill there are references to Hamilton's participation. An entry of June 14, 1790, ascribes to Robert Morris the statement that "Hamilton said he wanted one vote in the Senate and five in the House of Representatives; that he was willing and would agree to place the permanent residence of Congress at Germantown or Falls of the Delaware [Trenton], if he (Morris) would procure him those votes." But the Pennsylvania delegation was hopelessly divided between the Delaware and the Susquehanna claimants for the site, and Hamilton had to seek elsewhere for the votes he needed. He eventually effected the winning combination through support drawn from what at the start seemed the least promising quarter—the Virginia delegation—and, what seems stranger still, in view of their subsequent relations, he did this by the aid of Thomas Jefferson.

While the movement was going on that resulted in the meeting of the Philadelphia convention Jefferson was in France, where he was left in a precarious situation by the bankruptcy of the Continental Congress. In these circumstances he formed such strong national principles that he argued that "when any one State in the American union refuses obedience to the Confederation by which they have bound themselves, the rest have a natural right to compel them to obedience." [1] He went so far as to say: "There never will be money in the treasury till the Confederacy shows its teeth. The States must see the rod; perhaps it must be felt by some one of them." [2] When he took the post of Secretary of State under Washington he began his duties with high views of authority. Maclay describes a visit of Jefferson to the Senate chamber to advise a lump appropriation for the diplomatic service to be apportioned according to the discretion of the President. From Jefferson's correspondence at the time of the defeat of the Assumption Bill, it appears that he feared that the effect would be disastrous. He wrote to James Monroe, June 20, 1790, that, unless the measures of the Administration were adopted, "our credit will burst and vanish, and the States separate to take care everyone of itself." The South Carolina delegation had given plain notice that that was what that State would have to do if the war debt it had contracted was not assumed by the general government. Unless this were done all the war-ravaged States would lose by staying in the Union, since that would withdraw from their control revenue resources which they would otherwise possess. Jefferson saw that, if States loaded with debt by the war were left in

---

[1] Jefferson to De Meusnier, January 24, 1786.
[2] Jefferson to Monroe, August 11, 1786.

the lurch to save themselves as best they could, the Union would promptly break up. Hamilton availed himself of these anxieties to make a bargain by which Jefferson was to get enough Southern votes to carry assumption in return for enough votes from Hamilton's adherents to select the Potomac site for the national capital. Jefferson himself may have proposed the deal. He certainly outlined its features in his letter to Monroe and he personally attended to the actual negotiation. The terms were settled at a dinner given by Jefferson to which he invited Madison and Hamilton. As a sop to the Pennsylvania delegation it was decided that the national capital should be removed to Philadelphia for a stay of ten years, after which it should be on the eastern side of the Potomac River in a district ten miles square to be selected by the President within certain bounds. In consideration of Hamilton's support of this arrangement Jefferson and Madison agreed to facilitate the passage of the Assumption Bill. The Virginians got the goods first, but the bargain was loyally fulfilled on both sides. The Residence Act was approved July 16, 1790; the funding and assumption measures, now combined in one bill, became law on August 4. It was a narrower and rigider scheme than was first proposed by Hamilton. The changes made did not improve the measure, but Hamilton had to put up with them on the principle that half a loaf is better than no bread. Although a party to the bargain, Madison could not himself reverse his attitude on the issue, and his vote was recorded against assumption, but matters were arranged so that two Virginia members from Potomac districts changed their votes, enough to carry assumption by thirty-two ayes to twenty-nine nays.

The compromise upon the Assumption Bill not only ended a crisis which threatened to wreck national authority at the outset, but it also produced a receptive disposition in Congress of which Hamilton availed himself for a series of great measures. On December 14, 1790, he offered his plan for establishing a national bank, submitted as a further compliance with the order of the House requiring him to report plans for restoring the public credit. Here again he had to combat prejudices, which he instanced and considered in detail, such as that banks "serve to increase usury, tend to prevent other kinds of lending, furnish temptations to overtrading, afford aid to ignorant adventurers who disturb the natural and beneficial course of trade, give to bankrupt and fraudulent traders a fictitious credit which enables them to maintain false appearances and to extend their impositions, and that they have a tendency to banish gold and silver from the country." All these accusations are examined with a thoroughness that makes the report a masterly treatise upon the functions of banks. Such was the effect of the report that the bill incorporating the Bank of the United States had rather an easy passage through Congress. It originated in the Senate and was reported to the House from the committee of the whole, without amendment. But when the question was on the passage of the bill Madison opposed it on the ground that the Constitution did not expressly authorize Congress to grant charters, and that to assume such power by implication would "go to the subversion of every power whatever in the several States." Madison's argument had so little effect that the report preserved in the *Annals of Congress* notes that "the House discovering an impatience to have the main question put," the yeas and nays were then taken and the vote was thirty-nine to twenty in favor of the bill.

When the act reached Washington for his approval both the Virginia members of the Cabinet—Randolph, the Attorney-General, and Jefferson, the Secretary of State—took Madison's position that the Constitution did not warrant such an enactment. Washington seems to have been moved by this advice, for he requested Madison to prepare a veto message for him. But on February 16, while Madison was at work upon it, Washington referred the case to Hamilton with the request that he would consider the objections raised and give his opinion upon them. Madison handed in his draft of a veto message on the 21st. On the 23d Hamilton submitted his famous "Opinion as to the Constitutionality of the Bank of the United States," prepared in just one week.   It is safe to say that there is no other instance in which a great monument of jurisprudence was so rapidly erected.   In his letter of transmission Hamilton remarked that the opinion had "occupied him the greatest part of last night."   But the opinion itself bears no mark of haste.   Terse in diction and concise in method, it is so complete in its analysis that it is over 11,000 words in length, sustained in power, and solid in argument throughout.   In it Hamilton developed the doctrine of implied powers, which was later adopted by the Supreme Court and is now generally admitted to be an essential incident of genuine authority.   This doctrine was thus stated by Hamilton, the italics being his own:

Now it appears to the Secretary of the Treasury that this *general principle* is *inherent* in the very definition of government, and *essential* to every step of the progress to be made by that of the United States, namely: That every power vested in a government is in its nature *sovereign*, and includes, by *force* of the *term*, a right to employ all the *means* requisite and fairly applicable to the attainment of the *ends* of such power, and which are not precluded by restrictions and exceptions specified in the Constitution, or not immoral, or not contrary to the *essential ends* of political society.

He proceeded to support this proposition by copious instances, largely of a practical nature, showing that without such a principle of conduct "the United States would furnish the singular spectacle of a *political society* without *sovereignty*, or of a *people governed*, without government." The cogency of Hamilton's argument was eventually shown by the experience of his principal opponents—Jefferson and Madison—during their terms as President. Stress of practical necessity forced them to Hamilton's position after they had caused immense mischief to their country as well as great annoyance to themselves by their opposition to it.

Hamilton's argument was so convincing to Washington, after careful examination, that he rejected the advice of Randolph, Jefferson, and Madison, and signed the bill. The principles laid down by Hamilton thereafter guided Washington's administration. Although Washington was still pressed with strict-construction arguments he ceased to pay much attention to them. When Jefferson argued at a cabinet meeting that there was no constitutional authority for establishing a military academy, Washington cut short the discussion by saying that he would recommend such action to Congress and "let them decide for themselves whether the Constitution authorized it or not."

On January 28, 1791, Hamilton sent to the House a report on the establishment of a mint. He began with a powerful statement of the variety and disorder of the existing circulating medium, a medley

of foreign coins having no fixed and uniform standard of value.   He observed:

> In order to a right judgment of what ought to be done,
> the following particulars require to be discussed:
> 1st. What ought to be the nature of the money unit of
> the United States?
> 2d. What the proportion between gold and silver, if
> coins of both metals are to be established?
> 3d. What the proportion and composition of alloy in
> each kind?
> 4th. Whether the expense of coinage shall be defrayed
> by the Government, or out of the material itself?
> 5th. What shall be the number, denominations, sizes,
> and devices of the coins?
> 6th. Whether foreign coins shall be permitted to be
> current or not; if the former, at what rate, and for what
> period.

As might be expected from such an exhaustive
classification, the report is a complete dissertation
upon coinage problems.   It is a striking example of
Hamilton's habit of going to the bottom of every
subject before stating his conclusions, for he did not
have any great innovation to recommend.   His
plan virtually took the situation as he found it and
made the best of it.   The English pound, although
still nominally the unit of account, had been practically superseded by the Spanish dollar, but coins
of that denomination had no settled or standard
value.   Hamilton took the prevailing rating of the
dollar as the actual money unit, disregarding the

old value of the dollar as fixed by Spanish law, with the express purpose of keeping unimpaired existing contracts based upon the current rating of the dollar. So likewise he retained both gold and silver as full legal tender and fixed a ratio corresponding to the commercial ratio. However, he remarked, with a prescience since abundantly attested by events: "As long as gold either from its intrinsic superiority as a metal, from its greater rarity, or from the prejudices of mankind, retains so considerable a preeminence in value over silver, as it has hitherto had, a natural consequence of this seems to be that its condition will be more stationary. The revolutions, therefore, which may take place in the comparative value of gold and silver, will be changes in the state of the latter, rather than in that of the former."

As regards the scale of value in the coinage, he recommended the decimal system, which in fact had been adopted by the Continental Congress on August 8, 1786, although it had not gone into effect. Jefferson was strongly in favor of this system, which indeed met with quite general acceptance. As to devices upon the coins, Hamilton contented himself with remarking that they "are far from being matters of indifference, as they may be made the vehicles of useful impressions." He did not make any particular recommendations under this head in his report, but the bill as passed by the Senate contained a provision that coins should bear a representation

of the head of the President during whose administration they were issued, and it is presumable that
this was in accord with Hamilton's idea. This provision was energetically attacked in the House as a
servile imitation of the practice of monarchies. It
was in vain pointed out that the House amendment
striking out this instruction "left the matter entirely
to the judgment of the artist, who may form such an
emblem as suits his fancy." The amendment was
carried by twenty-six yeas to twenty-two nays,
Madison voting in the affirmative, and, although the
Senate was disposed to insist upon the clause, it
finally had to submit to the will of the House. The
result is the queer, totemistic character of the designs of American coinage. The heads of Presidents
and other public men now appear in profusion upon
the note issues of the United States, but not according
to any settled plan, and Hamilton's sensible idea of
making the devices "vehicles of useful impressions"
has yet to be utilized. It cannot be doubted that
devices corresponding to Presidential terms of office
would be a valuable source of historical instruction,
whereas the existing system is one of sheer caprice.

On December 5, 1791, Hamilton sent to the
House his famous report on manufactures, references
to which have been continual in the tariff controversies that form so great a part of the political history of the United States. It is generally claimed
to be a vindication of the protective policy, and so

it is, in consideration of the actual circumstances in which the United States was placed, but at the same time no stronger statement can be found of the argument in favor of free trade than that which the report presents at the outset. Hamilton remarked that the opponents of protection might reason as follows:

To endeavor, by the extraordinary patronage of government, to accelerate the growth of manufactures, is, in fact, to endeavor, by force and art, to transfer the natural current of industry from a more to a less beneficial channel. Whatever has such a tendency, must necessarily be unwise; indeed, it can hardly ever be wise in a government to attempt to give a direction to the industry of its citizens. This, under the quicksighted guidance of private interest, will, if left to itself, infallibly find its own way to the most profitable employment; and it is by such employment that the public prosperity will be most effectually promoted. To leave industry to itself, therefore, is in almost every case, the soundest as well as the simplest policy. . . . If, contrary to the natural course of things, an unseasonable and premature spring can be given to certain fabrics, by heavy duties, prohibitions, bounties, or by other forced expedients, this will be to sacrifice the interests of the community to those of particular classes. Besides the misdirection of labor, a virtual monopoly will be given to the persons employed on such fabrics; and an enhancement of price, the inevitable consequence of every monopoly, must be defrayed at the expense of the other parts of the society. It is far preferable, that those persons should be engaged in the cultivation of the earth, and that we should procure, in exchange for its productions, the commodities with which foreigners are able to supply us in greater perfection, and upon better terms.

Hamilton expressed much sympathy with this opinion. He observed: "If the system of perfect liberty to industry and commerce were the prevailing system of nations, the arguments which dissuade a country, in the predicament of the United States, from the zealous pursuit of manufactures, would doubtless have great force. It will not be affirmed that they might not be permitted, with few exceptions, to serve as a rule of national conduct. In such a state of things, each country would have the full benefit of its peculiar advantages to compensate for its deficiencies or disadvantages. If one nation were in a condition to supply manufactured articles on better terms than another, that other might find an abundant indemnification in a superior capacity to furnish the produce of the soil. And a free exchange, mutually beneficial, of the commodities which each was able to supply, on the best terms, might be carried on between them, supporting in full vigor the industry of each."

But no such ideal situation existed. "The regulations of several countries, with which we have the most extensive intercourse, throw serious obstructions in the way of the principal staples of the United States. . . . Remarks of this kind are not made in the spirit of complaint. It is for the nations whose regulations are alluded to, to judge for themselves, whether by aiming at too much they do not lose more than they gain. It is for the United States to consider by what means they can render themselves least dependent on the combinations, right or wrong, of foreign policy. . . . If Europe will not take from us the products of our soil, upon terms consistent with our interest, the natural remedy is to contract, as fast as possible, our wants of her."

Having thus made clear the grounds of the national policy he recommended, he proceeded to discuss its economic basis. He first considered the sources of the wealth of nations, the effects of diversification of industry, and the social consequences; next came a detailed examination of the resources of the United States, and the particular means by which they might be developed. He urged: "Not only the wealth, but the independence and security of a country, appear to be materially connected with the prosperity of manufactures. Every nation, with a view to those great objects, ought to endeavor to possess within itself all the essentials of national supply. These comprise the means of subsistence, habitation, clothing, and defence. The possession of these is necessary to the perfection of the body politic; to the safety as well as to the welfare of the society. The want of either is the want of an important organ of political life and motion; and in the various crises which await a state, it must severely feel the effects of any such deficiency." History has given impressive testimony to the justice of these observations.

The report, although extensive in its scope, has such conciseness and unity that it is impossible to offer any summary that can do it justice. In it Hamilton's genius shines with a brilliancy that places it alongside the report on the public credit in greatness of statesmanship. If it had appeared as a scholastic treatise instead of as a public document, it would figure as a classic of political economy, produced at a time when that science was almost inchoate. Its foundations had indeed been securely laid by Adam Smith, the first edition of whose *Wealth of Nations* appeared in 1776, but its influence was not manifested in English politics until 1792, when Pitt avowed his acceptance of its principles. Hamilton appreciated the work from the first, and he is known to have written an extended commentary upon it some time in 1783, during his first term as a member of the Continental Congress, but this is among the many Hamilton papers that have been lost. In one place in the report on manufactures he quoted a passage from Adam Smith on the economic reactions of transportation facilities. But there is no resemblance between the two works in style and method. Hamilton moved on his own lines and his report is the product of his own thought. In some measure it might even be described as a rejoinder to Smith, the weight of whose argument, as is well known, was in favor of free trade. This Hamilton doubtless had in mind when he observed: "Most general theories, however, admit of numerous exceptions, and there are few, if any, of the political kind, which do not blend a considerable portion of error with the truths they inculcate." Smith admitted that particular considerations might traverse the general principles he advocated, as, for instance, after condemning the Navigation Act as adverse to the national prosperity, he abruptly remarked: "As defence, however, is of much more importance than opulence, the act of navigation is, perhaps, the wisest of all the commercial regulations of England." This consideration which Smith dismisses with curt mention is drawn out at length with great power in Hamilton's report, not merely as concerns navigation, but in respect of the whole subject of national policy. But at the same time it should be observed that Hamilton's dissent from the principles of free trade was not based upon rejection of them in the abstract. His point was that the statesman has to deal with things as they are and not as they ought to be. His protective policy is connected with particular needs and circumstances, and is hence no hard-and-fast rule, but is subject to modification as needs and circumstances change.

Although the policy recommended in this report has since become a perennial source of controversy

in American politics, it did not excite active opposition when it was presented. Indeed, that policy
had already been adopted by Congress, although
more as a result of casual drift than of deliberate
purpose. Before Hamilton took office a tariff act
had been passed, with a preamble that included
"the encouragement and protection of manufactures" in its statement of purpose. The enactment
was prompted by the immediate need of revenue,
but Madison, who had charge of the bill, admitted
amendments of an avowedly protectionist character.

The series of great state papers that have been
described were all transmitted to the First Congress,
with the exception of the report on manufactures,
which was sent in at the opening of the first session
of the Second Congress. The measures devised
by Hamilton established the public credit upon such
solid foundations that it was able to sustain shocks
from incompetent management after his retirement
that would otherwise have been fatal. There is
no greater illustration of the proverb that republics
are always ungrateful than the return made to him
for his splendid services. He was subjected to fero-
cious persecution, pursued with untiring malignity,
and every art of calumny was employed to load his
name with obloquy, with such success as still to
give color to our political literature. He met every
attack with dauntless courage and triumphant energy, and he left the public service not because he

was overcome but because he was starved out. It is impossible to find in all history any other statesman who accomplished so much with such small means, and who received so slight a reward for his labors.

CHAPTER XVIII

THE ANTI-HAMILTON CAMPAIGN

IMMEDIATELY after their defeat on the Bank Bill, Madison and Jefferson took steps to provide themselves with a newspaper organ. Hamilton's conclusive opinion was transmitted, February 23, 1791. On the 28th Jefferson wrote to Philip Freneau offering him a clerkship in the State Department, with the assurance that "it requires no other qualification than a moderate knowledge of the French," and that "should anything better turn up" in the department that "might suit" Freneau, he "should be very happy to bestow it so well." At that time Freneau was arranging to start a newspaper in New Jersey. Madison went to see him and induced him to set up his newspaper in Philadelphia. Writing to Jefferson, May 1, 1791, Madison said: "I have seen Freneau and given him a line to you. He sets out for Philadelphia today or tomorrow." The result of the conferences which took place was that Freneau accepted the clerkship and made arrangements by which his newspaper was established in Philadelphia in time for the next session of Congress. The first number of the *National Gazette* appeared on October 31, 1791. Attacks upon the Administration began in it December 8, 1791, and continued thereafter until October, 1793, when the publication was discontinued soon after Jefferson left the Cabinet. Madison was a contributor almost from the start, furnishing articles on such topics as "Consolidation," "Money," "Government," "Charters," "Parties," "British Government," etc. They were calm in tone and decorous in language, but were calculated to produce vague impressions that public affairs were going wrong and that corrective action was desirable.

In addition to retaining Freneau's services, it appears that efforts were also made to get the aid of Thomas Paine. Writing to Jefferson, July 13, 1791, Madison said: "I wish you success with all my heart in your efforts for Paine. Besides the advantage to him which he deserves, an appointment for him, at this moment, would do good in various ways." About this time Paine produced his "Rights of Man," with the publication of which Jefferson was connected in a way which he did not expect and which considerably embarrassed him. An edition of Paine's pamphlet appeared with a letter of approval from Jefferson, who wrote at once to Washington explaining that it had been meant as a private letter— "to my great astonishment, however, the printer had prefixed my note to it, without having given me the most distant hint of it." Paine did not get an appointment, and the affair doubtless had much to do with the bitter attacks which he made later upon Washington.

In making these arrangements Jefferson and Madison do not appear at the outset to have had any distinct plan of opposition to the Administration, but simply had in view the strengthening of their political influence. The principal mark of their censure was not at first Hamilton, but was John Adams, the Vice-President, who had been publishing some newspaper articles which both Jefferson and Madison characterized as an attack upon republican principles. Adams figured prominently, in their correspondence in the summer of 1791, as the propagator of political heresies, but at this time there was no unfriendly mention of Hamilton. Both Jefferson and Madison seemed to be reluctant to make an issue of Hamilton's financial policy, for they had been a party to it through the aid they gave to the passage of assumption. Their original expectation was that the storm it had raised would soon blow over. On July 31, 1790, Madison wrote to his father that, although he had voted against assumption, he had felt "that there was serious danger of a very unfavorable issue to the session from a contrary decision, and considered it as now incumbent on us all to make the best of what was done. The truth is that in a pecuniary light, the assumption is no longer of much consequence to Virginia, the sum allotted to her being about her proportion of the whole, rather exceeding her present debt." Jefferson's correspondence shows positive favor to assumption. He wrote, June 27, 1790, that "a rejection of the measure . . . will be something very like a dissolution of the government." In a letter of July 4 he remarked: "The funding business being once out of the way, I hope nothing else may be able to call up local principles." On July 25 he wrote that "the measure was so vehemently called for by the State creditors in some parts of the Union that it seems to be one of those cases where some sacrifice of opinion is necessary for the sake of peace." On August 4 he wrote that the struggle over assumption "really threatened, at one time, a separation of the legislature *sine die*," and he remarked: "It is not foreseen that anything so generative of dissension can arise again, and therefore the friends of the government hope that, this difficulty once surmounted in the States, everything will work well." Writing on November 26, 1790, he remarked that assumption "is harped on by many to mask their disaffection to the government on other grounds," but the government was "too well nerved to be overawed by individual opposition." On December 29, 1790, he wrote a very friendly letter to Hamilton, in which he expressed the hope that it would be "taken as an advance towards unreserved communications for reciprocal benefit."

Everything indicates that for upward of a year after the passage of assumption Madison regarded it with indulgence, while Jefferson took credit to himself for having tided the government over a dangerous crisis. But the agitation did not subside. In December, 1790, the Virginia Legislature adopted fiery resolutions condemning both funding and assumption. These resolutions laid down the platform on which both Madison and Jefferson eventually took their stand. The financial policy of the government was censured as being an imitation of British policy, and as a violation of the constitutional principle "that every power not granted was retained by the States." The resolutions appealed to Congress "to revise and amend" the Public Credit Act, and "repeal, in particular, as much of it as relates to the assumption of the State debts." Jefferson was then loath to mount that platform, but as time went on he felt increasing anxiety about foreign policy, and he became ardently desirous of establishing a strong party interest on the side of the French revolutionary government. But it became manifest that among the means he could employ to push his party interest none was so available as opposition to the Funding and Assumption Act which had been passed through his own agency. Here was a pretty hobble; but Jefferson was able to twist out of it. He excused himself on the ground that he did not know what he was doing; that he "was most

ignorantly and innocently made to hold the candle"
to Hamilton's game. The discredit to his intelligence he relieved by saying that he had then only
recently arrived in the country, "a stranger to the
ground, a stranger to the actors on it."

It is impossible to reconcile this statement with
the statements contained in Jefferson's own letters
written at the time the deal on the Potomac site
was pending; and furthermore, with Madison at
his elbow, he could not have suffered from lack
of information. It is equally impossible to reconcile with contemporary evidence the account which
Jefferson eventually gave of the effect of the passage
of the act. As soon as "the form in which the bill
would finally pass" had been indicated, wrote Jefferson, "the base scramble began. Couriers and
relay horses by land, and swift sailing pilot boats by
sea, were flying in all directions. Active partners
and agents were associated and employed in every
State, town and country neighborhood, and this
paper was bought up at five shillings and even as low
as two shillings in the pound, before the holder knew
that Congress had already provided for its redemption at par. Immense sums were thus filched from
the poor and ignorant."

Inasmuch as Hamilton's proposals were communicated to Congress on January 14, 1790, and the
Assumption Bill did not become law until August
4, nearly seven months intervened during which

knowledge of the Government's intention could be diffused among the people. Moreover, there was nothing new about the proposals. They had been discussed in the Continental Congress, and as a member of that body Madison himself had argued in favor of assumption. The formidable opposition that developed in Congress certainly gave opportunity to speculators by clouding the prospects of government paper, but purchasers had to take a risk, since the passage of the Public Credit Act with the assumption feature was not assured until Jefferson himself put his shoulder to the wheel. Nothing like the scene of concerted activity described by Jefferson, writing long after the event, can be found in contemporary documents. There are references to speculative activity in Madison's correspondence shortly after the enactment, but nothing to justify the picture which Jefferson drew after his change of front. The psychology of the situation is, however, readily intelligible. It frequently happens that when shifts of interest take place, stirring the feelings and energizing the will, the memory is impressed into the service of the new state of the mind and thus becomes capable of rearranging past events in conformity with present views.

Jefferson and his adherents now made use of every possible means to break Hamilton's influence and discredit his management. Hamilton was attacked in the press, harassed in Congress, and in-

trigued against in the Cabinet. Jefferson himself
has recorded how he labored with Washington to
inspire distrust of Hamilton. An entry in *The
Anas* notes that the writer told the President that
"the department of the Treasury possessed already
such influence as to swallow up the whole executive
powers," and that the popular discontents had
"only a single source," Hamilton's policy.

Hamilton hit back vigorously, and to this is due
the clearest account that exists of the politics of the
time. In a long letter, May 26, 1792, to Colonel
Edward Carrington, of Virginia, Hamilton gave a
detailed account of the political situation from the
beginning. In it he showed that originally Madison
and himself had been in entire agreement on funding and assumption, and that he had been slow to
believe that Madison had both changed his views
and become personally unfriendly. "It was not
till the last session," wrote Hamilton, "that I became unequivocally convinced of the following truth:
that Mr. Madison, cooperating with Mr. Jefferson,
is at the head of a faction decidedly hostile to me
and my administration; and actuated by views,
in my judgment, subversive of the principles of
good government and dangerous to the union, peace,
and happiness of the country."

Hamilton's characteristic habit of getting to the
bottom of every subject he discussed is strongly
marked in this letter. He made no use of the easy

retort that was open to him of showing that Jefferson himself was a participant in the measures now assailed, but he traced the animosity of Jefferson and Madison to its source in their characters and circumstances, and he gave this portrayal of the nature of their proceedings:

It is possible, too, (for men easily heat their imaginations when their passions are heated) that they have by degrees persuaded themselves of what they may have at first only sported to influence others, namely, that there is some dreadful combination against State government and republicanism; which, according to them, are convertible terms. But there is so much absurdity in this supposition, that the admission of it tends to apologize for their hearts at the expense of their heads. Under the influence of all these circumstances the attachment to the government of the United States, originally weak in Mr. Jefferson's mind, has given way to something very like dislike in Mr. Madison's. . . . In such a state of mind both these gentlemen are prepared to hazard a great deal to effect a change. Most of the important measures of every government are connected with the treasury. To subvert the present head of it, they deem it expedient to risk rendering the government itself odious; perhaps foolishly thinking that they can easily recover the lost affections and confidence of the people, and not appreciating, as they ought to do, the natural resistance to government, which in every community results from the human passions, the degree to which this has been strengthened by the organized rivalry of State governments, and the infinite danger that the national government once rendered odious, will be kept so by these powerful and indefatigable enemies. They forget an old, but a very just though a coarse saying, that it is much easier to raise the devil than to lay him.

This acute criticism is not only a fine piece of political psychology, but it is also entitled to rank as political prophecy. The Civil War was logically the outcome of principles originally advanced in the war against Hamilton.

The Carrington letter was undoubtedly meant to call Jefferson and Madison to public account in their own State for their behavior. It was written to be shown about and, according to the customs of the times, it was a more direct challenge to them than a newspaper article would have been. At that time, both in England and America, it was considered undignified to go into journalism in one's proper person; a pseudonym was the rule even when the actual authorship was generally known. But the Carrington letter bore Hamilton's signature and it might readily have been the beginning of a direct controversy, but Jefferson and Madison were too cautious to be drawn. Jefferson countered in a letter to George Mason, of Virginia, arraigning the financial policy of the Government as a scheme of corruption, having for its ultimate object "to prepare the way for a change from the present republican form of government to that of monarchy, of which the British constitution is to be the model." The letter was virtually an indictment of Hamilton's policy drawn out under twenty-one heads, and this particularity turned out to be an advantage to Hamilton. What he most desired was that charges against him should be given some definite shape so that he could meet them, and this favor Jefferson's letter happened to supply. Mason gave Washington a copy and Washington transmitted the charges to Hamilton with a request for his "ideas upon the discontents here enumerated." Hamilton replied seriatim, expressing himself with marked warmth, as to which he remarked: "I have not fortitude enough always to bear with calmness calumnies which necessarily include me, as a principal agent in the measures censured, of the falsehood of which I have the most unqualified consciousness." The objections which Hamilton had to meet as to the propriety of loans, funding operations, and banking facilities are now so obsolete that the main impression left by examination of the documents is the absurdity of the elaborate case framed by Jefferson. It was a pointless argument to expatiate upon the burden laid upon the Government by the funding scheme unless some other way could be instanced for disposing of obligations that the Government could not meet. Now there was another way—that of simply ignoring them, and the only logical ground of complaint against Hamilton was that he did not take that way, which was repudiation. But Jefferson did not venture to take that ground, so it was easy for Hamilton to brush away his cavils by pointing out that "The public debt was produced by the late war. It is not the fault of the present government that it exists, unless it can be proved that public morality and policy do not require of a government an honest provision for its debts." Nevertheless there was a strong feeling, among men of all parties, that Hamilton might have avoided that issue and let the Revolutionary debt sink itself through inattention to it, thus starting the new government without any burden of debt. Even in the Federalist ranks there was rather a grudge against Hamilton that he was so determined to rake up and pay off the old obligations, and this accounts for much of the detraction he had to endure from some who figured as his allies.

The only effect of the cabinet attacks, so far a Hamilton was concerned, was to fortify his position in Washington's esteem; but Washington himself was so disturbed by the continual dissension that he wanted to retire from public life. This did not at all suit Jefferson's book. What his faction desired was that Washington should stay on but should act in their interest. Although it is now known, since his private correspondence is accessible, that Washington was strongly in favor of assumption, he judged it wise to practise strict reticence as to his own views, as the original conception of the Presidential office was that it should be above and beyond party spirit, like royalty. English political thought still colored men's thoughts, and the object of Jefferson's manœuvres was what in England would have been called a change of ministry. What this practically meant in the American situation was that Hamilton should be put out of office, whereupon, it was thought, Washington would naturally be guided by the advice of his Virginia associates—Jefferson, Madison, and Randolph. Washington went so far in his plans for retirement that he asked Madison to prepare a farewell message for his use; but the whole Virginia set now labored to induce him to consent to re-election, and he reluctantly consented.

The election over, the Jefferson cabal adopted new tactics. Instead of working directly upon Washington, they now planned to reach and move him through the action of Congress. In this scheme they were greatly aided by the conditions that had been established in Congress. Among the consequences of the exclusion of the Administration from the floor of Congress is the loss by Congress of intelligent control of its own business. Had Hamilton had the opportunity of confronting his accusers the growth of such fable as now collected about his plans and proceedings would have been impossible. Every one knows the difference between saying things to a man's face and behind his back. The latter is the Congressional method, and the only way in which matters can be brought to an issue is by the slow, cumbersome method of resolutions of inquiry and committees of investigation. Such means can be readily employed for purposes of sheer partisan annoyance, and there are innumerable instances of this character in the history of Congress. The evil has been aggravated by patronage developments. The creation of committees furnishes plausible occasion for numerous clerkships and other subordinate offices to be distributed by Congressional favor. Activities of this order are now very marked as a political campaign comes on, and they constitute one of the greatest abuses of American politics. This partisan machinery had its origin in the war on Hamilton. His enemies sought to break him by a series of Congressional attacks, concerted in secrecy with the advice and assistance of Jefferson and Madison. They obtained an ally in Congress who possessed exceptional courage, energy, and address.

William Branch Giles, of Virginia, was a lawyer who was as fearless as Hamilton himself in confronting opposition. British debt cases had been a marked feature of his practice, in the teeth of Virginia law prohibiting actions of this class, but Giles took the position, first maintained by Hamilton, that the Peace Treaty of 1783 prevailed over any opposing State law, and he pressed his cases with energy and success on the basis of a national jurisdiction in conflict with the Virginia statutes. This course was not calculated to secure political popularity, but he sheltered himself by the plea of professional duty, and on other matters he cultivated popular support with such success that he got into the First Congress at a special election to fill a vacancy. When he took his seat the Assumption Bill had been passed, but he followed Madison's lead in unsuccessful opposition to the Bank Bill. He was re-elected to the Second Congress and during its sessions displayed so much energy and audacity that Madison stepped aside to allow him to lead in the war on Hamilton. After some preliminary skirmishing a grand attack was made on January 23, 1793, when Giles presented a series of resolutions, in drafting which he had had the assistance of Jefferson and Madison. He supported them in an adroit speech in which he said that they had grown out of the embarrassments he had met with in trying to comprehend the statements of the Secretary of the Treasury respecting foreign loans. He submitted calculations suggestive of discrepancies, which he admitted might be removed by explanations but which at least showed that the House needed more information than it had.

The tact and moderation of this speech had such an effect that the resolutions were adopted without serious opposition, although, so far as Giles's claim of ignorance was well founded, it was an exposure of the defective procedure of the House. Could Hamilton have come before the House he could at once have supplied all the information it needed and all the explanations it desired. As it was he had to meet a heavy demand upon the resources of his department. The resolutions called for particulars of all loans, names of all persons to whom payments had been made, statements of semimonthly balances between the Treasury and the bank, and an account of the sinking-fund and of unexpended appropriations, from the beginning until the end of 1792. In effect, the resolutions required Hamilton to complete and state all Treasury accounts, almost to date, and to give a transcript of all the particulars. But the Treasury accounts were in such perfect order, and so great was Hamilton's capacity for work, that the information called for was promptly transmitted, in reports dated February 4, 13, and 14.

In completing the heavy task laid upon him by his enemies, Hamilton observed that the resolutions "were not moved without a pretty copious display of the reasons on which they were founded," which "were of a nature to excite attention, to beget alarm, to inspire doubts." This remark was taken as ground for a charge that he was "guilty of an indecorum to this House, in undertaking to judge of its motives in calling for information." Nothing was found amiss in the accounts; on the contrary, examination showed exactness, clearness, and order throughout.   But on February 28, 1793, Giles moved nine resolutions, charging Hamilton with violation of law, neglect of duty, and transgression of the proper limits of his authority.   The resolutions did not propose impeachment or, indeed, any action by Congress whatsoever, further than that "a copy of the foregoing resolutions should be transmitted to the President of the United States."   The proceedings virtually amounted to a declaration of want of confidence, with the expectation that Washington would be thereby constrained to remove Hamilton from office.

Hamilton felt keenly the disadvantage he was under in not being allowed to face his accusers on the floor of the House.   In the circumstances the best he could do was to supply his friends with material for use in the debate.   A speech delivered by William Smith, of South Carolina, was in fact written by Hamilton, and it bears the marks of his style. In it he exclaimed what injustice it was to "condemn a man unheard, nay, without his having even been furnished with the charges against him!"

The charges were intrinsically so weak that they could not stand up under discussion.   The imputations of wrong-doing rested upon mere cavils.   It could not even be alleged that any public interest had sustained actual harm.   It became so manifest that the resolutions were founded on nothing more substantial than spite that Giles could not hold his forces together. After the third resolution had been defeated by a vote of forty to twelve, an attempt was made to withdraw the others, but the House insisted upon consideration. One by one the remaining resolutions were voted down by increasing majorities, until only seven members voted with Giles at the last, among them James Madison. It was a signal triumph for Hamilton and an occasion for deep chagrin with Jefferson and Madison. Jefferson held that the judgment of Congress might be revised at a future session and efforts to overthrow Hamilton were steadily continued.

CHAPTER XIX

THE INFLUENCE OF THE FRENCH REVOLUTION

IN the course of his criticisms upon Jefferson and Madison, in his Carrington letter of May 26, 1792, Hamilton said:

In respect to foreign politics, the views of these gentlemen are, in my judgment, equally unsound and dangerous. They have a womanish attachment to France and a womanish resentment against Great Britain. They would draw us into the closest embrace of the former, and involve us in all the consequences of her politics; and they would risk the peace of the country in their endeavors to keep us at the greatest possible distance from the latter. This disposition goes to a length, particularly in Mr. Jefferson, of which, till lately, I had no adequate idea. Various circumstances prove to me that if these gentlemen were left to pursue their own course, there would be, in less than six months, an open war between the United States and Great Britain. I trust I have a due sense of the conduct of France towards this country in the late revolution; and that I shall always be among the foremost in making her every suitable return; but there is a wide difference between this and implicating ourselves in all her politics; between bearing good will to her and hating and wrangling with all those whom she hates. The neutral and the pacific policy appears to me to mark the true path to the United States.

278

The records made in *The Anas* show that Hamilton did not err in his estimate of the extent of Jefferson's partiality to France. The enthusiasm he had contracted for the revolutionary movement while resident in France during its early stages, while it had a philanthropic complexion, he carried with him into Washington's Cabinet and it colored his official behavior. He himself noted, on December 27, 1792, that the duty of the United States to support France against England and Spain was the "doctrine which had been my polar star." Numerous entries show that it was a satisfaction to Jefferson to record the energy and persistence with which he took the French side in any discussion of the subject in the meetings of the Cabinet.

Shortly after Hamilton had beaten the Jefferson faction in Congress a crisis was brought on by the breaking out of war between France and England. An able and experienced diplomatist, Edmond Genêt, was sent out to claim the United States as an ally and to use her territory as a base of operations against England. Genêt landed at Charleston, April 8, 1793, receiving an enthusiastic welcome, and he was so prompt and energetic that within five days he had opened a recruiting station at which American seamen were taken into the French service; he had commissioned American vessels as French cruisers, and he had erected the office of the French consul into an admiralty court to deal with the prizes that were being brought in.

Washington was at Mount Vernon when the news reached him. He at once called a meeting of the Cabinet and set out to Philadelphia to attend it. He arrived there on April 17, and the next day he laid before the members of the Cabinet thirteen questions upon which he desired their advice. Jefferson noted that the questions were in Washington's own handwriting, "yet it was palpable from the style, their ingenious tissue and suite, that they were not the President's, that they were raised upon a prepared chain of argument, in short, that the language was Hamilton's and the doubts his alone." In Jefferson's opinion they were designed to lead "to a declaration of the Executive that our treaty with France is void." Jefferson was right as to Hamilton's authorship. At a time when Jefferson had no advice to give save that it would be well to consider whether Congress ought not to be summoned, Hamilton had ready for Washington's use a set of interrogatories which subjected the whole situation to exact analysis. The critical questions were these:

Shall a proclamation issue for the purpose of preventing interferences of the citizens of the United States in the war between France and Great Britain, &c.? Shall it contain a declaration of neutrality or not? What shall it contain?
Are the United States obliged, by good faith, to consider the treaties heretofore made with France as apply-

ing to the present situation of the parties? May they either renounce them, or hold them suspended till the government of France shall be *established?*

The issues thus clearly stated involved some nice questions of international obligation. There were two treaties between France and the United States, both concluded on the same day. One provided that the ships of war of each country should defend the vessels of the other country from all attacks that might occur while they were in company. Each country had the right to use the ports of the other, either for regular ships of war or for privateers and their prizes, which were to be exempt from any examination or detention, "but they may hoist sail at any time and depart." All vessels of either country were entitled to refuge in the ports of the other, with entire freedom for repair and the purchase of supplies, but it was expressly provided that such hospitality should not be extended to vessels of an enemy of either country. The accompanying instrument, entitled a treaty of alliance, was a mutual guarantee of territory, "forever against all other powers." These broad rights and privileges were supplemented in 1788 by a convention which provided for consular jurisdiction over cases involving treaty rights. Genêt thus had large warrant for his activities, if the treaties were still binding. They had been made with the King of France, whose head had been sliced off by the guillotine. The

French revolutionary government held that his engagements fell with his head and that they were free to decide what treaties of the old monarchy should be retained and what rejected. It was their policy to retain the American treaties, and Genêt was under instructions to use the United States not only as an ally against England but also as an instrument for restoring French colonial empire in America. To gain Canada, Louisiana, and the Floridas was among the objects of his mission. He counted upon obtaining funds through collection of the amount still due to France on the old loans to the United States. This remainder was then about $2,300,000, and now France made a demand for three million livres,—about $600,000,—promising that the entire amount would be laid out in the purchase of supplies in the American market. On February 25, 1793, Jefferson noted that all the members of the Cabinet were willing to grant this demand except Hamilton, who stood out for keeping to the stipulated terms, according to which only an instalment of $318,000 was then due.

On the question of a proclamation Jefferson now argued that it would be equivalent to declaring that the United States would take no part in the war, and that the Executive had no right to take this position since it was the exclusive province of Congress to declare war. Therefore Congress should be called to consider the question. Hamilton, who held that it was both the right and the duty of the President to proclaim neutrality, was strongly opposed to summoning Congress. In a brief note of the cabinet meeting he remarked that "whether this advice proceeded from a secret wish to involve us in a war, or from a constitutional timidity, certain it is such a step would have been fatal to the peace and tranquillity of America." Hamilton pressed his views with such force that Jefferson agreed that if the term "neutrality" were not employed a proclamation might be issued enjoining American citizens from all acts and proceedings inconsistent with the duties of a friendly nation. It was then unanimously decided that Congress should not be convoked in advance of the regular session. The proclamation was drafted by Attorney-General Randolph, who showed it to Jefferson to assure him that "there was no such word as neutrality in it." Although Jefferson raised no objection to the wording of the proclamation at the time, a few months later he referred to it in letters to friends as a piece of "pusillanimity," because it omitted any expression of the affection of America for France.

By its terms the proclamation was simply an admonition to American citizens to keep out of the war, with notice that they would be liable to prosecution for acts of a nature to "violate the law of nations." It is manifest that the question whether or not the treaties with France were still in force was of great practical importance. If they were, they were part of the law of the land and American citizens might claim immunity for acts done under cover of their provisions. Hamilton held that the treaty obligations should be suspended since a situation had arisen which made them inconsistent with a policy of neutrality. They contemplated only defensive war; but France had taken the offensive, thereby relieving the United States of her reciprocal obligations. Jefferson held that the treaty stipulations were still operative, for, even if they apparently required the United States to engage in the war, it did not follow that such would be the actual consequence. The possibility was "not certain enough to authorize us in sound morality to declare, at this moment, the treaties null." It is not at all surprising that with this ambiguity in the position of the Government, there was difficulty in giving practical effect to the proclamation. When proceedings were taken against Gideon Henfield, an American citizen who had enlisted to serve on a French privateer, Genêt came to his defense and obtained a jury verdict of acquittal, which was popularly regarded as a rebuke to the Administration and a victory for Genêt.

The whole country thrilled with enthusiasm in behalf of France. According to Chief Justice Marshall, "a great majority of the American people deemed it criminal to remain unconcerned spectators of a conflict between their ancient enemy and republican

France." Genêt's journey from Charleston to Philadelphia assumed the character of a triumphal progress. As he approached the city a procession was formed to escort him to his lodgings. Among John Adams's reminiscences is an account of "the terrorism excited by Genêt in 1793, when ten thousand people in the streets of Philadelphia, day after day, threatened to drag Washington out of his house, and effect a revolution in the government, or compel it to declare war in favor of the French Revolution and against England." Adams related that he judged it prudent to order a chest of arms from the war-office to be brought into his house to defend it from attack.

This account, written many years after the event, is no doubt accurate in its description of the alarm which the situation caused to a timid man. Letters written by Hamilton during all this excitement show that he viewed it with cool intrepidity. In May, 1793, he wrote that the number of persons who went to meet Genêt "would be stated high at a hundred," and he did not believe that a tenth part of the city participated in the meetings and addresses of Genêt's sympathizers. "A crowd will always draw a crowd, whatever be the purpose. Curiosity will supply the place of attachment to, or interest in, the object." Washington's own letters at this period show no trace of concern about his personal safety, but he smarted under the attacks on his motives. In Jefferson's *Anas,* under date of August 2, 1793, is an account of an explosion of rage over a print in which Washington was brought to the guillotine for crimes against liberty. According to Jefferson, Washington swore that "by God he had rather be in his grave than in his present situation; that he had rather be on his farm than to be made *emperor of the world;* and yet that they were charging him with wanting to be a king."

At the cabinet meeting of April 19 there had been a sharp difference of opinion as to the way in which Genêt should be received. Jefferson and Randolph were of opinion that the reception should be unconditional. Hamilton, supported by Knox, proposed that this notice should be given to Genêt:

That the Government of the United States, uniformly entertaining cordial wishes for the happiness of the French nation, and disposed to maintain with it amicable communication and intercourse, uninterrupted by political vicissitudes, does not hesitate to receive him in the character, which his credentials import; yet, considering the origin, course, and circumstances of the relations continued between the two countries and the existing position of the affairs of France, it is deemed advisable and proper on the part of the United States to reserve to future consideration and discussion the question, whether the operation of the treaties, by which those relations were formed, ought not to be temporarily and provisionally suspended; and under this impression it is thought due to a spirit of candid and friendly procedure, to apprise him beforehand of the intention to reserve that question, lest silence on the point should occasion misconstruction.

The even division of the Cabinet, coupled with the fact that the matter belonged to Jefferson's department, caused Washington to refrain from making a decision, the practical effect being that Jefferson had his way.   This left Genêt in a position to claim all the advantages conferred upon France by the treaties, and he took an attitude of indignant remonstrance at the duplicity of the American position.   Did not the United States have treaty engagements with France?   By what authority, then, did the Administration interfere with him in the enjoyment of his rights as the representative of France, and interfere with American citizens in their dealings with him?   "As long as the States, assembled in Congress, shall not have determined that this solemn engagement should not be performed, no one has the right to shackle our operations."

Genêt's argument turned against Jefferson the same points that Jefferson himself had been making in the cabinet meetings.   Jefferson replied that "without appealing to treaties, we are at peace with all by the law of nature;—for by nature's law man is at peace with man."   Genêt insisted with entire logical propriety that if the treaties were in force he was entitled to act in accordance with them, and he managed to engage in the French service a considerable fleet of American vessels.   On June 19 he was able to inform his government: "I am provisioning the West Indies, I excite the Canadians to break the British yoke, I arm the Kentukois, and prepare a naval expedition which will facilitate the descent on New Orleans." The last-mentioned enterprise is one which he had arranged with the famous frontier commander George Rogers Clark, who was ready to invade Louisiana if funds and supplies were provided. Genêt's intimacy with Jefferson was such that he talked to him about this enterprise. Jefferson complained that enticing officers and men from Kentucky to go against Spain "was really putting a halter about their necks," but he did not think he had any right to interfere, and he noted that Genêt "communicated these things to me, not as Secretary of State, but as Mr. Jefferson."

Genêt acted with such ability and energy that he might have used the United States as the Germans used Turkey, had not Hamilton stood in the way. Genêt's chief trouble for some time was only lack of funds, due to Hamilton's steady refusal to anticipate the maturing of the French loan. Everything else seemed to be going in Genêt's favor when on June 29, 1793, publication began of a series of eight articles signed "Pacificus." Although rapidly produced, in the midst of alarms, they are so dignified in style, elevated in thought, acute in analysis, and cogent in reasoning that they have taken classic rank as a treatise upon international rights and duties. The effect upon all people capable of serious thought was so marked that at Jefferson's instance and with his aid Madison attempted a reply, but desisted after producing five articles over the signature "Helvidius," making the familiar points of strict-construction theorizing as to executive limitations, but failing to reach the main point of what to do and how to do it. Neither Jefferson nor Madison was a match for Hamilton in debate, and public opinion now began to turn against them. For this they now blamed Genêt, who after all was only claiming treaty rights which Jefferson acknowledged. By July 7 Jefferson was writing to Madison that "Genêt renders my position immensely difficult." But, as Genêt was acting in the interests of his mission and not in Jefferson's interest, he continued to equip vessels in American ports to prey on British commerce. In his perplexity Jefferson, on July 12, actually wrote to Hammond, the British minister, requesting him not to allow such vessels to depart. Hammond naturally expressed surprise that he should receive such an application, since he had no control over their movements.

Among the vessels mentioned in Jefferson's letter was *The Little Sarah*, a British merchantman, which had been brought into Philadelphia as a French prize and was being refitted as a French privateer, its name changed to *Le Petit Démocrate*. This, proceeding brought on a crisis. Steps were taken to detain the vessel by force, but Jefferson protested and undertook to arrange with Genêt that the vessel should not sail until its legal status was decided, urging that the President would consult the justices of the Supreme Court, "whose knowledge of the subject would secure against errors dangerous to the peace of the United States, and their authority insure the respect of all parties."

Washington, harassed and confused by the dissensions in his Cabinet, had indeed decided to take this step. Hamilton was opposed to a proceeding which involved prejudgment on questions that might come before the court in due course of law, and which seemed to him to be an evasion of the proper responsibility of the Executive, but he took part in preparing the case. Of the twenty-nine questions submitted to the Supreme Court, Hamilton framed twenty-one, Jefferson seven, and Washington himself added one. The justices declined to answer. Jefferson then consulted Randolph whether they could not "prepare a bill for Congress to appoint a board or some other body of advice for the Executive on such questions." But expedients for dodging executive responsibility had by that time been exhausted. *Le Petit Démocrate* had meanwhile put to sea. Jefferson felt hurt and indignant over the way Genêt had treated him. He now joined with the rest of the Cabinet in demanding that Genêt should be recalled, and his despatch setting forth the reasons is a dignified and powerful presentation of the case. But at this very time Genêt was still strongly upheld by the Jeffersonian press. Freneau's

National Gazette maintained that, so far from over-stepping his rights, Genêt had really acted "too tamely"; had indeed been "too accommodating for the peace of the United States." Hamilton now again appealed to public opinion in a series of articles over the signature "No Jacobin," in which Genêt's behavior was reviewed. After five articles had appeared the series ended abruptly because Hamilton was stricken by the yellow fever which raged in Philadelphia that summer. But the battle was now won. A reaction had set in for which Jefferson laid the blame on Genêt's defiant bearing, "risking that disgust which I had so much wished should have been avoided."

CHAPTER XX

RETIREMENT FROM OFFICE

In a letter of July 31, 1793, at a time when his troubles with Genêt over *Le Petit Démocrate* were at their height, Jefferson wrote to Washington announcing his desire to resign at the close of the next month. Jefferson noted that Washington tried to dissuade him, and in the course of their conversation said that "Colonel Hamilton had three or four weeks ago written to him, informing him that private as well as public reasons had brought him to the determination to retire, and that he should do it towards the close of the next session. He said he had often before intimated dispositions to resign, but never as decisively before; that he [Washington] supposed he had fixed on the latter part of next session to give an opportunity to Congress to examine into his conduct."

It was a fact that Hamilton had become anxious to retire from public office; not that he flinched from its burdens and anxieties, but simply because he could not afford to stay. While he was being assailed as the manager of vast profiteering operations in finance, the actual, pitiful fact was that his pay was only $3,500 a year, about a fourth of what he might have been earning in his profession, meanwhile enjoying the respect of the community, whereas he was now a mark for calumny and slander. Although more than any other man he was establishing the new government on a solid and durable basis, he was accused of planning its overthrow and was the object of a vast concoction of fiction to that purport. Partisan spite goes to extreme lengths in American politics, but never has it been so wildly extravagant as in the case of Alexander Hamilton. The proverb that where there is so much smoke there must be some fire is often turned to account by American politicians in lighting a smudge to darken the reputation of an opponent, and Hamilton had to endure more of this sort of warfare than any other American statesman. So far as its immediate purpose was concerned—that of forcing him out of the Cabinet—it defeated its end by its own violence. He wanted to get out as soon as he decently could, but he did not intend to go until he had met and answered every charge that could be brought against him. If his enemies had desisted when the Giles charges in the Second Congress broke down, he would have resigned office soon thereafter. But when Giles tried to explain his defeat on the ground that the House had acted without due examination of the evidence, Hamilton made up his mind that he would not allow his enemies that excuse.

When the Third Congress met, December 2,

1793, the Jeffersonians were strong enough to elect the Speaker. Undeterred by the fact that his political enemies were now in full control, Hamilton addressed a letter to the Speaker saying that it had been suggested that at the previous session there had not been time enough for a full inquiry into his conduct. "Unwilling to leave the matter on such a footing, I have concluded to request the House of Representatives, as I now do, that a new inquiry may be, without delay, instituted in some mode, most effectual for an accurate and thorough investigation; and I will add, that the more comprehensive it is, the more agreeable it will be to me." Giles promptly took up the challenge and moved the appointment of a committee to examine the condition of the Treasury Department in all its particulars.

Pending action by the House, Hamilton's enemies got hold of a discharged clerk of the Treasury Department, with whose aid a new line of attack was opened. A memorial from Andrew G. Fraunces was laid before the House making charges to the effect that the payment of warrants had been delayed so that they could be bought up by speculators at a discount. Hamilton's request for an investigation was allowed to lie on the table, while publicity was given to Fraunces's tale and arrangements were made for proceeding with it by a select committee. Giles was a member, a circumstance which turned out to be to Hamilton's advantage, for, although

Giles was a hard, bold, resolute fighter, he was an erect and manly foe. He did not stab in the dark and he did not use poisoned weapons. When he looked into Fraunces's character and into the testimony that was offered he could not stomach either and he concurred in a report on Hamilton, finding that the evidence was "fully sufficient to justify his conduct; and that in the whole course of this transaction the Secretary and other officers of the Treasury have acted a meritorious part towards the public."

Giles still pressed his motion for further investigation of the Treasury Department, but upon different grounds from what he had urged before. Now he admitted that imputations upon the Secretary's integrity had been quite removed, and he held that "the primary object of the resolution is to ascertain the boundaries of discretion and authority between the Legislature and the Treasury Department." But by this time the House was sick of the whole business. The original purpose had been to force Hamilton out of office so as to leave Jefferson with an undisputed premiership in Washington's Cabinet, but Jefferson quit on December 31, 1793, while this matter was pending, and doubtless it was known that Hamilton too was going. Doubtless it was also known that Washington was sorry that he had consented to re-election and that he, too, would have been glad to resign if he could. The attack upon

Hamilton had been a complete failure; everybody knew that. All that remained of it was a proposal that the House should engage in vague schemes of departmental regulation which after all would not touch Hamilton but would descend upon his successor, who might even be one of their own set. The House became so reluctant to proceed with the business that when it came up, February 24, 1794, Giles and Page were the only speakers and both disclaimed any intention of reflecting upon Hamilton. The House rid itself of the matter by referring it to a committee. It was perfectly well understood that this was simply a decent burial; and that was the end.

Hamilton had once more defeated his enemies, and might now have marched out with all the honors of the victor on a hard-fought field; but conditions of such peril to the Government had now been developed that he was unwilling to leave until he had removed them. One of the counts of Jefferson's indictment of Hamilton's policy was that the excise law was "of odious character . . . committing the authority of the Government in parts where resistance is most probable and coercion least practicable." The parts thus referred to were the mountains of western Pennsylvania, where popular discontent promptly coalesced with the agitation carried on against Washington's neutrality policy. At a meeting of delegates from the election districts of Allegheny County, held at Pittsburgh, resolutions were adopted attributing the course of the Government "to the pernicious influence of stockholders," and declaring "that we are almost ready to wish for a state of revolution and the guillotine of France, for a short space, in order to inflict punishment on the miscreants that enervate and disgrace our Government." In the summer of 1794 this state of mind had produced its natural consequence in open insurrection. Writing to Governor Lee, of Virginia, Washington said that he considered "this insurrection as the first formidable fruit of the Democratic Societies."

It was not in Hamilton's nature to retire from office in the presence of such a situation. Writing to Washington, May 27, 1794, he said: "I some time since communicated an intention to withdraw from the office I hold, towards the close of the present session. This I should now put in execution but for the events which have lately accumulated, of a nature to render the prospects of the continuance of our peace in a considerable degree precarious. I do not perceive that I could voluntarily quit my post at such a juncture consistently with considerations either of duty or character; and therefore I find myself reluctantly obliged to defer the offer of my resignation."

The letter went on to say that if Washington had meanwhile made other arrangements he would be glad "to relinquish a situation opposed by the strongest personal and family relations, and in which even a momentary stay could only be produced by a sense of duty or reputation." But Washington was delighted to have him stay on, and at once wrote: "I am pleased that you have determined to remain at your post until the clouds over our affairs, which have come on so fast of late, shall be dispersed."

Although what has passed into history as the Whiskey Insurrection had now assumed a character that would have naturally brought it under the War Department, Washington left the arrangements to Hamilton. The principle on which Hamilton acted was that the force employed ought "to be an imposing one, such, if practicable, as will deter from opposition, save the effusion of the blood of the citizens, and serve the object to be accomplished." All the members of the Cabinet concurred in Hamilton's opinion except Attorney-General Randolph, who abounded in objection, protest, and warning. Hamilton's plans called for a force of 12,000 men, of whom 3,000 were to be cavalry. Some appearance of timidity and inertia in Pennsylvania State authority was effectually counteracted by measures which showed that the expedition would move even if Pennsylvania held back. The business was so shrewdly managed that without any direct pressure Pennsylvania fell obediently into line, and everything went off as Hamilton had planned. The insurgents were so cowed by the determined action of the Government that they submitted without a struggle.

Since it is in the nature of precaution that the more successful it is the less necessary it appears to have been, the completeness of Hamilton's success furnished his enemies with a new cry against him, and his costly military expedition that had no fighting to do was held up to public ridicule. But the truth is that any failure might have been fatal to the Government. Randolph was in a state of panic. Fauchet, the French minister, reported him as overcome with grief, declaring: "It is all over; a civil war is about to ravage our unhappy country." He applied to Fauchet for financial assistance; the fact was made public through the capture of Fauchet's correspondence by the British and Randolph retired from the Cabinet under a cloud.

Hamilton now felt free to press his own resignation, but not until any official desire to investigate his conduct had been fully satisfied. Under date of December 1, 1794, he wrote to the Speaker of the House that he had arranged with the President to resign his office on January 31, adding: "I make this communication in order that an opportunity may be given, previous to that event, to institute any further proceeding which may be contemplated, if

any there be, in consequence of the inquiry during
the last session into the state of this Department."
No notice was taken of this communication and
Hamilton took no further notice of the attitude of
the House, which had certainly placed itself in an
undignified position by its failure to take decisive
action in one way or another on Giles's resolution.
Hamilton addressed to the Senate his final report
on the public credit. On January 16, 1795, he wrote
that he had "prepared a plan, on the basis of actual
revenues, for the further support of public credit,
which is ready for communication to the Senate."
The body promptly called for it and it was transmitted on January 20. It is a masterly examination
of the whole field of national finance, presented with
such clearness, order, dignity, and power that it
ranks among the greatest of Hamilton's state papers.
In addition to preparing this long and comprehensive
report, in the midst of his arrangements for de-
parture, he also made a much briefer report to the
House of Representatives, making some valuable
suggestions for the improvement of the revenue. He
finished this on the day his resignation took effect,
and by the time it reached the House he was no
longer Secretary of the Treasury. He had laid
down the office in which he had established a new
nation upon firm foundations.

CHAPTER XXI

PRIVATE DIRECTION OF PUBLIC AFFAIRS

In considering the later events of Hamilton's career, it is apt to occur to one how much better it would have been for his reputation had he had nothing more to do with political management after quitting public life. From now on one must observe a lowering of his standard of behavior, a tolerance of methods and practices which once he would have scorned and which he admitted now, not through change of opinion as to their character, but through calculations of party advantage. But upon a broad view of the situation it is clear that it was practically impossible for him to disengage himself from politics. He was still a young man—only thirty-eight when he resigned the Treasury portfolio. His advice was sought continually, and situations developed that made irresistible appeals to his sense of public duty. The blemish to his reputation is not in that his public activity continued but in that he allowed it to produce a system of private direction of public affairs incompatible with any sort of constitutional government. Occasion and opportunity for such tactics had been supplied by the behavior of Congress in disconnecting itself from the Administration, thus insuring its own subjection to outside influence covertly exerted. The conditions thus created explain Hamilton's behavior, but do not justify it. His proper function was to rectify conditions, not to yield to them; and in so doing the great statesman declined into the intriguing politician, a character poorly suited to one of his frank disposition.

To this part of his career, however, belongs as brilliant an achievement in public service as any performed by him. In June, 1795, the Jay treaty was ratified by the Senate with the exception of an article relating to trade with the West Indies, an omission to which the British Government in the end made no objection. The Senate had decided to keep the treaty a secret, but one of the members furnished a copy to the opposition press and at once furious denunciation of it began. Up to this time Washington had acted in a routine way, contenting himself with a reference of the matter to the Senate, but the conditional ratification and the outburst of popular disapproval raised questions which perplexed him. He applied to Hamilton for his opinion, saying: "My wishes are to have the favorable and unfavorable side of each article stated and compared together; that I may see the bearing and tendency of them."

Hamilton's reply, written in New York, is dated only six days later than the date of Washington's letter written at Philadelphia, so his analysis must have been the work of a few days, but nevertheless it is an elaborate and comprehensive examination of a complicated case. He condemned the article relating to West Indian trade and approved the action of the Senate in rejecting it, but on the whole his judgment was strongly in favor of accepting the treaty as thus modified. Washington was very grateful, and in returning his thanks said: "I am really ashamed when I behold the trouble it has given you, to explore and explain so fully as you have done."

At this time Jefferson was active in encouraging attacks upon the Administration. He held that the treaty was an "execrable thing," an "infamous act, which is really nothing more than a treaty of alliance between England and the Anglo-men of this country against the Legislature and the people of the United States." Meetings were held all over the country at which the most violent language was used. In Philadelphia, on the 4th of July, there was a parade in which an effigy of John Jay, bearing insulting inscriptions, was borne through the streets and then publicly burned. In New York a mob gathered in Wall Street to denounce the treaty. Hamilton made an attempt to address them from the balcony of Federal Hall but was met by a shower of stones. "These are hard arguments to encounter," he remarked with a smile as he retired. The mob marched to Bowling Green and burned a copy of the treaty in front of Jay's official residence

as Governor of New York, an office to which he
had been elected before the treaty was published.
Many prominent citizens took part in these demonstrations. Brockholst Livingston, Mrs. Jay's
brother, acted as chairman of a committee which reported twenty-eight resolutions of particular censure.

As a matter of fact Jay had performed a difficult
task with great tact and skill. The Administration
was in a poor position for obtaining any favor from
the British Government, for under the impotent
government of the Confederation the various States
had contemptuously ignored the stipulations of the
peace treaty in behalf of British creditors. While
Jay was secretary of foreign affairs he had advised
the Continental Congress that our treaty engagements with Great Britain "have been constantly
violated on our part by legislative acts, then and still
existing and operating," and that the British Government could not therefore be blamed for delaying the
surrender of the western posts until the United
States had shown themselves able and willing to
fulfil their own obligations under the treaty. Col-
lisions had begun on the western frontier and the
two countries were plainly drifting into war, when
Washington decided to send a special envoy to deal
with all the points at issue. Washington's original
intention had been to send Hamilton, but was warned
that the Senate would not ratify the appointment,

and Hamilton himself proposed Jay as the fittest man for the task. Jay could have offered a plausible excuse for declining, as he was at that time chief justice of the Supreme Court, and he showed a fine patriotism in accepting. He remarked to friends that the circumstances were such that no man could frame a treaty with Great Britain without making himself odious to popular sentiment, and he accepted the mission under "a conviction that to refuse it would be to desert my duty for the sake of my ease, and domestic concerns and comforts." Of course, every treaty made by voluntary agreement must be arrived at on the principle of give and take, but popular sentiment in the United States had not yet been educated up to appreciation of the fact that independence brought loss as well as gain. The general feeling seems to have been that now that the war was over things would go on as before in matters of commerce and navigation; and there was great indignation that they should now be denied rights and opportunities they had enjoyed as British subjects. Their mood was strong for taking but not for giving, and, although Jay had really been remarkably successful in making gains, these of course fell short of the public desire, while the concessions he had had to make were regarded as monstrous.

Popular sentiment ran so strongly against the treaty that Washington was much perturbed, and in one of his letters to Hamilton he spoke of the pleasure he had felt on reading a newspaper article in which one "Camillus" announced his intention of discussing the treaty in a series of communications. "To judge of this work," wrote Washington, "from the first number I have seen, I augur well of the performance and shall expect to see the subject handled in a clear, distinct, and satisfactory manner." Washington's hope was abundantly fulfilled, for "Camillus" was none other than Hamilton himself. Once again he had come forward to face and subdue the passions of the hour by sheer intellectual might.

The Camillus series began on July 22, 1795, and were continued well into the following year, ending with the thirty-eighth number. They form a masterly treatise upon the foreign relations of nations and the nature of international law, and in dignity of style, force of reasoning, and breadth of vision the successive numbers are worthy of ranking with *The Federalist* series. The power and ability displayed had a marked effect in bearing down the opposition and effecting a conversion of opinion. It was in reference to this series that Jefferson declared that "Hamilton was a Colossus to the Anti-Republican party," and he implored Madison to take the field against him. Madison prudently declined, but what controversial ability Jefferson's followers could produce was massed against Hamilton. He wisely refrained from any rejoinder in his Camillus series, which keeps to high ground throughout; but to deal with particular antagonists he carried on another series over the signature "Philo-Camillus," driving them one after another from the field. Hamilton's course during the agitation over the Jay treaty is a marvellous exhibition of sustained intellectual power, and it should not be forgotten that he who did this mighty work had to snatch the time for it from his occupation as a lawyer, on which he was wholly dependent for the support of his family. Had it not been for his intervention, the House of Representatives might have broken the treaty. As it was there was a violent struggle, during which Madison and Giles argued against the treaty, but in the end the House stood fifty-one to forty-eight in favor of giving effect to it.

During the struggle Washington kept in close touch with Hamilton, looking to him for help that was bounteously given. Not long after this matter had been concluded Washington again sought Hamilton's help on a matter he had much to heart—the composition of a dignified and appropriate address to announce his retirement to private life. This Farewell Address, to give it the name it has always since borne, was not addressed to Congress but to his countrymen, to let it be known that he refused to be a candidate for re-election. The address occupied much of Washington's attention during the summer of 1796. In 1792, when Washington thought of declining a second term, he got Madison to prepare an address making that announcement. This draft, with notes and suggestions, Washington now transmitted to Hamilton. Hamilton, however, prepared an entirely new address, the first draft of which was an abstract of points to be made, twenty-three in number. Later, after a conference with Jay in which the Madison draft and Washington's notes on it were considered, Hamilton prepared a paper of changes and corrections, in effect constituting an alternative draft. Washington, however, preferred Hamilton's original draft, and upon that, with Washington's notes, suggestions, and corrections, the address was formed in the shape in which it was finally issued. Washington's own ideas controlled the substance; the literary form was supplied by Hamilton. In addition Hamilton drafted an important part of Washington's address to Congress at the opening of the session, December, 1796.

But while Hamilton was engaged in these high and noble activities he was also dipping into the mean puddles of journalism, not without an occasional splash from their mud. He began to write for the newspapers while a college boy and he kept on doing so the rest of his life. The many journals that appeared from time to time in the Federalist party interest received help from his pen, and the volumes now required for his acknowledged writings would be much swollen had all his fugitive pieces been preserved. William Cobbett, who wrote under the pseudonym of "Peter Porcupine,"—a name which fitly characterizes his barbed style—was assisted by Hamilton in establishing his *Weekly Political Register*—which appeared from 1794 to 1800, when, broken by libel suits, Cobbett quit the fray, returning to England to continue there his tempestuous career. In 1801 Hamilton, in conjunction with several prominent Federalists, established the *New York Evening Post*, one of the few journals of the period that became a permanent institution. Hamilton's connection with *The Post* was so close that all its feuds were scored against him, and he was a frequent contributor. The editor was William Coleman, a clever lawyer who for a short time was a partner of Aaron Burr. Coleman made no secret of the fact that the paper acted in Hamilton's interest, but he once told a friend that Hamilton never actually wrote a word for it, then adding, "Whenever anything occurs on which I feel the need of information I state the matter to him, sometimes in a note; he appoints a time when I may see him, usually a late hour of the evening. He always keeps himself minutely informed on all political matters. As soon as I see him he begins in a deliberate manner to dictate and I note down in shorthand; when he stops, my article is completed."

Hamilton's newspaper connections gave provocations that imparted special venom to the scurrilous attacks of which he was a perpetual target. He would never reply in his own person unless some charge was made against his personal integrity, on which he was as sensitive as a good woman is to her reputation for chastity. Then he would strike back at once and strike hard. In November, 1799, he had the foreman of a New York paper indicted for libel, and the defendant was fined $100 and sent to prison for four months.

To Hamilton's susceptibility on this point is due a disclosure that has made a nasty stain upon his reputation. Charges of the same kind spattered many of the leading men of the times. Jefferson was among those who suffered from them, but he wisely forebore to reply. The circumstances which involved Hamilton in open scandal display the meanness to which partisanship can stoop more than all other events in American political history, dirty as is its record in matters of this sort. In 1792 two men, Clingman and Reynolds, were arrested for subornation of perjury in attempts to obtain money on a claim against the Government. Speaker Muhlenburg, of the House of Representatives, interested himself in Clingman's behalf and was told by him that Reynolds had a hold on Hamilton. Muhlenburg who was one of Jefferson's adherents, told Abraham Venable and James Monroe. The three conferred with Reynolds and his wife, and obtained some papers attributed to Hamilton, which, insignificant in themselves, were exhibited as evidence corroborating a charge that Hamilton had been concerned with Reynolds in buying up old claims against the Government. The three then confronted Hamilton, who frankly avowed that he had had an intrigue with Mrs. Reynolds, and then showed conclusively that the charges they were investigating were wholly the product of malicious fabrication. The inquirers professed to be entirely satisfied by the explanations made, and the matter was then dropped, but Monroe kept copies of all the papers, with records of statements made by Clingman and Reynolds, which he turned over to one of his political intimates, who some years later gave a partisan journalist the use of them.

The charges were made public in 1797. Hamilton at once called upon the investigators of 1792 to make a statement of their findings. Both Muhlenburg and Venable complied, to Hamilton's satisfaction. Monroe quibbled and dodged, until Hamilton denounced his conduct as malevolent and dishonorable, adding that if he resented the characterization a challenge from him would be accepted; but Monroe refrained. Monroe seems to have believed that he had Hamilton in such a fix that he could not move further in the business, but it was not in him to know what such a man as Hamilton would do. There was no shame, no disgrace, that he would not endure rather than rest under any charge against his integrity. So he came out with the whole wretched business, telling in complete detail the story of his relations with Mrs. Reynolds. It was the old story—a woman who came with a sad tale to get a personal interview and who made use of the opportunity to get a new protector. Both she and her husband worked the affair for all they could get out of it. Hamilton told the whole story, appending all letters, papers, and documents having any connection with it, fifty-two in number, the whole making a bulky pamphlet. In it Hamilton quite justly observed that his desire to destroy this scandal completely led him to a more copious and particular examination of it than was really necessary, and every one must agree to his summing up of the case:

The bare perusal of the letters from Reynolds and his wife is sufficient to convince my greatest enemy that there is nothing worse in the affair than an irregular and indelicate amour. For this, I bow to the just censure which it merits. I have paid pretty severely for the folly, and can never recollect it without disgust and self-condemnation. It might seem affectation to say more.

The Reynolds pamphlet, while it will always preclude in Hamilton's case the mythic veneration that has collected about some politicians of that period who were really shabby fellows, did have the effect of stamping out for good and all slander as to Hamilton's honesty. The manliness with which he had faced every accusation affected even inveterate enemies. It was a significant mark of esteem when in April, 1798, the high-minded statesman, Governor Jay, asked Hamilton's permission to appoint him United States Senator to fill a vacancy that had occurred. Hamilton replied that his situation obliged him to decline the appointment, adding: "There may arrive a crisis when I may conceive myself bound once more to sacrifice the interests of my family to public call. But I must defer the change as long as possible."

The situation in which Hamilton stood at that time forbade the acceptance of any post that would interfere with his legal practice. On returning to New York after leaving Washington's Cabinet, he took a small house at 56 Pine Street, later removing to 58 Partition Street (now Fulton Street), thence to Liberty Street, near Broadway, and thence to 26 Broadway, where he lived until 1802. In 1798, in conjunction with his brother-in-law John B. Church, he leased a country house, near where some years later he acquired a tract of land and built a house, calling the place "The Grange," after the name of the ancestral home of the Hamiltons in Scotland. It was then considered to be far out in the country. The house he built is still preserved, but it has been removed from its original site, which was what is now the corner of 142d Street and Tenth Avenue. His home plans were in mind when he refused Jay's offer. His law practice brought him about $12,000 a year, then reckoned a large income, and he could not afford the loss he would have sustained by attendance in Congress, then about to shift from Philadelphia to Washington.

But, while the stress of these circumstances must be recognized, a situation resulted which had dire consequences. Hamilton's irresistible vocation for statesmanship now operated under conditions that produced an extraordinary system of cabal and intrigue the collapse of which wrecked the Federalist party. And yet it is scarcely possible to mention a particular in which Hamilton himself was in the wrong. Events moved with the inexorable sequence of a Greek tragedy, individuals seeming to be the mere counters of fate. It all started from a false situation which was not of Hamilton's creation. Washington had virtually forced upon him the office of managing director of the Administration. All the members of the Cabinet, as it took shape in Washington's second term, looked to him for help and guidance in every important emergency. During Washington's time the relation had the character of a frank and honorable intimacy. With the succession of John Adams it became covert and secretive, not by direct intention but by gradual acceptance of a false situation.

CHAPTER XXII

THE BREACH WITH ADAMS

ADAMS and Hamilton felt mutual dislike, dating from the time when Adams was prominent among the lawyer politicians who got control of the Continental Congress, and Hamilton was active in advocating measures to repress Congressional jobbery and mismanagement. Adams was a vain, irascible, garrulous pedant, in whose nature there was a mixture of habitual effrontery with physical timidity rarely found except among lawyers. His defects of character were well known to the Federalist leaders, who from the outset of his Administration regarded it as a party duty to humor and manage him for his own good. Wolcott, of Connecticut, wrote to his son, Hamilton's successor in the Treasury Department, that Adams was "a man of great vanity, pretty capricious, of a very moderate share of prudence, and of far less real abilities than he believes himself to possess," so that "it will require a great deal of address to render him the service which it will be essential for him to receive."

Adams's dislike of Hamilton derived additional bitterness from some features of the Presidential election of 1796. At that time the electors each voted for two candidates without designating who should be President and who Vice-President. Thomas Pinckney, of South Carolina, was associated with Adams on the Federalist ticket, and Hamilton recommended both to the solid support of the Federalist members of the electoral college. But Hamilton foresaw that Pinckney would receive Southern votes that would not go to Adams, and that if both were solidly supported in the North Pinckney would come out ahead and get the Presidency. The New York, New Jersey, and Delaware electors voted solidly as Hamilton had recommended, but South Carolina voted for Jefferson and Pinckney, and moreover Pinckney received scattering votes elsewhere in the South, which would have insured his election had he received the solid support of the Federalist electors in New England, but eighteen of them cut Pinckney to make sure that he should not slip in ahead of Adams, with the result of electing Jefferson as Vice-President. Adams received only three electoral votes more than Jefferson, and for the narrowness of this margin he blamed Hamilton, who was certainly in no way responsible for it, although he had anticipated the South Carolina straddle, and had made plans with a view to that occurrence. On the other hand, Adams felt so kindly toward Jefferson, his old Congressional chum, that expressions of satisfaction over Jefferson's election instead of Pinckney's came from the Adams circle. Jefferson made friendly advances to Adams and wrote to Madison suggesting that "it would be worthy of consideration whether it would not be to the public good to come to a good understanding with him as to his future elections." The Federalist leaders were dismayed on hearing that Adams was conferring with Jefferson as to the policy of the Administration before he had had any conference with his own Cabinet.

What Adams had in mind was not a bad idea had it been at all practicable. He thought a good impression might be made by sending a mission to France of exceptional weight and dignity, and he wanted Jefferson to go as its head. Jefferson of course declined, but was suave and tactful in his refusal. Adams then proposed Madison, and Jefferson undertook to see him about the matter; but soon reported that Madison too felt unable to accept the honor. Then at last Adams decided to confer with his Cabinet, whose members had meanwhile become alarmed at his behavior. Adams had taken over the Cabinet just as Washington had left it. All its members were devoted to Hamilton and were accustomed to seek his advice. They all began writing to him, telling him what was going on and asking his help in preparing measures, making Hamilton's office in New York a more important administrative centre than Adams's own office at the seat of government.

There is no sign that Hamilton used his influence
to do any harm to Adams.   In fact he cleared the
way several times to Adams's advantage, although
Adams did not know it.   The attitude of the Cabinet
was decidedly hostile to Adams's pet scheme of a
special mission to France.   It was Hamilton's advice that secured their approval of the project, and
he also brought his friends in the Senate to its support.   He prepared for Secretary Wolcott a scheme
of taxation by which the revenue could be increased
to provide for national defense, and he prepared
for Secretary McHenry, of the War Department, a
scheme of military and naval preparations which,
though it was not adopted in its entirety, greatly
augmented the resources of the Administration and
was the most important factor in producing more respectful treatment of American interests.   Although
he himself became a major-general in the army,
Hamilton's advice was strongly in favor of making
the navy the principal arm of national power.   The
French Government had characterized the Jay
treaty as a violation of American engagements with
France and had retaliated by seizing American
vessels, confiscating their cargoes, and imprisoning
hundreds of American citizens.   Adams's special
mission was received with insult and accomplished
nothing, but when the little American navy got
busy results followed that were impressive.   During
the two years and a half in which hostilities con-

tinued eighty-five armed ves els were taken and only one American vessel was lost in action, and that one had been originally a captured French vessel. Most of the vessels taken were privateers, but there were two hard-fought actions in which heavily armed French frigates were defeated. The value of the protection given to American commerce was demonstrated by the increase of exports from $57,-000,000 in 1797 to $78,665,528 in 1799.

Among the experiences of Adams's special mission was a notice that they should not receive a friendly reception unless they were prepared to give as a "douceur to the Directory," a sum of money amounting to about $240,000. The story of this affair was told in the famous X Y Z dispatches, so known from the letters used in the papers laid before Congress, in place of the actual names of Talleyrand's three agents in pressing the demand. A wave of indignation swept the country, and, although Jefferson argued that the French Government ought not to be held responsible for "the turpitude of swindlers," his party in Congress was soon reduced to a feeble and dispirited minority. Among the measures now taken was one authorizing the President to raise a military force of 10,000 men, the commander of which should have the services of "a suitable number of major-generals." There was nothing to suggest that this puny measure could supply an explosive to blow up the Federalist party,

but such was the effect, owing to Adams's peculi-
arities.

He started with a characteristic bungle. Without any inquiry as to whether the appointment
would be acceptable, he named Washington as the
commander. When the news reached Hamilton
he was much surprised, for he had supposed that
every public man knew that Washington would not
endure unceremonious treatment. He wrote at
once to Washington urging him to overlook the impropriety and give his consent. The only rational
explanation of the tortuous course which Adams now
pursued was that he meant to get the use of Washington's name while retaining for himself actual control over the arrangements. His letters plied Washington with bland assurances and vague generalities.
No one was less likely to be caught in that way than
one of Washington's deliberate and methodical habits
of action. He demanded exact stipulations as to
his powers, including the right to appoint his major-
generals. Adams avoided committing himself, but
he instructed Secretary McHenry to obtain Washington's advice, and Washington then recommended
as major-generals Hamilton, C. C. Pinckney, and
Knox, in that order of rank. Adams seemed to
assent and the nominations were sent to the Senate
in that order, but as soon as confirmation took place
it then appeared that he was in the sulks. He left
for his home at Quincy, Massachusetts, without

notice to his Cabinet, and when McHenry wrote to him about proceeding with the organization of the army he replied that he would act as soon as Knox's precedence was acknowledged, and that the New England States would not submit to the humiliation of having Knox's claim disregarded.

From August 4 to October 13 wrangling over this matter went on. Adams wrote to Washington that he had signed the commissions on the same day, in the hope "that an amicable adjustment or acquiescence might take place among the gentlemen themselves"; but, should this hope be disappointed "and controversies shall arise, they will of course be submitted to you as commander-in-chief." Adams wrote to McHenry that "there has been too much intrigue in this business, both for General Washington and for me"; that it might as well be understood that in any event he would have the last say, "and I shall then determine it exactly as I should now, Knox, Pinckney, and Hamilton."

It was a painful feature of the dispute to Hamilton that it put his interest in opposition to that of Knox, who while a member of Washington's Cabinet had always been Hamilton's firm adherent. Hamilton wrote to Washington saying that Knox indeed had cause for complaint, since his rank in the old army had been so much higher than Hamilton's own rank. To McHenry he wrote: "I am pained to occasion to him pain for I have truly a warm side for him, and a high value for his merits; but my judgment tells me, and all I consult confirm it, that I cannot reasonably postpone myself in a case in which a preference so important to the public in its present and future consequences has been given me." When news came that Knox would refuse an appointment that put him lowest in rank, Hamilton at once wrote to Washington, saying that he did not want to be the occasion of any embarrassment, and adding: "I shall cheerfully place myself in your disposal, and facilitate any arrangement you may think for the general good."

But Washington, although he liked Knox personally, was determined to have Hamilton as his chief assistant, and with good reason. Knox was now a stout, rubicund veteran, fond of jolly company and good cheer, which he enjoyed in profusion on the country estate in Maine to which he had retired. The importance of having a good organizer in the principal post was enhanced by the fact that Secretary McHenry, a physician by profession, had little knowledge of military affairs. Washington himself, when he made the appointment, characterized it as "Hobson's choice." So Washington insisted on his right to use his own judgment, as he had distinctly stipulated from the first.

For months the deadlock halted action. Adams was obstinate; Washington was immovable. The suspense finally became so intolerable that the

Cabinet acted without further consultation with the President about the matter. Secretary McHenry submitted to his colleagues all the correspondence in the case and asked their advice. They made a joint reply that "the Secretary of War ought to transmit the commissions, and inform the generals that in his opinion the rank is definitely settled according to the original arrangement." This was done, but Knox declined an appointment ranking him below Hamilton and Pinckney, although Hamilton wrote to him in a futile attempt to soothe his feelings. The letter is in every way creditable to Hamilton, both manly and tender, without any trace of insincerity or affectation. It was with entire truth he declared: "Be persuaded that the views of others, not my own, have given shape to what has taken place, and that there has been a serious struggle between my respect and attachment for you and the impression of duty."

While this wretched squabble was going on Hamilton was trying to repress the spirit of arrogance that now possessed the Federalist members of Congress. They acted as if their heads had been turned by success, and they enacted some imprudent laws. The period of residence required of an alien before he could be admitted to American citizenship was raised from five years to fourteen. The President was authorized to send out of the country "such aliens as he shall judge dangerous to the peace and safety to the United States." The state of public opinion probably sanctioned these measures, but such was not the case with the famous sedition act, which made it a crime to write or publish "any false, scandalous, or malicious statements about the President or either House of Congress." As soon as Hamilton heard of the presentation of this measure he wrote a warning letter to Secretary Wolcott, saying: "Let us not establish a tyranny. Energy is a very different thing from violence." Later on he wrote to Senator Sedgwick, disapproving of the act as passed, declaring "it seems to me deficient in precautions against abuse and for the security of citizens." The result verified Hamilton's prediction to Wolcott that "if we push things to an extreme, we shall then give to faction body and solidity." Just that thing happened. The alien and sedition laws gave the Jeffersonian party an issue on which they recovered their lost ground.

In communicating the X Y Z dispatches to Congress Adams declared: "I will never send another Minister to France without assurance that he will be received, respected, and honored, as the representative of a great, free, powerful, and independent nation." But later on he changed his mind and, without consulting his Cabinet, he nominated a minister to France. This unexpected action stunned the Federalists and delighted the Jeffersonians. "Had the foulest heart and the ablest head in the world," wrote Senator Sedgwick to Hamilton, "been permitted to select the most embarrassing and ruinous measure, perhaps it would have been precisely the one which has been adopted." Hamilton's mediation now again made a smooth course for Adams. While he thought Adams had taken an unwise step, he advised that "the measure must go into effect with the additional idea of a commission of three." The matter was settled in this way, much to Adams's gratification. By the time the commission reached France, Bonaparte was in power. The envoys were decently received and were able to make an acceptable settlement of differences between the two countries.

As the Presidential election approached, efforts, in which Hamilton took part, were made to find a substitute for Adams as the party candidate, but they proved unavailing, as New England still clung to Adams, since to let him go meant the loss of the Presidency for that section. There was some talk of bringing out Washington again, but if any hopes were really entertained in that quarter they were destroyed by his death on December 14, 1799. When word of these proceedings reached Adams the wrath that filled his bosom ever since he had been baffled in the matter of the army appointments now boiled over. He decided to rid himself of men whom he characterized as "Hamilton's spies." The first to be dismissed was McHenry, on May 5,

1800, after an interview in which—as reported by McHenry himself—Adams accused him of having "biassed General Washington to place Hamilton in his list of major-generals before Knox." On May 12 Secretary Pickering of the State Department was dismissed. Secretary Wolcott of the Treasury Department stayed on until the end of the year, when he resigned of his own motion. In thus reconstituting his Cabinet Adams was entirely within his rights. A President ought to have as his advisers those who have his confidence and with whom he feels disposed to confer, and Adams would have acted wisely if he had selected friends of his own at the outset. But his taking such action in the midst of a Presidential campaign was not an exercise of good judgment but was an outbreak of his bad temper. He then went from bad to worse by raging against Hamilton, and the style of his remarks may be imagined from the fact that years after, when he had had plenty of time to cool down, he referred to Hamilton as the "bastard brat of a Scotch pedlar." Talk of this sort might have been ignored as a characteristic specimen of Adams's behavior when in a rage, but he was foolish enough to attack Hamilton's integrity and patriotism, and at no time would Hamilton submit to that. When news came that Adams was now reiterating the old calumnies, Hamilton wrote to Adams asking whether it was true that Adams had "asserted the existence of a

British faction" of which Hamilton himself was said to be a member. Adams made no reply. Hamilton waited for two months, and then wrote again, declaring "that by whomsoever a charge of the kind mentioned in my former letter, may, at any time, have been made or insinuated against me, it is a base, wicked, and cruel calumny; destitute even of a plausible pretext, to excuse the folly, or mask the depravity which must have dictated it." Even this sharp language did not move Adams to reply. He could be a backbiter, but when called to account he took refuge in obstinate silence.

Hamilton's natural indignation now led him to commit a great political blunder. Since he had decided to support Adams as his party candidate his personal grievance should have been subordinated to his sense of duty, but so great was his indignation that his feelings escaped control, and he wrote a scathing analysis of "The Public Conduct and Character of John Adams," for distribution among a few leading Federalists. Although it advised support of Adams's candidacy, as the only feasible course in existing circumstances, it exhibited him as so unfit for the office that acceptance of him could be justified only as a choice among evils. Aaron Burr managed to get hold of a copy, and he made such use of portions that Hamilton felt obliged to publish it in full. It was more damaging to Hamilton himself than it was to Adams, for Hamilton had more to lose in reputation. Even Robert Troup, Hamilton's friend from boyhood, wrote: "The influence of this letter upon Hamilton's character is extremely unfortunate. An opinion has grown out of it, which at present obtains almost universally, that his character is radically deficient in discretion. Hence he is considered as an unfit head of the party." The letter did not really affect the result, as all the electors chosen in the Federalist interest voted for Adams, and a Jeffersonian majority in the electoral college had been assured by the State elections in Pennsylvania and New York before the letter appeared. The truth of the matter is that the result of the Presidential election was decided by the way in which Aaron Burr had previously outgeneralled and defeated Hamilton in New York.

CHAPTER XXIII

THE DUEL WITH BURR

AARON BURR's reputation has been so blackened, that it is hard to view the man as he really was; but one may get a just exhibition of his character from Chesterfield's *Letters*, for Burr fully realized the ideal therein portrayed, both in its merit and in its defect. He had the poise, address, polish, courage, and fortitude of the type, together with its self-centred nature and epicurean morality, attained in his case by intellectual emancipation from the tradition which he had inherited from an eminent line of Puritan ancestors. Only a year older than Hamilton, Burr showed almost as brilliant capacity in his school-days, and in 1775, about the same time that Hamilton joined the Continental Army in New York, he took part in Benedict Arnold's march on Quebec as a volunteer. In that unfortunate expedition Burr showed ability, courage, and resourcefulness of the highest order. Returning to New York, he was for a time one of Washington's aides, but disliking the confinement he effected a transfer to General Putnam's command and was active in the battles about New York and the retreat through New Jersey. In 1777 he had risen to the rank of lieutenant-colonel, and was in actual command of a regiment detailed for scouting duty in New Jersey. It was while thus engaged that he first met Mrs. Prevost, the widow of a British officer, who eventually became his wife. The marriage, which took place in 1782, is certainly evidence that Burr was capable of disinterested attachment, for she had neither wealth, position, nor beauty, and was about ten years his senior; but she had intelligence, refinement, and charming manners, and he appears to have been a devoted husband. The fact that his wife was an English woman was a circumstance used against Burr in the abominable party warfare of the times.

Burr, who was small in stature like Hamilton himself, was so broken in health by rough living in the field that in 1779 he resigned his commission. He was well established at the Albany bar at the time Hamilton was beginning his studies, but when the migration to New York took place, in 1783, Hamilton stood with him in the first rank of lawyers. Burr was elected to the Assembly in 1784 on a ticket which included some of Hamilton's friends. He was then generally classed with the violent Whigs, who favored a policy of proscription, but when Hamilton began his brilliant and effective campaign against that policy, Burr did not join in the fray but dropped out of politics for the time. He was so quiescent in the struggle over the adoption of the

Constitution that he could be counted on neither side. Hamilton subsequently characterized Burr's conduct in that emergency as "equivocal." In 1788 Burr allowed his name to be put upon a legislative ticket presented by the defeated Antifederalists, but he was not active in the canvass and he may have been actuated merely by a desire to serve friends who were striving to keep alive their party with a view to the future. In 1789, by one of those twists which the factious character of New York politics could produce at any time on occasion, Burr figured with Hamilton, Troup, and others of Hamilton's friends on a committee selected to support the candidacy of Judge Yates for Governor. Burr's action was regarded to be a straightforward display of personal friendship. He was grateful to Yates for kind services when Burr was starting in the law, and he never failed to do what he could for Yates thereafter. Hamilton's motive was, however, merely to use Yates's candidacy to split the Antifederalist vote and thus defeat Clinton, but Clinton defeated the formidable combination by a narrow majority, obtained through the circumstance that his home county, Ulster, gave him an almost unanimous vote. Clinton, with a shrewd magnanimity which goes far to explain the popularity which six times elected him Governor, selected Burr as his Attorney-General, the appointment taking effect in September, 1789.

Hamilton appears to have remained on good terms with Burr until 1791, when General Schuyler came up for re-election to the United States Senate. No candidate appeared in opposition to him, and his was the only name presented, but when the vote was taken there were more nays than ayes. So far as one can judge, in a case where there is nothing of record to go upon, the result was due to personal antipathies excited by Schuyler's vehement partisanship. Somebody had to be chosen, and one of the Senators proposed Burr, the vote resulting twelve to four. When the news reached the House Burr was put in nomination there too, and he received a majority of five votes, thus winning the election.

Although a letter of Schuyler's refers to Burr as "the principal in this business," the available evidence indicates that the unexpected result was a chance concentration of favor owing to Burr's high social and professional standing and to the fact that he was regarded as a moderate man in politics, standing apart from the regular factions. John Adams, in one of his familiar letters, wrote: "I have never known the prejudice in favor of birth, parentage, and descent more conspicuous than in the case of Colonel Burr." In substituting Burr for Schuyler the members of the legislature did not in the least feel that they were lowering the quality of State representation at the national capital. But the defeat of his father-in-law seems to have supplied Hamilton with a grudge against Burr that was pursued with the constancy of a Scottish clan feud. Close examination of Hamilton's correspondence leaves no doubt that his feeling against Burr had in it personal enmity as well as antagonism on public grounds. He is severely critical of the behavior of Madison and Jefferson, but he preserves his dignity; when he speaks of Burr he falls into reviling. This spirit does not crop out in his correspondence until after Burr was preferred to Schuyler in the senatorial election. Then Burr is described as a thoroughly unprincipled character, "for or against nothing, but as it suits his interest or ambition"; and Hamilton declared, "I feel it to be a religious duty to oppose his career."

Hamilton constantly acted in this spirit toward Burr, and his behavior was such that, according to the manners of the times, he gave ample provocation for the duel in which their rivalry culminated. Indeed, it may be said that for years before the fatal meeting they carried on a political duel in which Hamilton was at a disadvantage through the warmth of his feelings, while Burr acted with a cool calculation which gave him superior ability as a tactician. At that time only freeholders with an estate of £100 above all liens had the franchise. In 1789, out of a population of 324,270 in the State, the poll was only 12,353. Hence New York politics were largely under the control of a few influential families. Any change in the attitude of the Livingstons, the Schuylers and the Clintons had political consequences. Conditions were favorable for the crafty diplomacy in which Burr excelled.

Although the records are so meagre that positive statement is scarcely warranted, Burr does not appear to have pursued a factious course as a member of the United States Senate. No complaint against him on that score is made in Hamilton's correspondence. Although generally classed as Antifederalist, Burr seems to have occupied rather an independent and detached position with respect to party politics, and he certainly obtained a reputation for calmness and moderation that extended beyond all party bounds. Early in 1792 there was a movement in the Federalist party in New York in favor of splitting the Antifederalist vote by taking up Burr as a candidate against Clinton, but Hamilton's influence was successfully exerted against the scheme. After the election, Clinton nominated Burr as judge of the Supreme Court of the State, but the office was declined. Such a succession of public honors as had come to Burr, together with the ability and dignity with which he behaved, caused him to be nationally regarded as a rising man. In the Presidential election of 1792 one of the South Carolina electors cast a vote for him in preference to John Adams as Vice-President, and in 1796 Burr received thirty electoral votes.

In later years, John Adams related that when Burr's term in the Senate expired he was loath to continue law practice and would have rejoiced in an army appointment. Adams proposed to Washington that Burr should be appointed brigadier-general in the army then being organized. According to Adams this arrangement was defeated through Hamilton's influence. If this be true,—and such evidence as is available supports Adams's opinion,— Burr was not allowed to escape from a position of professional and political rivalry to Hamilton in New York. If Hamilton supposed that he could crush Burr he made a sad miscalculation. For the moment Hamilton's power seemed to be secure. John Jay had been elected Governor in 1795 and he was re-elected in 1798 by what in those times was reckoned a large majority. Although Burr was elected to the Assembly from New York City in 1798, on coming up for re-election in 1799 he was heavily defeated and as the Presidential election of 1800 came on the Federalist party was in power both in city and State. The prospects of the opposition were poor, when Burr took charge of the campaign, which he managed with consummate skill. After much negotiation he made up a ticket headed by ex-Governor Clinton, with Brockholst Livingston as an associate, thus allying two great family connections. General Horatio Gates was brought out of his retirement to draw to the ticket feelings and sympathies inspired by the War of Independence. Every name on the ticket was picked with a view to personal influence, and Burr himself shrewdly refrained from including his own name in the list of city candidates, although at the same election he figured as a candidate in Orange C unty.

So powerful was the combination which Burr's management effected that it swept everything before it in the election. Hamilton's ticket was heavily defeated, and so great was the shock that his character gave way under it. As soon as it became clear that a legislature had been elected that would choose Presidential electors favorable to Jefferson, he wrote to Governor Jay proposing that the outgoing legislature should be convoked in special session to pass a law requiring Presidential electors to be chosen in districts by popular vote. In this way the defeated Federalists might still get some of the New York electoral votes, and Hamilton urged that "in times like these in which we live, it will not do to be overscrupulous." Jay filed the letter with the indorsement, "Proposing a measure for party purposes which it would not become me to adopt."

The loss of the New York electoral votes defeated Adams and yet did not elect Jefferson, by reason of the complications of the electoral system. The original draft of the Constitution provided that the President should be elected by Congress, which arrangement would have given the United States a constitution much like the present constitution of Switzerland. But the small States feared that this would put the Presidency in the continual possession of the large States, and to remove such objection the scheme of the electoral college was proposed and accepted as a fair compromise. It was supposed that this would advantage the small States, because in each State the electors should vote for two persons, only one of whom could be a citizen of that State, thus insuring some distribution of the vote on general considerations. But the scheme never worked according to this theory, and its complications have always been troublesome and, indeed, perilous. It is plain that when the electoral colleges began to vote solidly under a party mandate there would be a tie between the persons voted for. This is just what happened in the election of 1800. The electoral votes of the Jeffersonian Republican party were all cast for Jefferson and Burr, so the election did not decide who should be President and who Vice-President. The Constitution provides that in case no one receives a majority in the electoral colleges the House of Representatives shall make the choice for President, each State delegation to cast one vote. A House of Representatives elected two years before, when popular sentiment was running in favor of the Federalists, now had the say as between Jefferson and Burr. There was a strong movement among the Federalists in favor of preferring Burr, and to counteract this Hamilton wrote letters to his friends in Congress attacking Burr, whom he described as a man of daring, energy, inordinate ambition, without probity, a voluptuary by system, sunk in debt, and yet indulging himself in habits of excessive expense, with great talents "for management and intrigue, but he had yet to give the first proofs that they are equal to the act of governing well." An unpleasant feature of these letters is their telltale character. One finds no analysis of Burr's public record such as Hamilton made in writing against Jefferson and Madison; but instead one is told of Burr's profligate sentiments avowed in private talk, as, for instance, that he quoted with gusto Napoleon's saying that "great souls care little for small morals."

To a large extent Hamilton's judgment of Burr's character was verified by his subsequent career, but, at the time Hamilton was denouncing Burr as a man without moral principle, Burr himself was behaving in a way that looked very like inflexible honesty. Before the actual result of the voting by the electoral colleges was known, Burr wrote to a friend in the House of Representatives that, if it should turn out to be a tie, "every man who knows me ought to know that I would utterly disclaim all competition" with Jefferson for the Presidency. He added: "As to my friends, they would dishonor my views and insult my feelings by a suspicion that I would submit to be instrumental in counteracting the wishes and expectations of the United States. And I now constitute you my proxy to declare these sentiments if the occasion should require."

Language could not be more plain and straightforward than was used in this letter, and as it was made public it clearly defined Burr's position as one of opposition to any attempt to defeat Jefferson. According to Hamilton, this position was a piece of deep finesse, based upon the expectation that rather than take Jefferson the House would accept Burr without any effort or commitment on his part. But how can this view be reconciled with the existence of those great talents for intrigue which Hamilton ascribed to Burr? Examination of the evidence leaves scarcely a doubt that had Burr been willing to negotiate he could have been elected President. Hamilton's attacks seem to have been so ineffectual in arresting the drift of party sentiment in Burr's favor that one may infer that Hamilton's views of Burr's character were not accepted by men who also were in a position to form their views on personal knowledge. Hamilton refers to their favor as "a mad propensity," but the fact is significant that acute and well-informed men should have had this propensity in spite of his strong censure. Senator Bayard, of Delaware, to whom Hamilton wrote the most severe of his letters against Burr, replied that "the means existed of electing Burr, but this required his co-operation." This Burr steadfastly declined to give. Hamilton himself, in giving an account of the situation to a New York friend, wrote: "I know as a fact that overtures have been made by leading individuals of the Federal party to Mr. Burr, who declines to give any assurances respecting his future intentions and conduct." Some such assurances were, however, given in behalf of Jefferson, who was elected President through the action of some of the Federalist members in refraining from voting at all. Before the deadlock was broken a Federalist member of the House, William Cooper, father of the famous novelist, wrote from Washington, "Had Burr done anything for himself he would long ere this have been President." After it was all over Senator Bayard wrote to Hamilton that this result was not obtained until it had been "completely ascertained that Burr was resolved not to commit himself."

It does not seem possible to reconcile Burr's behavior under such great temptation with Hamilton's characterization of him as a man whose "sole spring of action is an inordinate ambition," and who is "wicked enough to scruple nothing." That such opinions were not held by other Federalist leaders is shown by the fact that respect for Burr remained strong among the Federalists despite Hamilton's efforts. Three years later, when Burr came out as an independent candidate for governor of New York, Hamilton wrote: "It is a fact to be regretted, though anticipated, that the Federalists very extensively had embarked with zeal in the support of Mr. Burr." Hamilton thought of bringing out a Federalist candidate, but finding that impracticable, his influence was exerted in favor of the regular Republican candidate and Burr was defeated.

Although he must have been well aware of Hamilton's activity against him at every turn, Burr seems to have avoided personal enmity and always bore himself with his habitual dignity and composure. In one of his denunciatory letters Hamilton remarked: "With Burr I have always been personally well." Of course Burr would have called Hamilton to account for the attacks upon his character had they been publicly made; but Burr made no move so long as they were confined to private correspondence, although their tenor had become a matter of common fame and a spiteful newspaper put the query, "Is the Vice-President sunk so low as to submit to be insulted by General Hamilton?"

During the political campaign a letter had been published in which Doctor Charles D. Cooper said that Hamilton declared Burr to be a dangerous man, adding: "I could detail to you a still more despicable opinion which General Hamilton has expressed of Mr. Burr." Apparently Burr did not hear of this publication at the time, but six weeks after the election he received notice of it. He sent a friend to Hamilton with a copy of the publication, together with a note in which Burr observed: "You must perceive, Sir, the necessity of a prompt and unqualified acknowledgment or denial of the use of any expressions which would warrant the assertions of Mr. Cooper." Hamilton was taken by surprise, as he had not before heard of Cooper's letter. He asked time for consideration and did not reply until two days later. He was in a difficult position, as the letter did not really misrepresent him. The gist of his long reply was that he could not consent "to be interrogated as to the justness of inferences which others might have drawn from what he had said of a political opponent in the course of fifteen years competition," but he stood "ready to avow or disavow, promptly and explicitly, any precise or definite opinion which I may be charged with having declared of any gentleman." Burr replied that a dishonorable epithet had been applied to him under the sanction of Hamilton's name, and the sole question was whether Hamilton had authorized this application, either directly or by uttering expressions or opinions derogatory to his honor. Hamilton replied that he had "no other answer to give than that which has already been given." This closed the correspondence between the principals, and the affair now passed into the hands of their seconds, who carried on further correspondence without modifying the attitude of the principals, and, according to the manners of the times, the two men being what they were, a duel was the necessary consequence.

The correspondence closed on June 27, 1804, but time was allowed for the principals to put their affairs in order before the duel. So it happened that Burr and Hamilton met as courteous tablemates on the 4th of July at the annual banquet of the Society of the Cincinnati, of which both were members. It was noted that while Burr's habitual reserve was more intense than usual, Hamilton's characteristic animation rose to a pitch of gayety. He was urged to give the company the old ballad, "The Drum," which was one of his songs on occasions of merry-making. He seemed unusually reluctant to comply, but finally yielded. He had a rich voice and he sang with impressive effect the verses which told how a recruiting sergeant knocked at the parson's door, and said:

> "We're going to war, and when we die
> We'll want a man of God near by,
> So bring your Bible and follow the drum."

While Hamilton was singing Burr leaned upon the table looking up into his face until the song was done.

One of Hamilton's last acts was to prepare a

statement as to his motives in meeting Burr. In it he admitted that his "animadversions on the political principles, character, and views of Colonel Burr have been extremely severe," and that while he certainly had strong reasons for what he said, it is possible that in some particulars he may have been influenced by misconstruction or misinformation. He added:

It is also my ardent wish that I may have been more mistaken than I think I have been; and that he, by his future conduct, may show himself worthy of all confidence and esteem and prove an ornament and a blessing to the country. As well, because it is possible that I may have injured Colonel Burr, however convinced myself that my opinions and declarations have been well founded, as from my general principles and temper in relation to similar affairs, I have resolved, if our interview is conducted in the usual manner, and it pleases God to give me the opportunity, to reserve and throw away my first fire, and I have thoughts even of reserving my second fire, and thus giving a double opportunity to Colonel Burr to pause and reflect. It is not, however, my intention to enter into any explanations on the ground. Apology from principle, I hope, rather than pride, is out of the question.

Hamilton left two farewell letters to his wife. One, written on July 4, ended with "Adieu, best of wives—best of women. Embrace all my darling children for me." In the night before the duel he bethought him of Mrs. Mitchell's kindness to him in his youth, and he wrote again to commend her to his wife's good offices. This letter closed with "Adieu, my darling, darling wife."

The meeting took place at seven o'clock, Wednesday morning, July 11, at Weehawken, on the west bank of the Hudson, then a noted duelling-ground. They fought at ten paces. Lots were drawn as to choice of position and as to giving the word, Hamilton's second winning in both cases. Hamilton was shot in the right side; Burr was untouched. Hamilton died the next day at two o'clock in the afternoon, aged forty-seven years and six months.

CHAPTER XXIV

APPARENT FAILURE

In 1797 Hamilton received from Scotland a family letter making inquiries expressive of the interest of the family home stock in his fame and achievements. In response he gave an account of his career, in which he said that he entered public life because, having promoted the movement for a new Constitution, he conceived himself to be under an obligation to lend his aid toward putting the machine in some regular motion, and hence he accepted Washington's offer to undertake the office of Secretary of the Treasury. He continued:

In that office I met with many intrinsic difficulties and many artificial ones, proceeding from passions, not very worthy, common to human nature, and which act with peculiar force in republics. The object, however, was effected of establishing public credit and introducing order in the finances.

Public office in this country has few attractions. The pecuniary emolument is so inconsiderable as to amount to a sacrifice to any man who can employ his time with advantage in any liberal profession. The opportunity of doing good, from the jealousy of power and the spirit of faction, is too small in any station to warrant a long continuance of private sacrifices.

This was a mood that became more confirmed in Hamilton's mind as time went on, and on some occasions swerved his conduct from the chivalric ideals that ordinarily governed it. The strongest instance is that unworthy letter to Jay proposing a partisan trick to set aside election results. Another instance of low calculation was a letter to Senator Bayard, in 1802, in which Hamilton proposed that an association should be formed to be denominated "The Christian Constitutional Society," its objects to be "the support of the Christian religion; the support of the Constitution of the United States." No man would have so thoroughly disdained such claptrap as Hamilton himself when acting in his proper character, and it is noticeable that he made no attempt to push the precious scheme of making religion a political stalking-horse. The notion was doubtless the outcome of a mood of discouragement such as occasionally afflicted him in the latter part of his career. It was in such a mood, during the same year, that he wrote to Gouverneur Morris:

Mine is an odd destiny. Perhaps no man in the United States has sacrificed or done more for the present Constitution than myself, and contrary to all my anticipations of its fate, as you know from the very beginning, I am still laboring to prop the frail and worthless fabric. Yet I have the murmurs of its friends no less than the curses of its foes for my reward. What can I do better than withdraw from the scene? Every day proves to me more and more that this American world was not made for me.

When Hamilton reviewed his career, with calculation of results rather than in that spirit of chivalry whose heroic and generous action is disdainful of profit, there was much in it that looked like failure. Against the remonstrances of his nearest friends he had given up his law practice, exposing his family to poverty, to lift the public business out of bankruptcy, and his own recompense had been calumny, persecution, and loss of fortune. His principal opponent in matters of administrative policy had shown such superior address in all the arts of popularity that he had reached the Presidency and was now victoriously sweeping away all rivalry to his mastery over the succession to that office. The Government itself had been given a twist that had frustrated the constitutional design of direct administrative proposals, and had introduced a system of committee management which was in effect a return to the methods of the Continental Congress. "Committees are the ministers," wrote Fisher Ames to Hamilton in 1797, "and while the House indulges a jealousy of encroachment in its functions which are properly deliberative, it does not perceive that these are impaired and nullified by the monopoly as well as the perversion of information by these committees." The vices which Hamilton had noted in the old system—"tedious delays, continual negotiation and intrigue, contemptible compromises of the public good"—had reappeared in the new system, with increased virulence. With no regular means existing by which Congress should be confronted by responsibilities exactly defined and decisively submitted, the electorate had nothing to go upon save vague impressions as to the general disposition of candidates, and pretense and blandishment were more serviceable than integrity and ability. Such conditions gave the utmost possible scope to the arts of cajolery that are the traditi nal bane of popular government, and in those arts Hamilton was so unskilful that as an electioneering tactician he was a sorry failure. To this on his own account he was indifferent, as he was quite free from envy, but he regarded the situation as a defeat of the purpose of the movement to form a more perfect union. Still he did not despair. In the same letter in which he acknowledged to Morris his acute disappointment, he added: "The time may ere long arrive when the minds of men will be prepared to *recover* the Constitution, but the many cannot now be brought to make a stand for its preservation. We must wait a while."

It is a satisfaction to note that when facing death his old chivalric spirit was in full possession of his soul. Among his papers was found a statement, undated, but manifestly of recent composition, in which he computed that he was actually worth about £10,000, and yet he feared that if anything should happen to force the sale of his property it might not even be sufficient to pay his debts. He gave particulars to show that the obligations he had contracted had been warranted by his circumstances, but to protect friends who had from mere kindness indorsed his paper discounted at the banks, he had thought it justifiable to secure them in preference to other creditors. While this might save them from eventual loss it would not exempt them from present inconvenience. "As to this," he said, "I can only throw myself upon their kindness and entreat the indulgence of the banks for them. Perhaps the request may be supposed entitled to some regard."

In conclusion the statement makes this noble declaration: "In the event which would bring this paper to the public eye, one thing at least would be put beyond doubt. This is that my public labors have amounted to an absolute sacrifice of the interests of my family, and that in all pecuniary concerns the delicacy no less than the probity of conduct in public stations has been such as to defy the shadow of a question." He went on to show that he had not enjoyed the ordinary advantages incident to military services. Inasmuch as he was a member of Congress when the matter of the claims of army officers was up, he formally relinquished all his own claim in order that he might occupy a disinterested position in effecting a settlement. Nor did he obtain from the State of New York the usual allowance of lands, although he had "better pretensions to the allowance than others to whom it was actually made."

The shock of Hamilton's death to his family was enhanced by the fact that it was added to other deep afflictions.   Less than three years before, his oldest son, Philip, who more than any of the other children is said to have resembled Hamilton in mental endowment, was mortally wounded in a duel at the same place where Hamilton himself fell later. The oldest daughter, Angelica, a beautiful and accomplished girl, suffered so great a shock from her brother's death that her mind was impaired, and she was under her mother's assiduous care when the family was again stricken by the loss of its head, together with impending poverty.   There were six other children, ranging from eighteen years of age to five.   Friends raised a fund to protect the estate, and General Schuyler gave his daughter such help as his heavily burdened family situation permitted, but he too died a few months later.   The widow had to dispose of the country home she and her husband had planned together, and she went to live in the city, where she had a hard struggle to keep the family together and provide for the education of its younger members.   Congress, acting with characteristic tardiness, passed a law in 1816 to give her the same commutation for back pay as had been allowed to other officers of Hamilton's rank, and with accrued interest from 1783 the sum amounted to $10,609.64, affording great relief to Mrs. Hamilton in her necessities. For Hamilton's expenses in equipping his company of artillery in the Revolutionary War, no reimbursement was ever made.

An object on which Mrs. Hamilton's heart was set and which she never ceased to pursue during the rest of her long life was the vindication of her husband's reputation as a statesman; but in this matter also she had to endure singular affliction, for whenever she made arrangements for a biography something would happen to frustrate the plan. Her first choice was the Reverend John M. Mason, who had delivered an impressive funeral oration before the Society of the Cincinnati. He collected some materials for a biography and kept that purpose in view for some years, but eventually abandoned it. In 1819 Mrs. Hamilton made some arrangements with a Mr. Hopkinson,—probably Joseph Hopkinson, of Philadelphia, author of "Hail, Columbia,"—but in some way the negotiation miscarried. In 1827 Timothy Pickering took the matter in hand, but had not gone further with it than to collect some material when he died. In 1832 Mrs. Hamilton wrote to a daughter: "I have my fears I shall not obtain my object. Most of the contemporaries of your father have also passed away." Nevertheless she did not relax her efforts, but kept writing to leading Federalists all over the country to collect all the facts she could about her husband's public services. Accounts of her old age describe her as a little, bright-eyed woman, of erect figure and brisk ways, retaining in her conversation much of the ease and brilliancy of her youth. Finally, at her pressing request, her fourth son, John Church Hamilton, accepted the task of preparing a biography. The two volumes of his *Life of Alexander Hamilton* appeared from 1834 to 1840. He also arranged his father's papers, and in 1849 his collection was purchased by Congress and was published under his editorial supervision. Thus Mrs. Hamilton had the satisfaction of seeing an object of such dear interest accomplished at last. She died in 1854, aged ninety-seven, her mind remaining perfectly clear until a few days before her death.

John Church Hamilton began his pious task with reluctance, due, as he said in the preface to his first volume, to "a deep conviction of my incapacity, the want of the necessary preparatory studies, and a distrust of the natural bias of my feelings." The two volumes he produced during his mother's lifetime brought the story of his father's life down to the period of the constitutional convention. By that time his studies had so enlarged his knowledge of American history that he decided to shift from biography to history in carrying on his work. The result was his *History of the Republic of the United States of America, as Traced in the Writings of Alexander Hamilton and His Contemporaries,* in seven massive volumes, published from 1857 to 1861. The work is written with dignity and ability, but its plan, taken in connection with the natural bias of feelings which, as he had anticipated, he was unable to escape, revived all the old controversies and detracted from the true greatness of Hamilton's statesmanship by exhibiting it merely in its provincial setting. It naturally engendered reply in the same spirit. The motive of Randall's voluminous *Life of Thomas Jefferson* is pointedly indicated by the author's remark that Jefferson left no son to be so "deeply interested in his mere personal defense" as to be willing "to swell pamphlets to books to roll back the tide of personal vituperation on his assailants." An abiding fashion was set for treating the early history of the republic as a drama of creation in which Hamilton and Jefferson figured as Ormuzd and Ahriman, but along with common agreement in this view went violent difference of opinion as to which was which.

Among the unfortunate consequences of this standing controversy was that it diverted attention from the need of further research into the particulars of Hamilton's life. The family collection of matter with which John Church Hamilton began his labors was large but not exhaustive, and he does not appear to have added to it materially, editorship and interpretation of the great mass already in hand fully occupying his time. His publications supplied the material used by various biographers until Professor William Graham Sumner's *Alexander Hamilton* appeared in 1890. In this he did not furnish any new data, but he gave a masterly portrayal of the features of American public life in Hamilton's time, thus supplying for the first time the proper background for a correct view of Hamilton's career. The obscurity which surrounded Hamilton's birth and childhood was not cleared away until Mrs. Atherton made a minute investigation of the West Indian scene in collecting material for her vivid and interesting historical novel *The Conqueror,* 1902. Nothing but a meagre and scrappy account of Hamilton's home life had appeared up to 1910, when a grandson, Allan McLane Hamilton, published *The Intimate Life of Alexander Hamilton,* a work whose completeness, sincerity, fairness, and grace make it an entirely worthy treatment of its theme. This work wisely avoided consideration of Hamilton's public career, and it was not until Frederick Scott Oliver's *Alexander Hamilton* appeared in 1916 that his achievements were disengaged from their provincial setting sufficiently to be estimated on a scale of world values. This splendid work marks the beginning of a new era in Hamilton biography, in which the old controversies fall into the background as among the local incidents of a career whose importance lies in the universal value of the constructive principles he discerned, developed, and applied. The old view, which insists on regarding Hamilton simply as a protagonist in a struggle between broad and strict principles of constitutional construction, between national and State authority, is really a piece of narrow, obtuse provincialism; and so too is the latest antithesis, produced by the revolutionary spirit of the present time, which regards the struggle as essentially one between capitalism and agrarianism. It is impossible to fit Hamilton's career into such a framework, as will plainly appear when mythology is discarded and actual facts are considered.

CHAPTER XXV

REVISED ESTIMATES

It is important to remember that Hamilton was never in full accord with the party with which he acted, and throughout his career he experienced detraction from party associates, including some who were among his intimates. The matter does not become fully comprehensible until the elements of the constitutional movement are considered. The starting-point of all fair judgment upon the situation after the Revolution is that attachment to English constitutional principles still continued to be the master influence over political thought. When at the beginning of the struggle with Great Britain Jefferson wrote, "It is neither our wish nor our interest to separate from her," he expressed a sentiment held by all the leaders. Although the events of the war, and particularly the necessity of accepting the condition on which alone the alliance of France could be obtained, forced the American leaders to abandon the distinction they had originally drawn between loyalty to the Crown and submission to taxes laid by the British Parliament, and induced them to issue the Declaration of Independence, they still continued to believe that the English constitutional system was the best practical solution of the problem of combining liberty with order that had been reached in all the long history of mankind. This belief presided over the constitutional movement. Jefferson held it as strongly as Hamilton and avowed it just as distinctly. The admiration for the English constitution expressed by Hamilton does not account for the charge of monarchical sympathies brought against him, for that was the common state of feeling. His fear lest the republican experiment should fail was too generally held to supply matter for particular indictment. None such was ever filed against Benjamin Franklin, although he repeatedly declared in the constitutional convention that "the government of these States may in future times end in monarchy." The truth of the matter is that the Hamilton myth originated in divisions and cross-purposes among men who had a common regard for English constitutional principles, but who differed somewhat as to the nature of those principles and also differed widely as to their application under American conditions.

The deepest cleavage was with respect to the position of the States. Hamilton was in favor of giving the national Executive power to appoint the State Governors; Madison was in favor of giving the federal administration "a negative in all cases whatever, on the legislative acts of the States, as the King of Great Britain heretofore had." Hamilton's plan would have put the States in about the same position as the royal colonies had been; Madison's, in about the same position as the charter colonies. In both cases the subordination was to be complete, and in any event it was inevitable if federal authority was to be securely established. Madison's plan has virtually prevailed, through extension of the authority of the federal courts on lines laid down by Madison himself in the legislation of the First Congress, in opposition to Hamilton's views. Hamilton held that the federal judiciary might be established by embracing the State courts in the system, under the supervision of the Supreme Court of the United States. That this plan was feasible is shown by the fact that it has been successfully introduced in some countries—notably in Switzerland. Madison, however, insisted on a distinct system throughout, his main argument being that in some of the States the courts "are so dependent on the State legislatures, that to make the federal laws dependent on them would throw us back into all the embarrassments which characterized our former situation." Had Hamilton's plan been adopted the subordination of the States to federal authority could scarcely be greater than it is now, and means would have existed for a more harmonious, economical, prompt, and efficient system of administering justice than is possible with two separate systems.

It seems to be now the general opinion that

Hamilton's plan of federal appointment of State Governors would have been fatal to State authority. An elaborate note in Senator Lodge's edition of Hamilton's *Writings* says that "this arrangement would have crushed the States." It is impossible to arrive at any fixed conclusion in discussing what might have been, but it may at least be observed that the plan has had no such result in the constitutional system from which Hamilton took the idea. The English plan of executive appointment of all governors is still in operation, and English commonwealths in all parts of the world do not appear to be inconvenienced thereby in their possession of self-government. Much light will be cast upon this subject if one shall seriously consider which in reality possesses greater power of action—a Canadian province or an American State?

Another deep cleavage was over the extent to which the Government should be subjected to the control of public opinion. What in general the upper classes in society were most intent upon was protection for their own interests, and they were bent upon securing this through assertion of constitutional privilege and by limitation in grants of power. They wanted an executive strong enough to keep order, but not strong enough to interfere with their privileges. In Hamilton's opinion they were inclined to go to lengths that were neither wise nor just. So early as 1777, when the first constitution of the State of New York was framed, he had differences with Gouverneur Morris on such matters, and when the Constitution of the United States was in the making such differences were renewed. Morris favored the accumulation of power in the custody of the Senate, which is a marked feature of the Constitution of the United States, and he expressed the hope that the Senate "will show us the might of aristocracy." Madison had virtually the same thought, when he said that the Senate "will guard the minority who are placed above indigence against the agrarian attempts of the ever-increasing class who labor under the hardships of life, and secretly strive for a more equal distribution of its blessings." Hamilton did not dispute that there were advantages to be gained through the political influence of wealth and social position, but he was not willing to give it supremacy. Madison's *Journal* notes that he expressed himself "with great earnestness and anxiety" to the effect that "the House of Representatives was on so narrow a scale, as to be really dangerous, and to warrant a jealousy in the people, for their liberties." Hence he favored an executive strong enough to keep every class, high or low, rich or poor, subdued to justice, and a representative assembly that would give the entire mass of the people an effective control over the Government. In the constitutional scheme he drafted in 1787 members of the Senate and also Presidential

electors were to be chosen by districts, apportioned
in a ratio to the basis of representation in Congress,
upon a suffrage limited by property qualifications
such as were then general. But the number of
senators should never be in larger ratio to the number of representatives than forty is to one hundred,
and the representatives were to be elected "by the
free male citizens and inhabitants of the several
States comprehended in the Union, all of whom, of
the age of twenty-one and upwards, shall be entitled
to an equal vote." Perhaps none of Hamilton's
recommendations were so shocking to his associates
as this one of manhood suffrage. Agreement was
then almost universal that suffrage ought to be confined to freeholders. James Madison's last political
battle was fought over this issue, when in 1830, with
the aid of James Monroe and others of the elder
statesmen, he succeeded in retaining the freehold
qualification in the Virginia constitution, thus excluding from the franchise about 80,000 white male
citizens of his State.

Hamilton's proposal to give the President a ten-
ure of office during good behavior, with power to
appoint State Governors, and with an unqualified
negative upon legislation, should be viewed in conjunction with the democratic control over the authority of both President and Senate which he sought
to provide in the House of Representatives. His
scheme was really nothing more than a democratized

version of the English constitution. If the provision of an unqualified negative over legislation looks autocratic, it should be considered that it cannot be so in reality, in view of the presence and activity of a genuinely representative assembly. Actual experience with this very provision, which is still a traditional feature of the English constitution, although now quite dormant, shows that it has no tendency toward absolutism in practice.

Hamilton's advocacy of broad authority was based upon democratic principles. He told the New York Convention, in the course of his fight for the adoption of the Constitution: "There are two objects in forming systems of government— safety for the people, and energy in the administration. When these objects are united, the certain tendency of the system will be to the public welfare. If the latter object be neglected, the people's security will be as certainly sacrificed as by disregarding the former." Hence he opposed Bills of Rights, on the ground that a good constitution is itself "in every rational sense and to every useful purpose a Bill of Rights"; and, moreover, that "they would even be dangerous," through the handle they would give for arrogant interpretations. "After all," he told the New York Convention, "we must submit to this idea, that the true principle of a republic is that the people should choose whom they please to govern them. Representation is imperfect in proportion as the current of popular favor is checked." In fine, Hamilton held that since in every form of government power must exist and be trusted somewhere, able to cope with every emergency of war or peace, and since the extent of emergency is incalculable, therefore, public authority is not really susceptible of limitation. If limitation be imposed, the effect is not to stay the exertion of power under stress of public necessity, but is rather to cause it to become capricious, violent, and irregular. The true concern of a constitution is therefore not limitation of power, but is provision of means for defining responsibility.

The constitutional ideal aimed at by Hamilton may be fairly described as plenary power in the administration, subject to direct and continuous accountability to the people, maintained by a representative assembly, broadly democratic in its character.[1] This ideal, although it anticipates a situation which since his time has been apparently the goal of democratic progress, was intensely obnoxious to conservative sentiment when Hamilton presented it. In that day a respectable republic was conceived of as being necessarily antidemocratic in its structure. According to Madison the essential distinction between a democracy and a republic "lies in the

---

[1] Expressions of opinion to this purport are found in many places in Hamilton's writings. They appear with particular distinctness in Nos. 23, 31, and 84 of *The Federalist*, and in a brief but comprehensive form in a letter to Timothy Pickering, September 18, 1803.

total exclusion of the people in their collective capacity from any share in the latter." Hamilton's dissent from the ideas and principles of the conservative reaction which produced the Constitution, not only explains how it was that his associates regarded him as monarchical and antirepublican at heart, but also how it was that he played so unimportant a part in the convention itself. The stream ran so strongly in favor of security to right and privilege by partition of authority that it was impossible for him to stem it effectively. The Constitution was not what he desired, but he at once accepted it as "the best that the present views and circumstances of the country will permit," and he applied all his powers to the task of putting it in motion. These facts amply explain the misunderstandings which harassed Hamilton in his own day and have been perpetuated even to our own times. If one's opinion be no longer taken from tradition but shall be formed upon the evidence, much material will be found in support of the belief that Hamilton was in advance of his times in comprehension of democratic principles of government and in knowledge of the proper application of them. So much depends upon the point of view that estimates of the value of Hamilton's ideas will probably keep changing with the times. It is noticeable that in England, where democratic progress has taken place on the lines which Hamilton anticipated, his statesmanship is rated higher than in the United States, in which there is still great reliance upon the partition of power, and upon impediments to action which Hamilton condemned as constitutional frailties apt to have fatal consequences. As to these matters history has yet to give complete instructions.

A habit of thought which obscures the truth about them both is that which views Hamilton and Jefferson as the champions of opposing theories of government. The only element of truth in this is that Hamilton took the realistic view of human nature, which holds that it cannot possess freedom save through moral discipline, while Jefferson inclined to the romantic view that humanity is naturally inclined to be good and kind if well treated, and that the country is best governed that is governed the least. One of the few strokes of satire to be found in Hamilton's writings is an allusion to the "enthusiasts who expect to see the halcyon scenes of the poetic or fabulous age realized in America." Jefferson did not think a modest realization of hopes of this order impracticable if the country should keep to plain, simple ways of living. In his *Notes on Virginia,* he said: "While we have land to labor, let us never wish to see our citizens occupied at a workshop or twirling a distaff. . . . Let our workshops remain in Europe. It is better to carry provisions and material to workmen there than to bring them to the provisions and materials, and with them

their manners and principles. . . . The mobs of
great cities add just so much to the support of pure
government as sores do to the strength of the human
body." He brought up this point again when writing to Madison about the new Constitution. He
said: "I think our governments will remain virtu-
ous for many centuries, as long as they are chiefly
agricultural; and this they will be as long as there
shall be vacant lands in any part of America. When
they get piled up upon one another in large cities,
as in Europe, they will become corrupt as in Europe."

It was certainly natural for one holding such
ideas to view with alarm Hamilton's measures for
developing banking, commercial, and manufacturing
interests, but it is a mistake to regard Jefferson as
either democratic in his principles or as antagonistic
to authority in his practice. His notion of a proper
Constitution was one "in which the powers of government should be so divided and balanced among
several bodies of magistracy as that no one could
transcend their legal limits without being effectually checked and restrained by the others." While
the constitutional convention was at work he wrote
to Madison suggesting that, to give stability to
jurisprudence, "it would be well to provide in our
constitution that there shall always be a twelve-
month between the engrossing of a bill and the
passing of it." His views as to the relations of
federal and State authority seem to have varied in

correspondence with his party interest. Strict consistency is rare among politicians the world over. But Hamilton was undoubtedly right when he wrote that Jefferson "was generally for a large construction of executive authority and not backward to act upon it in cases which coincided with his views."[1] Under the Virginia dynasty, which Jefferson founded, the Government was weakened through attempts to reduce it to rustic dimensions, but its federalist character was perpetuated. This was so notorious that Madison felt impelled to excuse it on the ground that with Republicans in charge of affairs things might be allowed that were justly regarded as dangerous while the Federalists were in power.[2] On the whole, Jefferson's career was more a help than an obstruction to the success of Hamilton's measures. It was Jefferson's timely aid that passed the Funding and Assumption Bill, and his success as a party leader was of immense value in reconciling popular sentiment to a constitutional system which the high-flying Federalists had been making odious, in spite of Hamilton's warnings.

It has often been remarked that Hamilton's writings afford little evidence of esteem for Washington, and it must be allowed that on Hamilton's side the usual relation was one of formal respect rather than

[1] Hamilton to James A. Bayard, January 16, 1801.
[2] Madison to William Eustis, May 22, 1823.

sincere affection. Something of this is accounted for by the fact that Washington was a much older man, and that his manners never encouraged familiarity in any one, but in addition there is evidence of imperfect sympathies which long stood in the way of full understanding. There is much to support Jefferson's claim that originally Washington was more disposed to confide in him and in Madison than in Hamilton. The attitude of neutrality which Washington thought prudent for him to maintain during the struggle over Hamilton's financial measures would naturally strike Hamilton as cold indifference, and the frequency with which Hamilton had to repel attacks upon him made privately to Washington must also have wounded him.[1] In the course of the Treasury investigation it became a question whether certain arrangements made by Hamilton had been actually authorized by Washington as Hamilton had claimed. As to this Washington wrote such a non-committal letter that Hamilton sent a reply protesting with considerable warmth at the way he was being treated.[2] But Washington was more and more drawn to Hamilton through experience of his powers and their relations eventually became those of the most cordial and

[1] See his letter to John Jay, December 18, 1792.
[2] Hamilton to Washington, April 9, 1794, vol. III, p. 190, Lodge's edition of *Hamilton's Writings*.

trustful intimacy. When Hamilton resigned his office Washington's feelings broke through his habitual formality of phrase. He wrote to Hamilton in terms of fervent affection and esteem, and Hamilton's reply was equally cordial. Washington's regard for Hamilton remained warm and active for the rest of his life, and Hamilton made proper response, but one gets the notion that Washington was fonder of Hamilton than Hamilton was of him, which in view of all that had happened is not surprising.

If one can escape the glamour that Hamilton's brilliancy is apt to produce and be able to view him simply as a brother man, it is not hard to see that his character was distinctly of what was once a well-marked Scottish type. It was a type which, in its idealism, in its gallantry, and in its self-sufficiency, has been depicted by a great artist whose nativity gave him special insight of Scottish character. Hamilton is an Alan Breck with a genius for statesmanship. Stevenson's hero in *Kidnapped* did not face tremendous odds with greater courage or in higher spirits than did Alexander Hamilton in accomplishing his mission. And in both one notes the same traits: generosity, devotion, promptness, daring, pride, conceit, touchiness, pugnacity, shrewdness, acumen, and inexhaustible energy—a mingling of high and low such as may be found only in characters built on a grand scale, with the bold irregularity of a mountain range.

His talents were great but not unequalled. In philosophy and eloquence he is so inferior to Burke that there is no basis for comparison; but in Burke's writings we have the polished result of skilful artistry, while Hamilton's writings were hastily produced as mere incidents of his political activity. In an age when heavily structured style was in fashion, his pen was easy, rapid, and fluent, slipping at times into some negligence of diction but always vivid and impressive. As he wrote only as current events prompted, it never occurred to him to put his ideas into systematic form, and his political philosophy comes out only in the way of side-lights upon concrete particulars. It is precisely this that gives *The Federalist* such permanent value as a political treatise. The matters with which it deals are just such as always crop out in forming a system of government, and it abounds with maxims for practical guidance.

Hamilton's inferiority as an electioneering tactician is easily accounted for. The case exemplifies the Italian proverb that the eagle is not good at catching flies. But nothing accounts for his genius for statesmanship. Its power is manifest; but its nature is inscrutable. There was nothing in his antecedents, in his education, or in his experience to explain the piercing vision into the springs of political action, the clear discernment of means for practical attainment of purpose, which he displayed from the first. Of political ambition in a personal way he was singularly devoid, except in the military line, his rank in which was matter for concern such as he never seems to have felt about purely civic honors. There is a singular concentration of purpose in his public career, which is the secret of its vigor and consistency. All his thought and effort were addressed to the great question which he propounded in the first number of *The Federalist:* "Whether societies of men are really capable or not of establishing good government from reflection and choice, or whether they are forever destined to depend for their political constitutions on accident and force." The answer is not yet quite clear, but it is quite clear that the greatest contribution to political method on the side of free agency is that which was made by Alexander Hamilton. Anticipating biological principles unknown to the age in which he lived, he stated the law of political development to be that "Every institution will grow and flourish in proportion to the quantity and extent of the means concentred towards its formation and support." [1] That principle guided his statesmanship and the result has demonstrated its efficacy beyond even his own large

[1] *The Federalist*, No. XI.

calculations. It still remains the only safe principle that political theory has supplied to political practice, and his success in discovering and applying it puts Alexander Hamilton among the greatest statesmen the world has produced.

INDEX

Adams, John, his slur on Hamilton's birth, 4; his panic, 70; antagonism to democracy, 84; charged with unrepublican principles, 262; succeeds to the Presidency, 314 *et seq.*; his character, 315; makes overtures to Jefferson, 316 *et seq.*; appoints Washington to command of army, 320; antagonizes Washington's selection of officers, 321; is overruled by his Cabinet, 323; sends another mission to France, 324 *et seq.*; dismisses cabinet ʲofficers, 324 *et seq.*; his rage against Hamilton, 326; is denounced by Hamilton, 327; loses the Presidency, 328; his regard for Burr, 332, 335

Adams, Samuel, 145, 166, 191

Algerine corsairs, 179

Alien and Sedition Laws, 323 *et seq.*

Allison, William, 80

Ames, Fisher, 215, 219, 227, 348

André, Major, 108

Antifederalists, plans of, 206; efforts to defeat the Constitution, 207; attitude of, in Congress, 212

Army, Continental, pay of, 147; grievances of, 154; disbandment of, 155

Arnold, Benedict, 70, 107

Asgill, Captain, 134 *et seq.*

Asia, British man-of-war, 40 *et seq.*

Assumption Bill, 233 *et seq.*, 239, 241, 245

Atherton, Mrs. Gertrude, 78, 355

Barbados, 18

Barlow, Joel, American poet, 177

Bayard, James A., of Delaware, 339, 347

Benson, Egbert, of New York, 178, 227, 239

Bible Society, American, 188

Bill of Rights, Hamilton's objection to, 363

Blackstone's *Commentaries*, 217

Bonaparte, Napoleon, 325

Boudinot, Elias, 20, 43, 227, 238

Brandywine, battle of, 58

Brown University, 151

Burgoyne, General, 61

Burke, Edmund, 96, 225

Burr, Aaron, Rev., 2

Burr, Aaron, guides Putnam's division, 47; defeated in election of 1785, 178; outgenerals Hamilton in election of 1800, 328; his character, 329; his military career, 329 *et seq.*; activity in New York politics, 331; elected to U. S. Senate, 332; antagonized by Hamilton, 334; his ability as a political tactician, 335; preferred to Jefferson by Federalists, 338 *et seq.*; refuses to negotiate for Presidency, 338 *et seq.*; assailed by Hamilton, 338; kills Hamilton in duel, 342 *et seq.*

Carrington, Edward, Col., 267, 269, 278

Chase, Samuel, of Maryland, denounced by Hamilton, 75

Chastellux, Marquis de, 106

Christian Constitutional Society, 347

Church, Mrs. Angelica, 104

Church, John B., 170, 313

Clinton, George, 74, 138, 159, 181, 182, 183, 185, 190, 199, 203, 204, 207, 218

Cobbett, William, 309

Coleman, William, 309

Commercial regulations, State difficulties over, 176; interstate negotiations on, 178; basis of call for constitutional convention, 180

Congress, Continental, its incapacity, 70 *et seq.*; Duché's opinion of, 72; Henry Laurens's account of, 72; its fondness for display, 73; Washington's opinion of, 73; its military policy, 76 *et seq.*; antagonizes Washington, 98; its financiering, 143 *et seq.*; proposes five-per-cent impost, 145; pay of its

375